THE OPEN HAND COOKBOOK

THE
OPEN
HAND
COOKBOOK

Great chefs cook for friends

Compiled and edited by
Robert C. Schneider

Illustrations by Deborah Zemke

POCKET BOOKS
New York   London   Toronto   Sydney   Tokyo

POCKET BOOKS, a division of Simon & Schuster Inc.
1230 Avenue of the Americas, New York, NY 10020

The recipe on page 8 is from *Cooking Bold and Fearless,* copyright Lane Publishing Co., Menlo Park, CA 94025

The recipe on page 20 is from *Joy of Cooking* by Irma Rombauer and Marion Becker (Bobbs-Merrill, 1975)

The recipes on pages 28-30 are from *The Food of Southern Italy* by Carlo Middione (William Morrow, 1987)

The recipe on pages 52-53 is from *The Italian Baker* by Carol Field (Harper and Row, 1985)

The recipes on pages 56-59 are from *The Wolfgang Puck Cookbook: Recipes from Spago and Chinois* (Random House, 1986)

The recipes on pages 121-124 are from *Jeremiah Tower's New American Classics* (Harper and Row, 1986)

The recipes on pages 155-160 are from *Chez Panisse Cooking* by Paul Bertolli with Alice Waters (Random House, 1988)
Copyright © 1988 by Alice Waters and Paul Bertolli

All are used by permission.

ISBN: 0-671-68064-1

First Pocket Books hardcover printing October 1989

10   9   8   7   6   5   4   3   2   1

POCKET and colophon are trademarks
of Simon & Schuster Inc.

Printed in the U.S.A.

Design and illustrations by Deborah Zemke.
Typography in Bembo by ATG/Ad Type Graphics, Sacramento, California.

To Ted Gietzen

CONTENTS

FOREWORD by Ruth Brinker xi

PREFACE by Gerald Jampolsky, M.D., and Diane V. Cirincione xiii

EDITOR'S INTRODUCTION by Robert C. Schneider xv

S P R I N G

A COASTAL BREAKFAST PICNIC by Heidi Haughy Cusick 3

A SPRING BREAKFAST WITH FRIENDS by Lindsey Shere 7

SPRING INTO SUMMER LUNCHEON by Jane Benet 9

A MEAL FOR FRIENDS WITH SPRING FEVER by Cindy Pawlcyn .. 13

A MOTHER'S DAY MENU by Patricia Unterman 17

AN INFORMAL EAST-WEST SPRING LUNCHEON by Ken Hom .. 21

A QUINTESSENTIAL CALIFORNIA SPRING MENU

    by Carlo Middione 27

AN ELABORATE DINNER FOR FRIENDS by Hubert Keller 31

BIRTHDAY BUFFET WITH CHAMPAGNE by Robert Reynolds 38

AN INFORMAL LATE-SPRING DINNER by Alice Waters 43

A SPRING DINNER FOR CLOSE FRIENDS by Carol Field 47

L.A. SUPPER by Wolfgang Puck 55

S U M M E R

A SUMMER LUNCH ON THE PATIO by Maggie Waldron 63

A SUMMER PICNIC by John Ash 67

A SUMMER MEAL FROM THE GRILL FOR FAMILY AND FRIENDS

    by Edward Espe Brown 71

A LIGHT LUNCH BY THE SEA by Lenee Arlen 78

A MIDDLE EASTERN BARBECUE by Loni Kuhn 81

AN INDIAN-SUMMER LUNCH ON BOARD by Arnold Rossman .. 87

A SUMMER DINNER WITH A SOUTHWESTERN TOUCH

    by Rick Cunningham 91

END-OF-SUMMER GRILL by Jay Harlow 99

A SUMMER MENU FOR FRIENDS

    by Rachel Gardner and Catherine Pantsios 103

SUMMER DINNER MENU by Peggy Knickerbocker 107

A SUMMER CHINESE DINNER by Harry and Eloise Lee 111

A SIMPLE SOUTHWESTERN DINNER FOR A SUMMER'S EVE

    by Deborah Madison 115

MENU FOR FRIENDS by Jeremiah Tower 120

MY OWN BIRTHDAY DINNER by Mary Risley 125

WEST VIRGINIA SUMMER SUPPER

    by Jacquelyn Buchanan-Palmer 129

SUMMER SUPPER AFTER THEATER OR BALLET

    by René Verdon 133

AN OREGON SUMMER'S MEAL FOR THE BEST OF FRIENDS

    by Allison Rodman 137

F A L L

A BENEVOLENT BREAKFAST MENU by Marion Cunningham 145

AN EARLY-FALL LUNCH by Laurie Schley 149

AN AUTUMN MENU FOR FRIENDS by Paul Bertolli 154

FAVORITE FLAVORS FOR FRIENDS by Amey B. Shaw 161

OUR SUNDAY DINNER MENU by Donna Grace Nicoletti 166

AN EARLY-FALL SUPPER by David Zafferelli 173

AN AMBITIOUS DINNER FOR FOUR by Judy Rodgers 179

A WINNING COMBINATION by Bradley M. Ogden 183

A FALL AFTERNOON GARDEN REVERIE

    by Ina Chun and Doug Gosling 189

A MENU FOR FAMILY AND FRIENDS by Rick O'Connell 196

GOING WILD FOR DINNER by Sammie Daniels 199

FALL MENU FOR FRIENDS SERVED AT HOME by Todd Muir 203

A HALLOWEEN DINNER by David Pellerito 208

A COLD-WEATHER DINNER by Carol Brendlinger 213

A DINNER AT HOME WITH FRIENDS by Fred Halpert 217

WINTER

A HOLIDAY BREAKFAST
by Phillip Quattrociocchi and Roberta Klugman 225

A SIMPLE MENU OF FAVORITE TASTES by John Schmidt 229

A WINTER LUNCHEON FOR GOOD FRIENDS
by Stanley Eichelbaum 233

A HEARTY WINTER LUNCH by Ron Clark 238

A SAVORY WINTER MENU by Nancy Jenniss Oakes 241

A LIVELY-FLAVORED MENU FOR FRIENDS by Karen A. Lucas 247

DINNER FOR A LOVED ONE by Joyce Goldstein 252

AN UNINTIMIDATING DINNER FOR FRIENDS
by Connie McCole 257

AN ITALIAN COUNTRY DINNER by Licia Demeo 262

A CONVIVIAL MENU by Annie Somerville 267

A WINTER DINNER FOR DEAR FRIENDS by Laura Chenel 272

A WINTER MEXICAN DINNER PARTY
by Heidi Insalata Krahling 277

A WINTER SUPPER FOR SOMEONE SPECIAL
by Robert C. Schneider 283

A NEW YEAR'S DAY DINNER by Chuck Phifer 288

AN EASTERN EUROPEAN DINNER by Amaryll Schwertner 291

INDEX 297

FOREWORD

Among the myriad problems faced by people with AIDS, getting meals is among the most critical. I understood this only after I watched a friend die and learned firsthand that there was no meal service for anyone stricken by this terrible disease.

I was compelled to launch Project Open Hand. Since the fall of 1985, the program has served two meals daily to anyone diagnosed with AIDS or ARC who has appealed to us for help.

From the beginning I wanted the meals to be an expression of the love I felt for my friend and by extension for all those living with this disease in the firm belief that love in itself is healing.

Ruth Brinker
Project Open Hand
San Francisco, California

PREFACE

This is a book of friendship and love. All of the contributors have shared generously — from their hearts — their gifts of cuisine to help those living with AIDS.

In our home there is a wall of photographs of open hands, taken over the years, to remind us each day to love and let go, to hold on to nothing and to recognize that our purpose here on earth is to reach out and help one another.

Project Open Hand is an organization that embodies these principles. Its mission is to provide meals to people with AIDS who have difficulty marketing and preparing meals for themselves. How appropriate it is that a share of the proceeds from this book will go to Project Open Hand to continue the circle of love.

This is a book about caring and giving. Let it inspire all of us to live each day resolved not to let fear impede our being compassionate and loving to each other. May *The Open Hand Cookbook* help to focus our lives on giving, loving, and forgiving so that we may be reminded that to give is to receive.

Gerald Jampolsky, M.D.
Diane V. Cirincione
The Center for Attitudinal Healing
Tiburon, California

EDITOR'S INTRODUCTION

The menus and recipes that comprise this collection have been contributed by some of California's most gifted chefs. They've been submitted in response to a request for a meal for good friends, a theme chosen to mirror the compassion and comfort so evident in the Open Hand program.

Cooking for loved ones can be an inspiring experience. It presents the opportunity to achieve another dimension of nourishment, something more elusive and subtle than simply the nutritional components of food. Good food prepared with love and care promotes health and well-being.

All of the contributors were free to select the season and setting for their menu. The unifying characteristics of these diverse menus are an emphasis on the impeccable freshness of ingredients; a straightforward approach in the manner of preparation; and an appreciation for natural, unadulterated tastes.

It's interesting to note that a number of the chefs have relied on such soul-satisfying dishes as polenta and risotto, where the hand preparing the dish is of greater importance in its execution than the ingredients. After all, in its purest form, polenta is simply corn flour and water in the proper proportions. Its true magnificence is imparted by the constant stirring of the cook for as long as it takes to get it to that perfect place.

I've included the menus of some friends and associates who, while not earning their livings as professional chefs, are splendid cooks and are intimately involved with food as growers, producers, writers, and teachers. My heartfelt thanks and appreciation to all of the contributors for sharing their creative processes with us, and to the volunteers and staff of Project Open Hand for their unabashed magnificence.

I wish to thank my friends for their encourage-
ment with this project and particularly Douglas
Chouteau, John Ferrone, John Fremont, and
Antonia Lamb. Special thanks to Michael Katz,
Deborah Zemke, and Bill Grose, and to Ted
Gietzen for his invaluable assistance.

Some Notes on Ingredients: For the most part, the
ingredients called for in these recipes are available in many markets. Some of the more exotic
salad greens can be difficult or impossible to find
at certain times of the year. If gardening is in
your blood, there is great satisfaction to be de-
rived from presenting a bountiful bowl of tender
greens, freshly picked from your window box
or backyard plot. Those items less common can
usually be found in major metropolitan areas,
especially in the appropriate ethnic market. One
of the most interesting aspects of cooking can be
locating a fine source or grower for the ingredients one desires. Time and patience are necessary to make this a rewarding endeavor. If
you're unfamiliar with certain ingredients, take
the time to do a little research. Finally, remember Escoffier: "Stay simple, cook simply."

Robert C. Schneider
Mendocino, California

S P R I N G

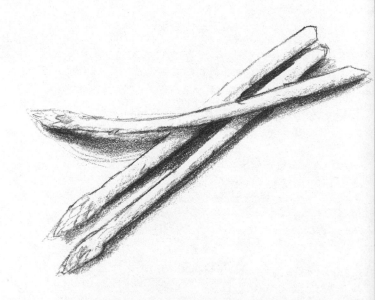

A COASTAL BREAKFAST PICNIC
by Heidi Haughy Cusick

Strawberry-Orange Smoothie

Spanish Potato Tortilla

Fruited Muffins

Coffee with Cream

serves four

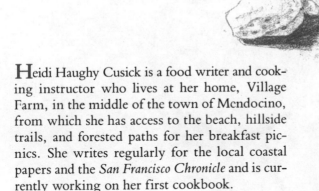

Heidi Haughy Cusick is a food writer and cooking instructor who lives at her home, Village Farm, in the middle of the town of Mendocino, from which she has access to the beach, hillside trails, and forested paths for her breakfast picnics. She writes regularly for the local coastal papers and the *San Francisco Chronicle* and is currently working on her first cookbook.

"A breakfast picnic begins with a short walk to a peaceful setting, usually on the Mendocino headlands overlooking the surf, or directly on the beach. The blanket is spread and the food laid out, the newspaper unrolled and the coffee poured. Paper plates are filled with the bounty from the basket, and a serenity falls that usually makes us wish we'd left the news at home.

"In the crisp air of morning the vitality of a new day is felt. We share our dreams, our schedules for the day, and the knife for spreading cream cheese on the muffins."

STRAWBERRY-ORANGE SMOOTHIE
serves four

Smoothies can be made with peaches, nectarines, pineapple, or any soft fruit that is in season. Just puree, add a little of your favorite juice, and enjoy.

1 ripe banana, peeled
2 oranges, peeled
10 strawberries
1/2 cup frozen orange
  juice concentrate
1½ cups water

1- ½ C orange juice

Cut banana into chunks and put in food processor. Puree. Section oranges, remove seeds, add to banana, and puree. Add strawberries and puree again.

Pour in frozen orange juice concentrate and blend for 30 seconds. Add water and blend for 60 seconds. Pour into thermos and pack.

SPANISH POTATO TORTILLA
serves four

This is a pretty basic tortilla, that wonderful tapa found on the bars in Spain and Portugal. You may add sliced artichoke hearts, tomatoes, ham, or any herbs that you love. It's delicious hot or cold, which is great because it can be made the night before.

Heat the oil in a 10- to 12-inch skillet until it is very hot. Add the potato slices, one at a time so they don't stick. Sprinkle with a little salt and turn to coat all the potatoes with oil. Continue cooking, turning occasionally, until the potatoes brown lightly. Add the onion and red pepper rings, reduce heat to medium, and cook until everything is tender, 6 to 8 minutes. Stir occasionally. Transfer potatoes, onions and peppers to a colander set over a bowl. Drain off excess (onion-flavored) oil, and reserve. Sprinkle the potatoes with salt.

Beat the eggs in a mixing bowl and add a little salt, the pepper, and chopped basil leaves. Gently stir in the potatoes, onion, and red pepper.

Heat 3 tablespoons of the reserved oil in the skillet. Pour in the egg mixture and spread the potatoes around evenly. Cook over moderate heat for about 2 minutes. Shake pan to prevent sticking. When tortilla is firm but not dry, cover the skillet with a flat plate and invert it onto the plate. Slide tortilla gently back into the pan, and cook for 3 minutes longer to brown the other side. Flip it back onto a plastic or heavy plate. Garnish with chopped parsley. For the picnic, cool slightly or overnight, seal in plastic wrap, and pack.

3/4 cup olive oil
3 large potatoes, peeled and sliced into 1/4-inch rounds
1 to 2 teaspoons salt
1 large onion, thinly sliced
1 red pepper, cored and thinly sliced into rings
4 large eggs
Freshly ground pepper
10 basil leaves
Freshly chopped parsley

FRUITED MUFFINS *makes 12 muffins*

I love bagels and cream cheese and homemade huckleberry jam on breakfast picnics, but these little gems are so moist and delicious, they are always a hit, especially with my kids.

1/2 cup boiling water
3/4 cup dried apricots, chopped
1/4 cup figs, chopped
1/2 cup prunes, chopped
2 eggs
3/4 cup milk
1/3 cup safflower oil
1/2 cup chopped walnuts, optional
2 cups unbleached flour
1/4 cup sugar
1 tablespoon baking powder
2 teaspoons cinnamon
1 teaspoon allspice
1/2 teaspoon salt

Preheat oven to 400° F. Grease muffin tin or line with paper liners.

Pour boiling water over apricots, figs, and prunes in a mixing bowl and set aside to plump.

Combine eggs, milk, oil, fruit mixture, and nuts in a large bowl. In another bowl, combine flour, sugar, baking powder, cinnamon, allspice, and salt. Make a well in the center of dry ingredients and add liquids all at once. Mix just until combined. Fill muffin tins 3/4 full.

Bake 20 to 25 minutes or until toothpick comes out clean. Remove muffins from tin and let cool on wire rack. Pack in plastic bag and take to the picnic.

A SPRING BREAKFAST WITH FRIENDS
by Lindsey Shere

Fresh Fruit Bowl

Orange Juice or Mimosa

Finnish Pancake

Real Maple Syrup

Homemade Jam or Preserves

Café au Lait

serves four

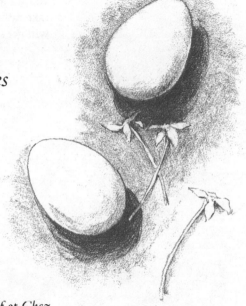

Lindsey Shere has been the pastry chef at *Chez Panisse* in Berkeley, California, since it opened seventeen years ago. She is the author of *Chez Panisse Desserts* (Random House, 1985) and co-owner of the *Downtown Bakery and Creamery* in Healdsburg, California.

"My husband and I lead very busy lives so our entertaining is usually done at the restaurant. But often the only time we can get together with friends is at breakfast, and this is a menu we have served many times. The Finnish pancake has been a family favorite with both children and grown-ups for thirty years and comes from the old Sunset book Cooking Bold and Fearless. *We usually also serve a bowl of seasonal fruit and fresh-squeezed orange juice with or without champagne."*

FINNISH PANCAKE *serves four*

3 eggs
2 cups milk
1/4 cup honey (preferably)
  or sugar
3/4 cup flour
1/4 teaspoon salt
4 tablespoons butter

Beat eggs and milk together. Beat in honey or sugar, then flour and salt. Melt the butter in a 9-inch iron frying pan until it sizzles, and immediately pour the batter into the hot pan in a circle around the center so butter will be pushed to the top and sides. Bake in a preheated oven at 425° F for 25 to 30 minutes or until the pancake is set and puffed and golden brown on top. Serve with maple syrup or homemade jam or preserves. If you want to serve more people, bake another pancake rather than making a larger one so everyone will get some of the crusty edges.

SPRING INTO SUMMER LUNCHEON by Jane Benet

Mussels in White Wine

Pepper-Stuffed Chicken Breasts

Oven-Fried Potatoes

Salad of Mixed Greens with Vinaigrette and Nuts

Lemon Meringue Pie

serves six

Jane Benet served as food editor of the *San Francisco Chronicle* for thirty-five years until 1988. She currently pursues a career as a food consultant and freelance food writer.

"My greatest pleasure is cooking good food for people I love, for family members and good friends. Feeding them is really what cooking is all about in my book, at least for home cooks.

"This meal is a particularly satisfying one to prepare and serve because it features such a diversity of favorite flavors. The mussels offer a deliciously subtle introduction, then the oven-fried potatoes are the perfect foil for the chicken dish because they are best used to sop up all the good juices.

"The salad can be as simple or as elaborate as desired. It will be equally good as a simple mixture of assorted lettuces, or with the addition of watercress, arugula, frisée, dandelion greens, or red mustard leaves. A bit of crumbled goat cheese makes a splendid addition. The dressing should be about four parts good olive oil to one part mild wine vinegar, and lightly seasoned with salt and pepper. It's nice, on occasion, to use walnut oil for the dressing and top the salad with a few toasted walnuts. Or use hazelnut oil and toasted hazelnuts.

"The lemon pie is the ideal dessert for the season, since it is both light and refreshing and serves as the bridge from spring to summer's fresh-fruit bounty."

MUSSELS IN WHITE WINE
serves six as first course

enlued

2 to 3 tablespoons butter
4 leeks, thinly sliced
2 shallots, peeled and
   sliced
Salt and pepper to taste
2 cups dry white wine
36 live mussels
1 cup heavy cream
Pinch of saffron
Crusty French bread

Melt butter over low to medium heat in a wide, shallow sauté pan that has a tight-fitting lid. Clean leeks, slice, and add to pan with the shallots. Turn to coat with butter, salt and pepper to taste, and then cover tightly and let "sweat" for about 10 minutes. Add wine and simmer, covered, about 10 more minutes.

Scrub and debeard mussels, add to pan, cover, and steam until they open. Remove mussels to very hot soup plates and keep warm. Bring contents of pan to a rolling boil. Add cream and saffron and cook for about 5 minutes, stirring. Ladle sauce over the mussels and serve immediately with crusty French bread to sop up the juices.

PEPPER-STUFFED CHICKEN BREASTS *serves six*

Pat chicken dry, place between sheets of plastic wrap, and pound out as nearly flat as possible. Arrange, smooth side down, on plastic and set aside. Preheat oven to 425° F.

Melt butter over medium to low heat in a sauté pan that has a tight-fitting lid. Add onion, cover, and "sweat" until barely tender, stirring a few times. Remove from heat and add peppers, capers, and half the cheese, combining well.

Divide mixture among chicken breasts, placing on uneven side, but don't cover completely. Overlap sides to make open-ended rolls. Place seam-side down in a buttered baking dish. Pour in vermouth, then sprinkle remaining Parmesan over each breast. Bake for 15 to 20 minutes, depending on size of chicken pieces. Remove to warmed plates and spoon pan juices over all.

Note: When prepared with oven-fried potatoes, these go on the upper rack above potatoes for the last 15 to 20 minutes of the potatoes' cooking time.

6 half chicken breasts, skinned and boned
3 tablespoons butter
1 small red onion, finely chopped
3 roasted red bell peppers, peeled, seeded, and chopped
3 teaspoons capers, drained and chopped
3 heaping tablespoons freshly grated Parmesan cheese
1/2 cup dry vermouth or chicken stock

OVEN-FRIED POTATOES

Allow one baking potato per person. Scrub, then cut each into eighths, lengthwise. Place wedges on a baking sheet, skin-side down, and sprinkle lightly with salt and pepper (cumin is good too). Place on lower rack of preheated 425° F oven and bake for 1 hour.

Note: These are great for sopping up juices from the chicken breasts.

LEMON MERINGUE PIE *serves eight*

1 baked 9- or 10-inch pie
   crust (see below)
1⅓ cups sugar
6 tablespoons cornstarch
2½ cups cold water
4 large egg yolks
2 tablespoons butter
1 teaspoon vanilla
Grated rind of 2 lemons
1/2 cup fresh lemon juice
Meringue (see below)

Combine sugar, cornstarch, and cold water in a medium-sized saucepan. Cook together until clear and bubbling, stirring all the while with a large whisk. Add egg yolks, butter, and vanilla. When bubbling again, add lemon rind and juice and stir well to combine all thoroughly. Pour filling into baked pie shell and top with meringue. Bake in a preheated 250° F oven until golden brown. Cool before serving.

1 cup all-purpose or
   unbleached flour
1 teaspoon sugar
1/4 teaspoon salt
1/2 cup shortening
   (lard is excellent)
1/4 cup cold water,
   or as needed

Pie Crust
Combine dry ingredients in a mixing bowl. Add shortening and cut it into the dry ingredients with a pastry cutter or two knives until it is in lumps the size of tiny green peas. Now add the water, stirring the dough to make sure it is of handling consistency. The amount of water may vary, but it is better to have the dough a tiny bit too moist rather than too dry. Wrap the pastry in plastic and allow to rest in the refrigerator for 40 minutes.

Preheat the oven to 400° F. Roll out the dough on a floured surface to a circle to fit a 9- or 10-inch pie pan, with enough extra around the edge to double back and make a stand-up edge for the crust, which should be fluted or crimped to make it stand above the edge of the pan. Prick the pastry all over with the tines of a fork, then line it with a sheet of foil, which in turn should be filled with beans, rice, or pie weights to cover the surface. Bake for 15 minutes, then remove foil and weights and return the shell to the oven and bake until golden, about 5 to 10 minutes longer.

Meringue

4 large egg whites
Pinch of salt
1/4 cup granulated sugar
1 teaspoon vanilla

Beat egg whites with salt until creamy. Add sugar gradually, beating all the while, then add the vanilla and beat until mixture stands in good peaks but is not dry. When spreading on pie, smooth it down to the edge of the crust all around so it won't shrink away as it cooks.

A MEAL FOR FRIENDS WITH SPRING FEVER
by Cindy Pawlcyn

Asparagus Risotto

Swordfish Braised with Baby Leeks and Tarragon

Gratin of Baby Artichokes

Strawberries with Sweetened Crème Fraîche

serves four

Cindy Pawlcyn has been working in professional kitchens since she was thirteen years old. She is currently executive chef and owner of five California restaurants, *Tra Vigne* and *Mustards Grill* in the Napa Valley, *Fog City Diner* and *Roti* in San Francisco and the *Rio Grill* in Carmel.

"This menu was prepared for friends with spring fever. The asparagus for the risotto should preferably be pencil-thin. I had originally planned to grill the swordfish, but it was raining too hard to start the grill so I braised the fish with baby leeks and fresh tarragon instead. The season's first strawberries were a treat for dessert."

ASPARAGUS RISOTTO *serves four*

2 tablespoons good
  olive oil
1/4 cup minced shallots
  or scallions
2 cups Arborio rice
1/2 cup dry white wine
3 cups water
1½ to 2 pounds pencil-
  thin asparagus, cut into
  2-inch pieces
Salt and white pepper
  to taste
2 tablespoons minced
  fresh mint
2 tablespoons minced
  chives
Grated Parmesan cheese

Heat the olive oil in a heavy-bottomed pan and add the shallots or scallions. Stir while cooking 2 to 3 minutes over medium heat, to soften without coloring. Add rice and stir to coat with oil. Add wine and cook till reduced, stirring constantly. Add the water one cup at a time and cook until absorbed. When adding the last cup of water, also add asparagus and remaining seasonings. Cook until liquid is absorbed and asparagus are crisp-tender.

Pour into bowls, sprinkle with freshly grated Parmesan, or let the guests grate their own over each bowl.

SWORDFISH BRAISED WITH BABY LEEKS AND TARRAGON *serves four*

**4 swordfish steaks
1 to 1½ inches thick
(approximately 7-ounce
portions)**

Combine all ingredients, mix well, and pour over swordfish steaks, coating both sides well. Marinate for 30 minutes.

Marinade:
**2 tablespoons finely
minced fresh lemon
grass
2 cloves garlic, peeled and
minced
Salt and fresh, coarsely
ground black pepper
to taste
1/4 cup olive oil
Juice of 1 lemon or lime
2 tablespoons fresh
tarragon, chopped
2 tablespoons fresh
parsley, chopped**

Drain excess marinade from swordfish. Melt 2½ tablespoons butter, and when it begins to foam, cook the fish for 2½ minutes per side. When turning the fish, add the leeks, let them soften a bit, and add the wine. When the wine comes to a boil, remove the fish to a large heated platter. To the wine and leeks, add the tarragon, salt, pepper, and 1½ tablespoons butter. Let butter melt into reducing wine, then pour over the fish.

**4 tablespoons unsalted
butter
Sauté pan large enough
for steaks to lie flat
(or use 2 pans)
6 baby or 2 large leeks,
well washed and
drained, cut into rings
1 cup white wine
2 to 3 tablespoons
tarragon, chopped
Salt and pepper to taste**

GRATIN OF BABY ARTICHOKES
serves four

2 tablespoons good
  olive oil
1/2 cup white wine
1/2 cup water
Salt to taste
Cracked white pepper-
  corns to taste
3 bay leaves
3 parsley sprigs
12 small artichokes
1 lemon
1/2 cup bread crumbs
1/2 cup grated Parmesan
  cheese
2 tablespoons minced
  Italian parsley
2 tablespoons butter

In a large pot, combine olive oil, wine, water, salt, cracked peppercorns, bay leaves, and parsley sprigs. Bring to a boil.

Peel back 4 to 6 outer leaves on artichokes and trim the bottom, then cut in half. Rub with a cut lemon to prevent darkening. Cook in wine/water mixture until knife tip will pierce heart without resistance. Drain and keep warm.

Butter an oven-proof gratin dish and place artichokes cut-side up in one layer. Combine bread crumbs, Parmesan, and minced parsley and sprinkle over artichokes, then dot with butter. Place under the broiler until golden and crispy, about 5 minutes.

STRAWBERRIES WITH SWEETENED CRÈME FRAÎCHE *serves four*

1 cup heavy whipping
  cream
3 tablespoons buttermilk
Sugar to taste
Vanilla extract
1 quart strawberries

Mix the cream and buttermilk well and let sit one night at room temperature. Mix in sugar to taste and a couple drops of vanilla extract. Beat until lightly thickened. Clean berries, and if they are large, cut in half. Mix well with the cream and serve in large bowls with large spoons. Your favorite chocolate cookies would be a nice complement.

CRABCAKES ON GREEN SALAD
serves six

1 pound fresh crab meat
1/2 cup garlic mashed
   potatoes (see below)
1/4 cup chopped chives
1 egg, beaten
Salt (if needed)
Cayenne pepper (until
   you can just taste it
   after a second or two)
1 cup freshly made bread
   crumbs
1/4 pound butter, clarified

3/4 pound Idaho or
   Kennebec potatoes
Salt to taste
3 cloves garlic
4 tablespoons butter

1 head baby escarole
2 heads young frisée
1 head of young red
   leaf lettuce
1 head of curly green
   leaf lettuce
Big handful of arugula
Any other young, small-
   leafed lettuces you wish

1/2 cup minced shallots
1/2 cup sherry vinegar
   (La Bodega sherry
   vinegar preferred)
1/2 teaspoon salt or to taste
Freshly ground pepper
1 cup light olive oil
1/2 cup extra virgin olive oil

Mix together crab meat, only 1/2 cup of the garlic mashed potatoes, chives, egg, salt, and cayenne. Add a scant 1/2 cup of the bread crumbs. The mixture should just hold together without being pasty. Form them into cakes about 1/2 inch thick and as large in diameter as you want them. Bread them generously in the remaining fresh bread crumbs. Sauté slowly in clarified butter until the outsides are golden and the insides are warm all the way through. Place cakes on a large, deep platter of assorted greens dressed in sherry-shallot vinaigrette.

Garlic Mashed Potatoes
Peel potatoes and cut into chunks. Cover with water, add salt and garlic. Bring to a boil and simmer until potatoes are soft.

Drain off all but 1/8 inch of water using a pot top to keep potatoes from falling out, saving some of the cooking water. Mash the potatoes and cooked cloves of garlic with butter. Add salt to taste. They should be moist mashed potatoes; add a little of the cooking water to thin them out if necessary.

Green Salad
Rinse and dry greens completely. Toss them in sherry-shallot vinaigrette so the leaves are coated and no dressing is left in the bottom of the bowl.

Sherry Vinegar-Shallot Vinaigrette
Combine first four ingredients in a large bowl. Whisk in olive oils and adjust seasoning.

A MOTHER'S DAY MENU
by Patricia Unterman

Crabcakes on Green Salad

Grilled Pacific Salmon

Italian Broccoli

Lemon Sponge Custard with Fresh Berry Sauce and Cream

serves six

Patricia Unterman is a chef and co-owner of the *Hayes Street Grill* in San Francisco. She also writes restaurant reviews for the *San Francisco Chronicle*. She is coauthor of four editions of *Restaurants of San Francisco*, a restaurant guide published by Chronicle Books.

"This is a Sunday-afternoon meal I serve every year on Mother's Day to a small group of friends who are mothers, their husbands, and kids. I choose only the foods I personally love, even if they don't quite go together, because it is Mother's Day, and I get to celebrate too. Since the occasion falls in the beginning of May, the menu stays almost the same year after year. There's always the first local salmon, bitter Italian broccoli or fresh fava beans, and a salad of many greens. Dessert is a bit of a problem because hanker after the first juicy fruits of summer, which haven't arrived. So my husband contributes his specialty, Lemon Sponge Custard made with Meyer lemons, a recipe straight out of Joy of Cooking, *and it hits the spot. Over each beautiful square he pours heavy cream and wild Oregon blackberry syrup. We have jars of it in the pantry a jelly that failed."*

GRILLED PACIFIC SALMON

Have your fishmonger cut 7-ounce portions of Pacific salmon filet. I like to grill it in my fireplace on a Tuscan grill over an oak-wood fire. It certainly can be done on an outdoor barbecue.

Make a hot fire but let it die down a little so it won't flame when you put the salmon on the grill. Brush the salmon with a little olive oil. Grill it bone-side down for about 4 minutes, then very gently loosen it with a spatula and flip over. Grill only until the fish warms all the way through. It should still be translucent in the center. It will keep cooking after you take it off the grill. Put it on a warm platter.

ITALIAN BROCCOLI

entered

Try to find small, perky stalks of Italian broccoli and trim off lower stems. We just use the upper third of the stalks with tiny flowers and the tender leaves. Like spinach, you put a huge pile of it in a pan and it melts down.

Heat up a generous amount of light olive oil in a large sauté pan. Throw in a tablespoon of finely minced garlic. Cook until just aromatic. Don't let it burn. Add lots of broccoli so it mounds up in the pan, some salt, and a pinch of hot red pepper flakes. Toss the broccoli in the oil and add about 1/2 cup of chicken stock. Bring to a boil, cover, and turn down heat and cook until broccoli is tender and not mushy. This can take anywhere from 5 to 10 minutes depending on the size of the broccoli and the amount of it in the pan. Italian broccoli should not be al dente. Taste the broccoli for salt. Put in a warm bowl and sprinkle with extra virgin olive oil. There should be lots of garlic, olive oil, and hot red peppers in the broccoli.

LEMON SPONGE CUSTARD *serves six*

3/4 cup sugar
1½ tablespoons butter
2 teaspoons grated
  lemon rind
3 eggs, separated
3 tablespoons flour
1/4 cup lemon juice
1 cup milk

Cream together sugar, butter, and lemon rind. Add egg yolks and beat well. Stir in flour a little at a time, alternating with lemon juice and milk. Beat egg whites until stiff but not dry and fold them into the mixture. Place the batter in a buttered 7-inch dish and set it in a pan filled with an inch of hot water. Bake at 350° F for about 1 hour, until set. Serve warm or cold with heavy cream and fresh berry sauce.

Fresh Berry Sauce
Put a pint of ripe blackberries, raspberries, or boysenberries into a sieve and press out their juice. Put the juice in a food processor and add sugar to taste. Process for a good half minute or so, to dissolve the sugar.

AN INFORMAL EAST-WEST SPRING LUNCHEON
by Ken Hom

Rice Paper Shrimp Rolls

Double Coriander-Ginger Light Cream Soup

5-Spice Roast Squabs with Rice-Wine and Butter Sauce

Curry Couscous with Fresh Chives

Green Salad with Sesame and Walnut Oil Dressing

Warm Chinese Pear-Apple Compote with Candied Ginger à la Mode

serves four to six

Ken Hom is the author of *Ken Hom's East Meets West Cuisine* (Simon and Schuster, 1987), *Ken Hom's Chinese Cookery* (Harper and Row, 1986), *Chinese Technique* (Simon and Schuster, 1981), and *Asian Vegetarian Feast* (William Morrow, 1988). His television series, *Ken Hom's Chinese Cookery*, has been shown throughout the world. Born in America, Ken Hom speaks several languages, studied medieval art history, and was formerly a professional photographer and freelance television producer. He divides his time between Berkeley, California, and Paris, France.

"This is a menu I would cook for my good friends. It is light, tasty, and enormous fun because I usually serve the spring rolls in the kitchen with champagne and then we go to the dining room for the rest of the meal with wines. This menu lends itself very well to informal dining, a casual part of the California scene."

RICE PAPER SHRIMP ROLLS
serves four to six   ✓

2 tablespoons kosher salt
16 medium–sized fresh
  shrimp, peeled and
  deveined
Salt and freshly ground
  pepper to taste
1 tablespoon olive oil
3 tablespoons fresh
  tarragon leaves
3 tablespoons freshly
  chopped scallions
3 tablespoons finely
  chopped sun–dried
  tomatoes
1-pound package Banh
  Trang rice paper
  rounds (available in
  Asian groceries)
2 cups peanut oil

Fill a large bowl with cold water, add 1 tablespoon of kosher salt, and gently wash the shrimp in the salt water. Drain and repeat the process. Then rinse the shrimp under cold running water, drain, and blot them dry with paper towels.

Combine the shrimp with the salt, pepper, olive oil, tarragon leaves, scallions, and sun-dried tomatoes. Mix well, and let the mixture sit in the refrigerator for about 1 hour, covered with plastic wrap.

When you are ready to make the spring rolls, fill a large bowl with warm water. Dip a rice paper round in the water and let it soften a few seconds. Remove and drain on a linen towel.

Place one shrimp with about 1 teaspoon of the filling on the edge of the rice paper. Roll the edge over the shrimp and filling at once, fold up both ends of the rice paper, and continue to roll to the end. The roll should be compact and tight, rather like a short, thick finger cigar about 3 inches long. Set it on a clean plate and continue the process until you have used up all the mixture. The spring rolls can be made ahead to this point; cover with plastic wrap and refrigerate for up to 4 hours.

Heat the peanut oil in a wok or deep frying pan until it is moderately hot, about 350° F, and deep-fry the spring rolls a few at a time. They have a tendency to stick to one another at first, so do only a few at a time. Drain the spring rolls on paper towels and serve at once. Makes 16 spring rolls.

DOUBLE CORIANDER-GINGER LIGHT CREAM SOUP *serves four to six*

Heat the butter, peanut oil, and sesame oil in a large sauté pan. Sauté the scallions, ginger, and shallots gently without browning for about 8 minutes. Add the ground coriander, sugar, chicken stock, salt and pepper. Mix well, bring the mixture to a simmer, and cook for 5 minutes. Remove from heat.

Stir in the heavy cream, fresh coriander, and chives. Ladle the soup into a blender in small batches and process until completely smooth. Slowly reheat the soup, add the butter pieces, stir well. Ladle the mixture into a soup tureen or individual bowls, garnish with coriander leaves, and serve at once.

2 tablespoons unsalted butter
2 teaspoons peanut oil
1 teaspoon Chinese sesame oil
1/2 cup finely chopped scallions
2 tablespoons finely chopped fresh ginger
1/2 cup finely chopped shallots
2 teaspoons ground coriander
1 tablespoon sugar
4 cups chicken stock
Salt and freshly ground pepper to taste
1/2 cup heavy cream
1/2 cup finely chopped fresh coriander (cilantro)
4 tablespoons finely chopped fresh chives
2 tablespoons unsalted butter, cut into small pieces
Fresh coriander leaves for garnish

5-SPICE ROAST SQUABS WITH RICE-WINE AND BUTTER SAUCE
serves four to six

4 to 6 squab or Cornish
  game hens, 12 to 14
  ounces each
1 tablespoon sesame oil

Marinade:
1 tablespoon 5-spice
  powder
2 teaspoons kosher salt
1 teaspoon Sichuan
  peppercorns, roasted
  and finely ground
2 tablespoons finely
  chopped orange zest

Sauce:
1/2 cup chicken stock
1/2 cup rice wine or dry
  sherry
2 tablespoons cold butter,
  cut into small pieces
2 tablespoons finely
  chopped scallions

Butterfly the squab by splitting them open along each side of the spine. Remove and discard the backbone. Flatten them out with the palm of your hand. Make two small holes on either side of the breastbone, and tuck their legs through. This will help hold the shape of the birds while they roast. Rub them with the sesame oil.

Combine the marinade ingredients and rub the squabs with this mixture. Place them in a flame-proof casserole or baking dish for 1 hour at room temperature. Preheat oven to 400° F. Roast the squab for 30 minutes, skin side up. Remove the squab from the dish and skim off any fat. Place the dish over a burner and deglaze with the chicken stock and rice wine, scraping the bottom of the pan as you stir. Reduce the liquid over high heat until only 1/2 cup is left. Remove the dish from the heat and whisk in the butter and scallions. Spoon a few tablespoons of sauce on individual plates and place the squab on the sauce and serve at once.

CURRY COUSCOUS WITH FRESH CHIVES *serves four to six*

Heat the olive oil in a medium-sized casserole, add the onions, and cook them gently over low heat for about 5 minutes without browning. Add the couscous, mix well, and continue to cook over low heat for another 2 minutes. In a separate pot, combine the stock, soy sauce, butter, curry, and sugar and bring the mixture to a boil. Add this to the couscous mixture. Mix well and remove from the heat. Cover tightly and let sit for about 20 minutes. Remove the lid, stir in the chives and apples, add salt and freshly ground white pepper to taste, and serve at once.

2 tablespoons olive oil
1/2 cup finely chopped onions
2 cups dried couscous
2 cups chicken stock
1 tablespoon dark soy sauce
1 tablespoon unsalted butter
2 tablespoons Madras curry paste or powder
1 teaspoon sugar
1/2 cup finely chopped fresh chives
1/2 cup finely diced peeled Granny Smith apples
Salt and freshly ground white pepper to taste

GREEN SALAD WITH SESAME AND WALNUT OIL DRESSING *serves four to six*

Rinse and thoroughly dry the salad greens. In a medium-sized stainless-steel bowl, combine the shallots, vinegar, salt and pepper. Slowly beat in the sesame and walnut oils. Add the greens and toss thoroughly. Serve at once.

4 to 6 cups young salad greens

Dressing:
3 tablespoons finely chopped shallots
1 tablespoon Chinese white-rice vinegar
Salt and freshly ground black pepper to taste
2 tablespoons Chinese sesame oil
2 tablespoons walnut oil

WARM CHINESE PEAR-APPLE COMPOTE WITH CANDIED GINGER À LA MODE *serves four*

1 vanilla bean, split in half
2 tablespoons sugar
1/2 cup sugar
1 cup water
2 pounds Chinese pear-apples or pears, peeled, pitted, and sliced
3 tablespoons unsalted butter, cut into small pieces
2 tablespoons finely chopped candied ginger
1 tablespoon lemon juice
1 pint of your favorite vanilla ice cream

Scrape the inside of the vanilla bean and combine with 2 tablespoons sugar and set aside. In a medium-sized skillet, combine the vanilla bean, 1/2 cup sugar, and water. Bring it to a boil and reduce by one-third. Remove the vanilla bean. Add the pear-apples, sugar/vanilla-seed mixture, and simmer for 5 minutes to warm. Whisk in the butter, a few pieces at a time. Then add the candied ginger and lemon juice, mix well, allow to cool slightly. Spoon into serving dishes and top with your favorite vanilla ice cream. Serve at once.

A QUINTESSENTIAL CALIFORNIA SPRING MENU
by Carlo Middione

Penne with Asparagus

Salmon in Parchment

Strawberry Soufflé

serves six

Carlo Middione is the chef/owner of *Vivande Porta Via* in San Francisco and is the author of *The Food of Southern Italy* (William Morrow, 1987).

"Friends must be counted among the essentials of life in the same way that breathing, eating, and making love are. It follows, then, that when you have a chance to be with friends, you can choose to make it a special occasion. Not lavishly, unless it is in the form of genuine friendliness, and not opulently, unless it is abundance of care and love. Then, you can concentrate on just being with your friends and making them comfortable and at ease.

"The following menu is one I have used successfully many times. Since I see my friends all too infrequently, I can serve it more than once . . . it gives them something to look forward to. If you do it often and make it a 'staple,' you can get really good at doing it. It's like playing your favorite Beethoven sonata on the piano, something you can do with confidence."

PENNE WITH ASPARAGUS *serves six*

1 pound thin, fresh
   asparagus
1/4 cup virgin olive oil
2 large garlic cloves,
   peeled, and well
   crushed
1½ pounds tomatoes,
   cored, peeled, and
   well crushed
14 ounces of penne
1 cup grated pecorino
   cheese, plus more
   for the table
2 large eggs
Salt to taste
Plenty of freshly
   ground pepper

Rinse the asparagus well, trim off the bottoms, and cut the tender stalks into 2-inch pieces. Cook it in a large amount of boiling salted water for 4 minutes or so. Drain and reserve, saving the water for later. Heat the olive oil in a large frying pan over medium heat, add the garlic, and fry it until it is deep gold. Add the tomatoes, and stir all the ingredients well. Cook the sauce for about 10 minutes, and keep it hot but not simmering.

Meanwhile, bring the asparagus water back to a boil and cook the penne really al dente. You should be able to actually chew them. When the penne are done, drain them, leaving in just a bit of the cooking water.

Mix the penne and the asparagus together in a large, heated casserole dish. Add the cup of cheese, and mix everything again. Break the eggs into a small dish, beat them lightly, add them to the penne and the asparagus, and mix once more. (Adding the cheese before the eggs creates a kind of insulation to keep the eggs from becoming too hot and curdling.) When you have a nice glossy, well-coated mass of penne, asparagus, cheese, and eggs, add the tomato sauce, and stir everything until it is well blended. Add salt and pepper to taste. Serve the penne on heated plates immediately and pass a bit more grated pecorino cheese at the table.

SALMON IN PARCHMENT *serves six*

Preheat oven to 375° F. Cut 6 pieces of parchment paper roughly 18 by 12 inches and fold the paper to 9 by 12 inches. Lay the parchment papers out so they open like a book. Brush some olive oil on the bottom of each piece and lay the salmon down on the oil very close to the fold, centered. Place a sixth of the zucchini, carrot, and squash alongside salmon. Scatter on the scallions and season with salt and pepper. Lay 2 basil leaves on each piece of salmon and seal the parchment by folding the two open edges of paper together, overlapping to make a tight seal. Aluminum foil is not a substitute for parchment.

Put the packages close together on a baking sheet and bake for about 9 to 11 minutes depending on the thickness of the fish. Put the cooked fish on hot plates off-center. Place a circle of 4 slices of cucumber off to the side and place the lemon crown in the center, or attractively arrange 4 wedges of tomato and some olives in place of the cucumber and lemon. You might even like both. Serve immediately. Each person should open the package by ripping open the top and tearing back the paper, eating out of the parchment.

Serve crusty bread at the table.

Parchment paper

4 tablespoons extra virgin olive oil

2¼ pounds salmon filet, cut into 6 pieces the same size and shape

2 medium zucchini, washed, trimmed, and julienned

1 large carrot, peeled and trimmed, julienned finely

2 yellow crookneck squash, washed, sliced diagonally 1/8 inch thick

2 scallions trimmed and sliced 1/8 inch thick

Salt to taste

Freshly ground black pepper to taste

12 large fresh basil leaves

24 medium slices of English cucumber and

3 lemons made into crowns; or

3 medium-sized tomatoes, cored, peeled, and cut into eighths and

12 or more Gaeta or Kalamata olives

STRAWBERRY SOUFFLÉ *makes six*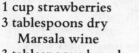
individual soufflés in 4-inch ramekins

1 cup strawberries
3 tablespoons dry
   Marsala wine
3 tablespoons brandy
2 tablespoons sugar, plus
   more for coating
   ramekins
4 egg whites at room
   temperature
4 tablespoons butter,
   or a bit more

Put the strawberries in a small bowl and sprinkle with the Marsala and brandy. Let macerate for about 2 or 3 hours in a warm place. When the fruit is soft, take it out of the bowl and squeeze out the liquid. Chop the fruit fine and put it back into the liquid. Add 1 tablespoon of the sugar and stir.

Place a rack in the lower third of the oven and preheat it to 350° F. Lightly butter six 4-inch tin or ceramic ramekins and dust them with granulated sugar. Set aside. Whisk the egg whites until they are very frothy and sprinkle in 1 tablespoon of sugar. If using a mixer, beat on medium speed to firm but supple peaks. Put about 1/2 cup of egg whites into the fruit mixture to soften it, then fold into the remaining egg whites. Quickly spoon the souffle mixture into the ramekins and put them onto a cookie sheet for easier, safer handling. Bake for 12 to 14 minutes or until they puff and slide up out of the ramekins 1 or 1½ inches above the rim. Quickly serve them or they will begin to deflate. However, if they deflate a little, they are still quite good and look very pretty.

Note: Since there is no roux base, you cannot add more fruit than specified because it will not suspend in the egg white mixture.

AN ELABORATE DINNER FOR FRIENDS
by Hubert Keller

*Chilled Tomato and Red Bell Pepper Soup
with Caviar*

*American Foie Gras and Roasted Apple
with Ginger Sauce*

*Braised Fennel à la Barigoule with
Vegetables and Herbs in Broth*

*Maine Lobster Mousseline with Black Chanterelles
and Flageolets with Lime Sauce*

*Frozen Nougat Flavored with Candied Fruits
and Pureed Mint*

serves four

Hubert Keller is executive chef de cuisine and
managing partner of San Francisco's *Fleur de Lys*
restaurant.

*"This is an elaborate dinner for friends. The menu will appear too generous to some
people, but I really believe that the best dinner party with friends needs a measure of
overflowing food, wine, and festivity.*

*"Once dinner starts and dish follows dish, the wine flows freely, the faces light up, and
the talk gets warmer, you and your friends feel happy sharing a wonderful time around
a table with delicious food and incredible wines."*

CHILLED TOMATO AND RED BELL PEPPER SOUP WITH CAVIAR *serves four*

4 fleshy sweet red bell peppers

3 tablespoons virgin olive oil

1 medium-sized onion, chopped

2 cloves of garlic, chopped

3 tomatoes, peeled, seeded, and chopped

Pinch of thyme

8 fresh basil leaves

1 teaspoon sugar

Salt and freshly ground pepper

1½ quarts white chicken stock

1 tablespoon sherry vinegar

3/4 cup heavy cream

20 watercress leaves for garnish (or 4 pinches chervil)

4 teaspoons beluga caviar or golden caviar

Preheat the broiler, coat the peppers with olive oil, and place them under the broiler and roast, turning frequently until the skin is blackened on all sides. When the peppers are charred, let cool slightly and peel off the black skin. (Peppers can be roasted directly over a gas flame.) Remove the stems, cut the peppers open, and remove the core and seeds. Chop the peppers.

In a medium saucepan, heat remaining 2 tablespoons of olive oil and cook the chopped onion until translucent, about 3 minutes. Add the chopped garlic, tomatoes, bell peppers, thyme, basil, sugar, freshly ground pepper, and salt. Keep cooking slowly for about 5 minutes. Add 1½ quarts of white chicken stock and bring to a boil over high heat. Reduce heat and simmer for 20 minutes. Transfer in batches to a blender and puree until completely smooth. Strain the soup into a mixing bowl, let cool, and set aside in the refrigerator.

Just before serving, stir in the vinegar, cream (if the soup should be too thick, thin it with extra cream), and season to taste with salt and pepper. Ladle the soup into 4 shallow-rimmed soup plates, and sprinkle with the watercress leaves or chervil. Place one teaspoon of caviar in the center of each serving.

AMERICAN FOIE GRAS AND ROASTED APPLE WITH GINGER SAUCE *serves four*

1 each carrot, leek, and celery to flavor the stock
7/8 cup chicken stock
1 foie gras of duck (about 1 pound)
Salt and pepper
1 apple
1 ginger root
Dash of vodka

Peel and slice the onion, carrot, and celery and place in a saucepan with the chicken stock. Boil to reduce by half. Strain and reserve.

Cut the foie gras into 4 slices. Season with salt and pepper. Peel the apple, cut into quarters, then slice thinly. Place the slices on a buttered baking sheet and place under the broiler to brown lightly. Set aside. Peel the ginger and cut it into thin julienne strips.

Fry the slices of foie gras, then remove from the pan and place on a platter. Pour the fat from the pan into a bowl and reserve.

Deglaze the pan with the reduced stock, add the ginger, and boil to reduce still further. At the last minute, bind the sauce with the fat saved from cooking the foie gras, add salt and pepper and the dash of vodka.

Spoon the sauce onto the dinner plates. Place a slice of foie gras on each plate, garnish the plates with the sliced apples, and serve.

BRAISED FENNEL À LA BARIGOULE WITH VEGETABLES AND HERBS IN BROTH *serves four*

1 onion
1 carrot
4 cloves garlic
6 fresh basil leaves
2 stalks celery
3 bulbs fresh fennel,
    quartered lengthwise
5 tablespoons olive oil
3 fresh laurel (bay) leaves
3 sprigs fresh thyme
Salt and freshly ground
    pepper
3 tablespoons sliced
    green olives
1 teaspoon finely
    chopped parsley
1 teaspoon finely
    chopped chives
4 tablespoons chopped
    tomatoes, peeled
    and seeded

Prepare the vegetables, slicing the onion and peeled carrot thinly. Finely chop two of the garlic cloves with the basil leaves. Cut the celery into julienne slices and rinse. Blanch the fennel in boiling, salted water for 2 minutes. Drain, refresh under cold water, and drain again.

Heat the olive oil in a saucepan. Add the onion and bring it to a golden blond color. Add the fennel, the celery, and carrot and cook together for 2 to 3 minutes. Add the laurel leaves, thyme, 2 whole cloves garlic, salt, and freshly ground pepper. Add just enough water to cover the vegetables. Bring to a boil, then lower the heat to barely simmering and continue cooking for 10 to 12 minutes. Add the green olives and continue simmering for 3 to 4 minutes.

Carefully remove the fennel from the broth, transfer it to a warm serving platter, and cover with aluminum foil or waxed paper to keep them hot the time (2 or 3 minutes) that you need to finish the sauce. Add the chopped garlic and basil, parsley, chives, and chopped tomatoes to the broth and bring to a boil over high heat. Stir slightly. Taste and adjust with salt and pepper if necessary. Gently spoon the sauce and vegetables over the fennel. Serve hot, or warm. I always give a spoon to the diners at the table to enjoy the sauce.

This dish has a pretty contrast of colors and a delightful taste that comes from the richness of the olives and the fennel, blended with all the fresh fine herbs and vegetables.

MAINE LOBSTER MOUSSELINE WITH BLACK CHANTERELLES AND FLAGEOLETS WITH LIME SAUCE
serves four

Bring a gallon of water to a boil. Add a bouquet garni, celery stalk, and one onion, peppercorns, and salt. Then poach the lobster for about 9 to 10 minutes. Remove the lobster from the court bouillon. Let the lobster cool, then break it in two, where the tail meets the body. With scissors, cut the soft part of the tail and remove the meat in one piece. Set aside. Break off the claws and carefully crack the shells and remove the meat. Save the lobster shell, the inside scales, and the roe for the lobster sauce.

Lobster Sauce
In a heavy pot, sauté the mirepoix for 5 minutes in 2 tablespoons of butter. Add the lobster shells, inside scales, and the roe, salt, cayenne pepper, and clove of garlic and cook for another 3 minutes. Add the cognac, white wine, a bouquet garni, and chopped tomatoes. Let simmer for 5 minutes and add water (or fish stock) just to cover. Cook slowly for 20 minutes. Strain the broth through a fine sieve into a sauce pot. Reduce the liquid by half and pour in 7 ounces of cream. Bring to a boil and add the chopped tarragon, lower the heat, and continue simmering to get the sauce to the right consistency. Adjust the seasoning.

Preheat oven to 275° F.

Place the flageolets in 1 cup of cold water. Add a pinch of salt, a bouquet garni, and an onion. Bring to a boil, then reduce the heat and allow to simmer for 2 hours or until the flageolets are tender. If the water evaporates during cooking, add boiling water.

3 bouquets garnis: parsley, bay leaves, thyme
1 celery stalk
2 medium onions
1 tablespoon black peppercorns
1 live lobster (1¼ to 1½ pounds)
1 cup ingredients for mirepoix: carrots, onions, celery, and white leeks, each finely diced
8 tablespoons sweet butter
Salt
Cayenne pepper
1 clove garlic
1/4 cup cognac
1 cup white wine
2 tomatoes, seeded and chopped
1½ cups heavy cream
1 tablespoon freshly chopped tarragon
1/2 cup dried green flageolets
6 ounces black chanterelles
1 tablespoon olive oil
1 tablespoon chopped shallots
5 ounces filet of sea bass
1 large egg
White pepper
2 limes: juice and zest
1/2 bunch chervil

(continued next page)

Sauté the black chanterelles in the olive oil over medium-high heat until they expel their liquid, about 3 minutes. Add one tablespoon of chopped shallots, salt, and freshly ground pepper and sauté for 2 more minutes.

Lobster Mousseline
Note: It is most important that all ingredients be thoroughly chilled before mixing.

Place the sea bass in a food processor. Process with about six on/off pulses until the fish is finely chopped. Add 1 whole egg, a dash of salt and white pepper. Mix together well. With the machine running, pour 5 ounces of cream through the feed tube. Season to taste.

Butter 4 soufflé dishes (4 ounces each). Put the mousseline into a pastry bag and squeeze into the molds, leaving a hole in the center. Fill the center with the lobster meat, cut into small pieces, mixed with 4 tablespoons of the lobster sauce. Top with the mousseline and tap gently against the work surface to settle the mixture and eliminate air bubbles. Put the molds in a pan and pour boiling water into the pan to halfway up the molds. Bake for about 20 minutes.

Lime Sauce
In a small sauce pot, mix the lime juice and 3 tablespoons of the broth from the flageolets. Bring to a boil, lower the heat, and whisk in 6 tablespoons of sweet butter, a few pieces at a time. Stir in the black chanterelles, the flageolets, and the lime zest. Check the seasoning.

Have ready four heated plates and pour the hot lime sauce in the center of each plate. Unmold the lobster mousseline and place on top. Garnish with the chervil. This is an extremely pure and clean dish in which you can taste the fine flavors of the lobster married with the taste of flageolets, black chanterelles, and lime.

FROZEN NOUGAT FLAVORED WITH CANDIED FRUITS AND PUREED MINT *serves fifteen*

This recipe should be prepared the day before serving for best results.

Place the 25 ounces of cream in a large mixing bowl and chill in the refrigerator.

In a small sauce pot, bring 3½ ounces of heavy cream to a boil and blanch the mint leaves in it for about 2 minutes. Blend the mixture in a blender until you obtain a bright green liquid. Remove and chill in the refrigerator.

Remove the chilled heavy cream and bowl from the refrigerator and beat with a whisk until whipped. Chill.

Place the egg whites in the bowl of an electric mixer or in a mixing bowl (not plastic or aluminum, and the bowl must be very clean for the eggs to obtain maximum volume). In a small saucepan, combine the sugar with 3½ tablespoons of water. Place the saucepan over low heat. At the same time, begin to beat the egg whites, at first slowly, then faster. Continue to beat the egg whites until stiff, while cooking the syrup until it reaches 250° F, or the soft-ball stage.

Reduce the speed of the beater to low and pour a thin stream of the hot sugar syrup into the egg whites. Continue beating at low speed until the mixture has cooled. Chill. At this point you should have the following: an Italian meringue (egg whites and sugar syrup), whipped cream, a chilled mint cream, and the candied fruit mix.

To assemble, gently fold, with a rubber spatula, the Italian meringue in the whipped cream, adding the fruit mix and the fresh mint cream, and blend together well. Pour the mixture into a terrine, filling the mold to the rim. Smooth the surface with a spatula, cover, and freeze overnight. Just before serving, invert the terrine on a flat, very cold plate and unmold. Slice the nougat with a bread knife and present with a raspberry sauce.

25 ounces + 3½ ounces heavy cream
10 to 12 mint leaves
3½ ounces egg white
7 ounces granulated sugar
7 ounces candied fruit mix

BIRTHDAY BUFFET WITH CHAMPAGNE
by Robert Reynolds

*Walnut Bread**

Goat Cheese and Lentil Spread

*Baked Salmon and Asparagus
with Raspberry Mayonnaise*

*Zucchini Pillows with Sweet
Peppers*

*Orange Genoise with
Strawberries in Red Wine*

serves twelve

*See recipe page 228.

Robert Reynolds is the chef/proprietor of *Le Trou Restaurant Français*. He is also a teacher offering courses and apprenticeships in San Francisco and France. He is coauthor of *From Brittany France to America* with Josephine Araldo (Addison–Wesley, Spring 1990).

"I love the idea of being able to cook at home after spending all my time in the restaurant kitchen. It brings me back to the very basic question of why I like cooking. The answer is the very special pleasure that can be found at the table in the presence of good friends. On my birthday I sent invitations for a buffet, birthday cake, and Saint George Distillery Kiwi Champagne. I wanted to be free to attend my own party so I put everything on the table before everyone arrived. I wanted it to be effortless."

GOAT CHEESE AND LENTIL SPREAD

Dice onions, carrot, and celery root to 1/4-inch mirepoix. Tie celery, parsley, thyme, and bay leaf into a bouquet garni. Put all ingredients including lentils into a large pot and cover with water (or stock). Bring to a boil, reduce heat, and simmer until lentils are done, about 2 hours. Drain lentils, add plenty of minced garlic and chopped parsley while lentils are still warm, then spread out lentils to cool. Place lentils in a bowl, mix in crumbled goat cheese thoroughly, seasoning with salt and pepper and adding olive oil sparingly. Spread on walnut bread or toast.

2 onions
1 carrot
1/2 cup celery root
1 stalk celery
6 sprigs parsley
6 sprigs thyme
1 bay leaf
1/2 pound lentils
Minced garlic
Additional parsley, chopped
1/2 pound goat cheese (e.g. Montrachet or Boucheron)
Salt
Pepper
Olive oil

BAKED SALMON AND ASPARAGUS WITH RASPBERRY MAYONNAISE
serves twelve

Raspberry Mayonnaise:
2 shallots, finely diced
1/2 cup dry white wine
   (or fish stock)
2 tablespoons raspberry
   vinegar, or
2 tablespoons red wine
   vinegar and
8 to 10 fresh raspberries
Salt
1 egg yolk
Freshly ground pepper
3/4 cup mild oil (e.g.,
   corn or peanut oil)
2 tablespoons raspberry
   eau-de-vie

36 stalks asparagus
5 pounds salmon filets,
   cut 2 inches wide into
   at least 12 pieces
Mixed salad greens,
   as available (butter
   lettuce, radicchio,
   redleaf, or arugula)

Put shallots, wine, vinegar (and fruit), and salt into a small saucepan and reduce to a total volume of 3 tablespoons. Put into blender or food processor, adding the egg yolk and freshly ground pepper. Turn machine on and add oil in slow drizzle. Flavor with raspberry eau-de-vie and refrigerate.

Prepare the asparagus by breaking stems, discarding base. Peel remaining stalks to below the tip. Bring enough water to cover asparagus to a boil with some salt. Add the asparagus and bring water back to a boil. Add a cup of cold water and bring water to a third boil. Test for doneness; asparagus should be cooked through but still crisp. If more cooking is required, add another cup of cold water and bring to a boil again. Then rinse under cool water, drain, and spread out to cool.

Preheat oven to 450° F. Arrange salmon filets on buttered surface of flat metal pan allowing space between filets for cooking. Salt very lightly and give a grind of fresh pepper. Set into the hot oven and cook until the flesh shows white, indicating that the albumen natural to fresh fish has cooked. Remove from the oven and allow to cool.

Prepare plates with a bed of salad greens at the center. Place cooked salmon on top of greens, garnish decoratively with asparagus. Use the raspberry mayonnaise as a sauce for the fish and the asparagus.

ZUCCHINI PILLOWS WITH SWEET PEPPERS *serves six*

Butter six 2-ounce ramekins. Lightly salt the peppers and sauté in olive oil until they render their juices and are cooked through. Garnish with garlic and parsley and set aside.

In a nonoxidizing skillet, heat olive oil, and add grated zucchini, onion, and salt. Cook until vegetables give off their liquid and it evaporates. Remove from heat, add ground pepper and 1 to 2 teaspoons herbes de Provence, and set aside to cool. In a mixing bowl, combine the eggs and cream and mix well. Add the cooked zucchini. Measure an equal amount into each buttered mold. Set into a bain-marie in a 300° F oven and cook for 40 minutes until set. Unmold and garnish with sautéed sweet peppers. Serve hot or cold.

2 sweet peppers, peeled and diced
Salt
Olive oil
Minced garlic
Chopped parsley
4 medium-sized zucchini, grated
1 onion, minced
Pepper
Herbes de Provence
3 whole eggs
1 cup heavy cream

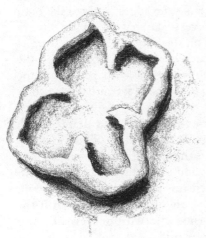

ORANGE GENOISE WITH STRAWBERRIES IN RED WINE
serves twelve

Cake:
6 eggs
1 cup sugar
Pinch of salt
1 cup sifted flour
2 tablespoons cornstarch
4 tablespoons melted
    butter
1/2 cup orange
    marmalade

Lightly butter an 11-by-16-inch sheet-cake pan, line with waxed paper, butter the paper, and dust with flour. Preheat oven to 375° F.

Beat the eggs, sugar, and salt in a mixer with a whip attachment for 10 minutes at high speed. Sift flour and cornstarch together. When eggs are finished whipping, sift 1/3 cup flour onto eggs and fold in carefully, then sift and fold in remaining flour. When completely combined, add melted butter and fold in. Pour batter into cake pan, reduce oven heat to 350° F, and bake for 15 to 20 minutes. Test for doneness by placing your finger on the center of the cake. If it leaves an impression, cake needs more time; if the cake springs back, it is done. Remove it from the oven.

Run a knife around the edges, invert cake onto a rack, then reinvert cake so it sits on the counter with the paper on the bottom. Spread a layer of orange marmalade over the surface and roll the cake while peeling the waxed paper. Wrap the roll in the paper loosely and set onto rack to cool.

Topping:
1 quart strawberries,
    rinsed, hulled, and
    halved
2 tablespoons honey
1/2 cup red wine
3/4 cup whipping cream
1/4 cup sour cream
    (without gelatin)
Grated orange rind

Put strawberries in a bowl and drizzle with honey. Allow to sit for a couple of hours so that the honey draws the liquid from the berries. Just before serving, add the red wine and mix well. Whip the two creams together in another bowl. To serve, top slices of the jelly roll with the strawberries, then the whipped cream, and finally the orange rind.

AN INFORMAL LATE-SPRING DINNER
by Alice Waters

Rocket Salad with Spring Scallions and Onions, Prosciutto, and Sieved Egg

Green Garlic and Potato Soup with Grilled Sourdough Bread

Cherry Compote

serves six

Alice Waters is founder of *Chez Panisse* restaurant in Berkeley, California. She is the author of *Chez Panisse Menu Cookbook* (Random House, 1982). Currently involved with issues relating to sustainable agriculture, she is also working on a children's cookbook.

"When you care about friends and family, you care about what they're eating. The way to ensure freshness, flavor, and purity of produce is to have a little garden of your own.

"I love to go out in the garden to find inspiration for dinner. In June, the rocket in my garden is plentiful and the onions are sweet. So I would begin the meal with those special ingredients. The prosciutto and sieved egg would help marry the flavors and give a little color."

ROCKET SALAD WITH SPRING SCALLIONS AND ONIONS, PROSCIUTTO, AND SIEVED EGG *serves six*

4 red scallions or shallots,
  finely diced
1/4 cup good red wine
  vinegar
Salt to taste
1/4 cup olive oil
6 handfuls rocket
  (arugula)
12 tiny scallions
Black pepper
6 very thin slices of
  prosciutto
4 eggs, hard–boiled
  and sieved

Macerate the diced scallions in the vinegar for 5 minutes with salt. Stir in the olive oil at the last minute (adding more or less depending on how vinegary you like it). Rinse the rocket and dry it well. Put it in a large bowl with the tiny scallions. Add the vinaigrette and freshly ground black pepper and toss gently. Put out on a large platter and garnish with prosciutto slices and sieved egg.

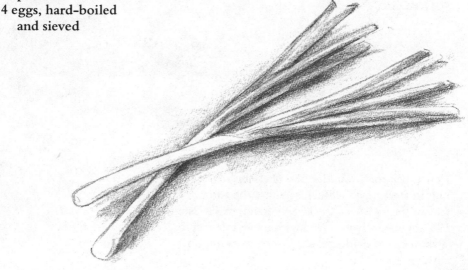

GREEN GARLIC AND POTATO SOUP
serves six

Melt the butter in a 6-quart noncorroding pot. Add the garlic and 1/4 cup of water. Bring to a simmer, cover tightly, and cook for 15 minutes. Then add the potatoes and remaining water and cook at a simmer for another 20 minutes. Add the chicken broth, return the cover to the pot, and allow to bubble gently for 20 minutes more.

Puree the soup in batches for 2 minutes in a blender. Pass it through a medium-fine sieve. Stir in the cream, salt, and pepper. Add the vinegar half a teaspoon at a time, tasting the soup after each addition before you add the next (some vinegars are more acidic and strongly flavored than others).

Reheat the soup gently and serve it in warm bowls with grilled sourdough bread.

2½ tablespoons unsalted butter
12 young garlic plants, 1/2 inch in diameter at the root end, white part only (8 ounces), sliced in half lengthwise
1/2 cup water
1/2 pound small red potatoes, peeled and quartered
3 cups light-bodied chicken broth
1/4 cup heavy cream
1½ teaspoons salt
Freshly ground black pepper
1 to 1½ teaspoons white wine vinegar
Grilled sourdough bread (see below)

Grilled Sourdough Bread
Use a country-style bread with a good crust (*levain* bread, slightly sour if possible). Cut it into 1/4-inch slices and grill over a medium fire on both sides (2 minutes each side, depending on the fire). Remove, drizzle with good olive oil, and rub with a bulb of new garlic.

CHERRY COMPOTE *serves four to six*

2 pounds black and
   yellow cherries
1/4 cup sugar
1 teaspoon kirsch
2 to 3 teaspoons balsamic
   vinegar

Put the cherries in a colander, pick out any bad ones, rinse, and stem. Put them in one layer in a heavy-bottomed, noncorroding sauté pan. If you haven't a pan big enough, cook the cherries in two or more batches. Sprinkle the fruit with the sugar and shake the pan over high heat for about 5 minutes, or until the sugar melts and the cherries feel a little soft when you press them. The sugar will make little white crystals on the cherries before it melts.

Sprinkle the cherries with the kirsch and vinegar and shake them for about 30 seconds longer. Scrape them with their juice into a container and chill or cool to room temperature, then let them stand at least an hour or two.

A SPRING DINNER FOR CLOSE FRIENDS
by Carol Field

Risotto with Artichokes

Arista (Pork Loin) with Rosemary, Garlic, Pepper, and Fennel Seeds

Peperonata

Pugliese Bread

Green Salad

Meyer Lemon Sorbet

serves four to six

Carol Field lives in San Francisco. Her passion for Italy and Italian food has led her to write *The Italian Baker* (Harper and Row, 1985), a compendium of the breads and sweets that come out of the Italian baker's oven, and *The Hill Towns of Italy* (Dutton, 1984), with Richard Kauffman, a book about the towns between Florence and Rome. She is a journalist who writes for a variety of national publications and is presently at work on yet another book about the food and culture of Italy.

"The times I best like cooking for friends are the simple lunches and dinners that usually start with four or six of us sitting in the kitchen talking and drinking a little wine, while I slice and sauté and stir things into simmering pots. What's cooking often depends on what's growing in our little city garden, because I like to make a meal from whatever it yields at the moment.

"There are a couple of different ways that I love to cook for friends. Sometimes I'm really up for spending half the day in the kitchen preparing food for people I love. There is something about the gift of the time and the sensuous rhythm of the cooking that is actually communicated in the meal itself. There I am, having a lovely time kneading the dough, grating the lemons, and rolling out a pastry crust as I stand in our wonderful light-filled kitchen. I've got Mozart playing in the background, there are wonderful smells and sizzling sounds, I'm tasting as I go to see how things are coming along, and all's right with the world.

"And other times I like being entirely impromptu, cooking with friends, especially Italians, who have taught me a lot about simple, delicious food. I have a great Italian friend who often arrives with a handful of ingredients he's picked up in his explorations of the city, and then he and I go to work at the stove. Once when I was in Tuscany, we went out to eat calda calda, *the special snack of their town, and the next time he came to San Francisco, he brought me the ground* ceci *flour, its essential ingredient. So we figured out how to make it in my kitchen, and we cooked it along with some thin stalks of asparagus that we drizzled with good Tuscan olive oil, poured glasses of dry Tuscan white, and sat in the garden feeling like kings."*

RISOTTO WITH ARTICHOKES
serves four to six

Snap off all the hard outer leaves of the artichokes, leaving only the really tender and edible inner leaves. Cut away the pointed tops of the leaves. Cut the artichokes into eighths and remove the chokes. Keep as much of the stems as you can, trimming and peeling them.

Sauté the artichokes in a pan with the oil and half the butter until they are lightly golden. Bathe with 6 tablespoons of water and cook them covered for about 20 minutes until they are soft.

In a separate pan, bring the chicken broth to a slow boil. Add the rice to the artichokes, stirring constantly for a few minutes, allowing it to absorb the oil and butter, then cook as for a risotto, adding about 1/3 cup boiling broth every few minutes, allowing it to be absorbed, and then adding more until you have used all the broth. Be sure to stir the rice every so often to keep it from sticking to the bottom of the pot.

As soon as the risotto is cooked, remove from the heat, add the rest of the butter, the Parmesan cheese, and salt and freshly grated pepper. Serve immediately with more Parmesan cheese at the table.

4 artichokes
3 tablespoons olive oil
4 tablespoons butter
6 tablespoons water
5 cups chicken broth,
   preferably homemade
1½ cups Arborio rice
3 tablespoons grated
   Parmesan cheese
Salt and pepper

ARISTA (Pork Loin) WITH ROSEMARY, GARLIC, PEPPER, AND FENNEL SEEDS *serves four*

4 tablespoons fresh
   rosemary
4 cloves garlic
4 tablespoons finely
   chopped Italian parsley
1 teaspoon fennel seeds
Salt and freshly ground
   black pepper
3 pounds pork loin, boned

Preheat oven to 375° F. Mix rosemary, garlic, parsley, fennel seeds, and salt and pepper either by hand or in a food processor.

Slice the boned pork loin open from the thin side toward the fat spine as if you were opening a book. Into the center put the mixture of chopped rosemary, garlic, parsley, fennel seeds, salt and pepper. Spread them evenly and then lace up the opening with skewers and string. Set in a lightly oiled roasting pan and roast for about 1½ hours at 375° F (30 to 35 minutes per pound until it reaches an internal temperature of 170° F).

PEPERONATA *serves four to six*

Peel the peppers by putting them in a 450° F oven and letting them char. Turn them from time to time so the entire surface becomes black. When they are finished, remove from the oven and close up tightly in a paper bag, allowing them to steam for 15 minutes. Their skins will now peel off easily. Slice into long strips.

While the peppers are in the oven, sauté the finely sliced red onion in the olive oil over low heat, allowing it to render its own juices and flavors slowly. Add the pepper slices and sauté for another 15 minutes until they are lightly browned. Add the chopped tomatoes and cook 15 minutes more. Sprinkle the balsamic vinegar into the mixture, cooking 4 to 5 minutes longer and serve hot or warm.

4 red peppers
4 yellow peppers
1 large red onion
1/4 cup good olive oil
3 ripe tomatoes, seeded and chopped
2 teaspoons balsamic vinegar

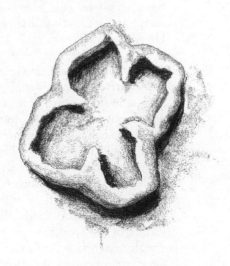

PUGLIESE BREAD *makes 2 large round,*
flat loaves or 3 smaller round loaves

1¼ teaspoons active dry
   yeast or
1/2 small cake fresh yeast
1/4 cup warm water
3 cups water, room
   temperature
4/5 cup biga starter
   (see next page)
7½ cups unbleached
   all-purpose flour
1 tablespoon plus
   1 teaspoon salt

Stir the yeast into the warm water in a large
mixer bowl and let stand until creamy, about 10
minutes. Add 3 cups water and the starter and
mix with the paddle until well blended. Add the
flour and salt and mix until the dough comes
together and pulls away from the side of the
bowl, 1 to 2 minutes. You may need to add another 1 to 2 tablespoons flour. Change to the
dough hook and knead at medium speed for 3 to
5 minutes. The dough will be very soft and elastic but will never pull entirely away from the
bottom of the bowl. If you want, finish kneading by hand on a floured surface with floured
hands until the dough loses its stickiness and is
soft and velvety, about 1 minute.

First rise: Place the dough in a lightly oiled large
bowl or plastic tub, cover tightly with plastic
wrap, and let rise until tripled, about 3 hours.
Do not punch down.

Shaping and second rise: Generously flour your
work surface, flour a dough scraper, and have a
mound of flour nearby for your hands. Pour the
dough out of the bowl, flour the top, and cut
into 2 or 3 equal pieces, depending on how many
loaves you are planning. Flatten each piece of
dough and roll it up lengthwise. Turn the dough
90 degrees, pat it flat, then roll up again. Shape
each piece into a ball by rolling the dough between your cupped hands, then push across the
surface of the worktable to pull the skin of the
dough taut. Place the loaves on floured parchment paper set on baking sheets or peels, cover
with a heavy towel or cloth, and let rise until
doubled, about 1 hour.

Baking: A half hour before baking, heat the oven with baking stones in it to 450° F. About 5 to 10 minutes before baking, flour the tops of the loaves and dimple them all over with your fingertips. The imprints will disappear but will keep the bread from rising crazily in the oven. Let stand 5 to 10 minutes. The loaves will feel as soft as a baby's bottom when ready to bake, although you will notice a bit of resistance in the dough. Sprinkle the stones with cornmeal. Italian bakers turn the doughs over into the oven very carefully with a swooping motion that scoops up some of the flour on the peel. You may prefer to slide the loaves onto the baking stones without turning them over, or if they are on baking sheets, the loaves can be baked directly on the pans. Bake until golden brown and crusty, about 50 to 60 minutes for the larger loaves, 30 to 35 minutes for the smaller ones. Check by knocking on the bottom of each loaf and listening for the hollow ring that indicates it is cooked through, but if you're in doubt, bake for the longer time indicated. Cool on racks.

Biga Starter

Mix together yeast and water until creamy. Add the flour and mix for 3 to 4 minutes. Let stand at least 24 hours.

1/4 teaspoon active
  dry yeast
1 cup and 1 tablespoon
  warm water (105° F)
2½ cups unbleached
  all–purpose flour

MEYER LEMON SORBET
serves four to six

Juice of 2 Meyer lemons
Grated rind of 2 Meyer
lemons
2/3 cup sugar
1/4 teaspoon grated
nutmeg
1½ cups light cream

Mix together the juice and grated lemon rind. Stir in the sugar and grated nutmeg and let the mixture stand for 5 minutes. Add the cream, stir well, and freeze in an ice cream maker, following the manufacturer's instructions. You could also pour the mixture into a freezer container and freeze until mushy. Remove and beat with electric beaters or with the steel blades in the food processor. Return and freeze thoroughly.

Take the sorbet out of the freezer about 5 to 10 minutes before serving.

L.A. SUPPER
by Wolfgang Puck

Mandarin Steak Salad

Alaskan Salmon with Ginger and Black Pepper

Celery Root Puree

Strawberry Shortcake

Strawberry Swirl Ice Cream

serves four

By blending fresh California ingredients and classical French training, Wolfgang Puck has been praised for his successful southern California restaurants, *Spago* in West Hollywood and *Chinois on Main* in Santa Monica. He has written *The Wolfgang Puck Cookbook: Recipes from Spago and Chinois* (Random House, 1986). *PosTrio*, his first restaurant in San Francisco, opened in April, 1989.

"I have always believed that the most important thing about any meal is the food, the wine, and the company, and not so much whether you have Limoges. I reserve evenings under the stars at the Hollywood Bowl for special friends. I bring the food and they bring the wine. Occasionally I like to bring china, silver, and glasses, but often I prefer paper plates, chopsticks, or just a plastic fork. I never prepare complicated food, yet people around us always look at our meal with a mixture of curiosity and longing."

MANDARIN STEAK SALAD
serves four

Mandarin Marinade:
2 tablespoons orange
    marmalade
1 teaspoon minced fresh
    ginger
1 clove garlic, minced
1/2 teaspoon freshly
    ground white pepper
Salt
1/4 cup fresh lemon juice
1/4 cup wine vinegar
1/4 cup fresh orange juice
1/2 teaspoon chili flakes
1/2 cup extra virgin
    olive oil

Vinaigrette:
5 to 6 tablespoons sherry-
    wine vinegar
1 tablespoon mandarin
    marinade
1/2 cup peanut or
    hazelnut oil

Salad:
1 1-pound flank steak or
    2 8-ounce New York
    steaks
Salt and freshly ground
    pepper
1/2 pound shiitake
    mushrooms
4 cups mixed salad greens,
    such as mâche, arugula,
    and curly endive

Prepare the mandarin marinade. In a sauté pan, combine all the ingredients, except olive oil. Bring to a boil, then simmer over high heat until reduced to thick consistency (about 10 minutes). Remove from the heat and let cool. Stir in the olive oil and reserve.

Prepare the vinaigrette. In a bowl, mix together all the ingredients, using only 1/3 cup oil. Correct the seasonings as necessary and set aside.

Season the steaks with salt and pepper and brush with some of the marinade. If you are using a grill, cook the steaks to medium rare and let rest for a few minutes. If you do not have a grill, heat a sauté pan and cook the steaks just a few minutes per side. The meat should be seared on the outside, but medium rare and juicy inside. Heat a small amount of the remaining oil in a sauté pan and sauté the mushrooms for several minutes, until al dente. Toss the salad greens with the vinaigrette and mound in the center of four dinner plates or one large serving plate. Place the mushrooms around the greens. Slice the steak at an angle and place on plates around the greens. Garnish with edible flowers or fresh herbs.

ALASKAN SALMON WITH GINGER AND BLACK PEPPER *serves four*

Heat 2 tablespoons butter in a sauté pan until foamy. Add shallot, garlic, and tomato and sauté for several minutes, or until shallot is translucent. Add wine and vinegar and continue cooking over medium heat until reduced by half. Add chicken stock and reduce again by half. Finish sauce with butter to desired consistency and season to taste with salt and freshly ground pepper. Keep warm. Mix together ginger and pepper. Season salmon with salt and coat with ginger-pepper mixture. Sprinkle with olive oil and grill or sauté salmon until desired doneness. Divide sauce among four warm dinner plates. Spoon equal amounts of celery puree into center of plates. Place salmon on top.

6 tablespoons unsalted butter
1 shallot, chopped
1 clove garlic, minced
1 tomato, peeled, seeded, and chopped
1/2 bottle Cabernet Sauvignon
2 tablespoons balsamic vinegar
1 cup chicken stock
Salt and freshly ground black pepper to taste
3 tablespoons chopped fresh ginger
3 tablespoons ground black pepper
4 Alaskan king salmon filets, about 6 ounces each
Olive oil
Celery root puree (see below)

CELERY ROOT PUREE

Chop the potato and celery root into 1-inch cubes. Boil in salted water for about 15 to 20 minutes until soft. Drain water and replace celery root and potato in pot. Add cream and simmer for about 15 minutes over medium heat, stirring occasionally to prevent sticking, until thickened. Remove from heat, add butter, salt, and pepper to taste. Process in food mill or for several seconds in a food processor until creamy, but not gluey.

1 medium baking potato, peeled
1 celery root (approximately 1½ to 2 pounds), peeled
1/2 cup heavy cream
2 tablespoons butter
Salt
Pepper

STRAWBERRY SHORTCAKE
serves ten

3 pints strawberries
2 to 3 tablespoons sugar
1 tablespoon lemon juice
1 teaspoon kirsch
1 teaspoon orange zest

Shortcakes:
2¾ cups pastry or cake
    flour
6 tablespoons sugar plus
    extra for top
1 tablespoon plus
    1 teaspoon baking
    powder
5 ounces unsalted butter
1 cup heavy cream plus
    extra for top
Strawberry swirl ice
    cream (recipe follows)

Rinse and drain berries. Remove stems and slice, gently toss with sugar, coating all the strawberries. Add lemon juice, kirsch, and orange zest and mix lightly. Set aside. Preheat oven to 375° F.

In a food processor, combine flour, sugar, and baking powder and process for a few minutes. Add the cold butter in small pieces and process until loosely mixed. Dough should *not* form a ball. With the motor running, add the 1 cup cream and stop processing before the dough forms a ball.

Turn out the dough onto a floured surface. Knead several times until dough comes together in a ball. Roll out into a disc 3/4 inch thick. Using a 2-inch biscuit cutter, cut 10 circles from the dough. Place cakes on a parchment-lined baking sheet. Brush the tops with the extra cream and sprinkle lightly with sugar.

Bake at 375° F for 5 minutes, then reduce heat to 350° and bake for 20 to 25 minutes, until cakes are firm to the touch. Remove cakes from baking sheet and split in half. Place bottom half on individual plates. Spoon ice cream onto cake. Top with a portion of the strawberries and the top half of the cake. Serve immediately.

STRAWBERRY SWIRL ICE CREAM
makes 2½ quarts

In a saucepan, combine the cream, milk, and vanilla bean and bring to a boil. Turn off heat, cover, and let steep for 15 minutes.

In a large mixing bowl, use a whisk or a rotary beater to beat egg yolks. Gradually add the sugar until the mixture is pale yellow and ribbons form when the whisk is lifted. Reheat the cream, pour over the egg yolks, stirring constantly. Return mixture to saucepan and cook over low heat, stirring constantly with a wooden spoon until the mixture thickens slightly and coats the back of the spoon. Return mixture to the mixing bowl and cool over ice. Strain through a fine mesh sieve. Set aside.

Puree strawberries in a food processor until smooth. Do not strain. Measure puree: you should have 6 cups. Add sugar, juice, and kirsch and process just until combined. Puree must taste slightly sweet to freeze properly. Add 1 to 2 tablespoons sugar if necessary. Combine puree with vanilla base. Freeze in an ice cream maker according to manufacturer's instructions. You may have to freeze the ice cream in two batches.

Vanilla Base:
1½ cups heavy cream
1/2 cup milk
1 vanilla bean, split and
   scraped
4 egg yolks
1/4 cup sugar

Strawberry Puree:
6 pints strawberries
1½ cups sugar
1/4 cup lemon juice
2 tablespoons kirsch

SUMMER

A SUMMER LUNCH ON THE PATIO
by Maggie Waldron

San Francisco Crabcakes

*Tiny Steamed New Potatoes
with Lemon Butter*

Red and Green Cabbage Slaw

*Warm Apple Cobbler with
Heavy Cream*

serves four

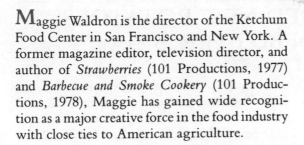

Maggie Waldron is the director of the Ketchum Food Center in San Francisco and New York. A former magazine editor, television director, and author of *Strawberries* (101 Productions, 1977) and *Barbecue and Smoke Cookery* (101 Productions, 1978), Maggie has gained wide recognition as a major creative force in the food industry with close ties to American agriculture.

"When our kids were small and attending the same school, Ruth Brinker and I often took turns at the feed lot. My Sara always loved staying at the Brinkers' for dinner. Ruth's warm and generous spirit prevailed over a constant stream of hippies, musicians, and poets. Her open hand has always been an extension of her genuine caring for all kinds of people."

SAN FRANCISCO CRABCAKES
serves four

3/4 pound cooked
  crab meat
1 cup dry bread crumbs
3 eggs, beaten
1/4 cup mayonnaise
2 tablespoons Dijon-style
  mustard
2 teaspoons Worcester-
  shire sauce
1/4 to 1/2 teaspoon hot
  pepper sauce
1/4 to 1/2 teaspoon
  cayenne pepper
1/2 teaspoon salt
1/3 cup chopped parsley
Vegetable oil, for frying
Additional beaten egg and
  bread crumbs to coat
  crabcakes
Lemon wedges for
  garnish

In a bowl, mix all ingredients except vegetable oil to blend thoroughly. Shape into 12 patties, 1 inch thick. Dip into additional beaten egg and coat with additional bread crumbs. Deep-fry, a few at a time, at 350° F until golden and crisp, or pan-fry over medium-high heat, turning once. Drain on paper towels. Serve with lemon wedges.

TINY STEAMED NEW POTATOES
WITH LEMON BUTTER *serves four*

12 to 16 small red
  potatoes (about
  1¼ pounds)
3 tablespoons butter
1 tablespoon lemon juice
1 tablespoon finely
  chopped parsley
Salt and freshly ground
  pepper to taste

In a saucepan, cook potatoes, covered, in 1 inch of boiling water just until tender, about 12 to 15 minutes. Drain, add butter and lemon juice to saucepan, and toss over medium heat for 2 to 3 minutes. Transfer to a serving dish. Sprinkle with parsley, salt, and pepper.

RED AND GREEN CABBAGE SLAW
serves six

Combine all ingredients except lettuce and paprika. Toss to blend thoroughly; chill. To serve,
spoon into lettuce cups and dust with paprika.

1 cup diced red and green
    bell pepper
3 cups finely shredded red
    and green cabbage
1/2 cup golden raisins
1/3 cup sliced green
    onions
1 medium carrot, peeled
    and shredded
Dill dressing (see below)
Butter lettuce cups
Paprika

Dill Dressing
In a small bowl, whisk together all ingredients
and season to taste with salt and pepper.

1/4 cup sour cream
1/4 cup mayonnaise
1 tablespoon red wine
    vinegar
1 teaspoon sugar
1 teaspoon prepared
    mustard
1 teaspoon dill weed
Salt and pepper to taste

WARM APPLE COBBLER WITH HEAVY CREAM *serves six*

7 cups peeled, cored, and very thinly sliced Granny Smith apples
2 tablespoons lemon juice
3/4 cup sugar
1/2 teaspoon cinnamon
1/4 teaspoon nutmeg
7 tablespoons unsalted butter
1 cup flour
2 tablespoons brown sugar
2 teaspoons baking powder
1/4 teaspoon salt
6 tablespoons milk

In a bowl, toss apples with lemon juice. Combine sugar, cinnamon, and nutmeg. Add to apples and toss. Arrange in an even layer in an 8-inch baking dish. Dot with 3 tablespoons of the butter and set aside. In a bowl, combine flour, brown sugar, baking powder, and salt. Mix to combine well. Add 4 tablespoons of butter cut into small chunks. Work butter into flour mixture with pastry blender until mixture resembles coarse meal. Gradually add milk while tossing with a fork. Gather into a ball and pat into a square to fit baking dish. Place dough over apples and tuck in around edges to seal. Brush top lightly with additional milk and sprinkle with additional sugar. Bake in preheated 425° F oven for 40 to 45 minutes until apples are tender and crust is nicely browned. Cool slightly. Spoon into serving dishes. Serve warm, drizzled with heavy cream.

A SUMMER PICNIC
by John Ash

*Santa Rosa Plum and White
Wine Soup*

*Romaine Leaves with Couscous
Salad*

*Smoked Game Hen with an
Oriental Touch*

*Strawberries in Melon Halves
with Yogurt and Date Sugar**

serves four

*Recipe not included

John Ash is chef/owner of *John Ash and Company*
in Santa Rosa, California. He teaches cooking
classes in Napa, at Santa Rosa Junior College,
and at his restaurant. John also hosts his own cooking talk show on KSRO in Sonoma County.

*"I like this menu and these recipes because they can all be done ahead of time, even the
day before. They are perfect for a picnic or a tailgate party and offer something a little
more luxurious than the usual fried chicken."*

SANTA ROSA PLUM AND WHITE WINE SOUP *serves four to six*

2 pounds ripe red or
    purple plums, pitted
    and coarsely chopped
1 cup dry white wine
1 cup fresh orange juice
1/2 cup sugar
1 cinnamon stick
4 white cloves
1 bay leaf
1/4 teaspoon freshly
    ground pepper
Big pinch of salt
Sour cream and fresh
    blueberries for garnish

Add all ingredients except garnish to a nonaluminum saucepan and bring to a boil. Skim any foam. Reduce heat and simmer for 15 minutes till plums are very tender. Discard cinnamon stick, cloves, and bay leaf.

Puree in food processor and strain through coarse sieve. Taste for seasoning and add more sugar if desired. The soup will taste less sweet when cold. Cover and refrigerate well.

To serve, ladle into mugs and garnish with a dollop of sour cream and fresh blueberries.

ROMAINE LEAVES WITH COUSCOUS SALAD *serves two to four*

Bring the stock to a boil and mix in the couscous. Cover and remove from heat; let stand for 5 minutes. Uncover and fluff with a fork and place in bowl. Cool to room temperature.

Mix remaining ingredients, except romaine, carefully together, then mix in cooled couscous.

Serve salad in crisp romaine leaves.

1 cup chicken stock
3/4 cup couscous
1 large ripe tomato, seeded and chopped
3 tablespoons chopped green onions
3 tablespoons chopped arugula or watercress
1 red or yellow bell pepper, chopped
2 tablespoons chopped and pitted oil-cured olives
4 tablespoons fruity olive oil
3 tablespoons lemon juice
2 tablespoons toasted pine nuts
Tender romaine lettuce leaves

SMOKED GAME HEN WITH AN ORIENTAL TOUCH *serves four to six*

3 game hens, halved with
  backbones removed

Marinade for Game Hens:
Grated zest of 1 lemon
Grated zest of 1 orange
1/2 cup soy sauce
1/2 cup oyster sauce
1/2 teaspoon fresh ginger,
  minced
2 garlic cloves
1 tablespoon fresh
  cilantro
1/4 teaspoon freshly
  ground black pepper
1 bay leaf
2 tablespoons honey

Sauce:
2 teaspoons vegetable oil
1 large clove garlic,
  minced
1 teaspoon fresh ginger,
  minced
1/4 teaspoon hot red
  pepper flakes
3 shallots, minced
1 tablespoon soy sauce
1 tablespoon red wine
  vinegar
2 tablespoons brown sugar
1½ tablespoons water
2 teaspoons sesame oil

Combine marinade ingredients in a food processor and blend well. Marinate game hens overnight in refrigerator.

In a kettle barbecue, use indirect method with a layer of foil on the grill between the hens and the coals. Barbecue/smoke hens for approximately 1 hour with vents nearly closed. Baste every 15 minutes with marinade. Add a few more coals after 30 minutes.

For sauce, add all ingredients except sesame oil to a saucepan, bring to a boil, and simmer for 5 minutes. Cool and then add oil.

As soon as hens are done, brush with sauce. Serve hot or cold.

A SUMMER MEAL FROM THE GRILL FOR FAMILY AND FRIENDS
by Edward Espe Brown

Grilled Eggplant and Red Pepper Salad

Grilled Corn with "Ancho" Chili Butter

Fresh Tomatoes

Pizza Bread

Fresh Berry Compote

serves four to six

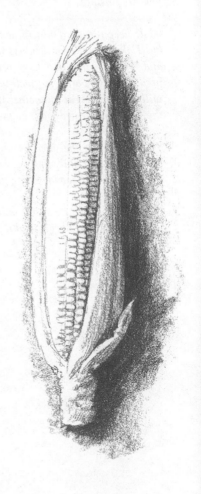

Edward Espe Brown is author of *The Tassajara Bread Book* (Shambhala/Zen Center, 1970), *Tassajara Cooking* (Shambhala/Zen Center, 1973), and *The Tassajara Recipe Book* (Shambhala/Zen Center, 1985). He is coauthor of *The Greens Cookbook* (Bantam, 1987) and has cooked at *Tassajara Hot Springs* restaurant and *Greens* restaurant in San Francisco. He currently teaches cooking classes, leads meditation retreats, and writes cooking columns for *The Yoga Journal*.

"Charcoal grilling is the focus of this meal, but the real agenda is that we get to do something together that nourishes one another, food-wise and friendship-wise. It's a great way to spend the afternoon or early evening, with everybody hanging around visiting, drinking mineral water (with bitters or whatever fits the mood), and cooking. Hosts and

guests alike share in the preparation and eating of the meal. Charcoal grilling is so immediately gratifying that somebody invariably volunteers to take charge. Of course, you want to do it yourself, so you let them persist a little before relenting.

"The other focus of the meal is the ingredients. Fruits and vegetables of the earth and sky, here they are in all their splendor. If you think some of your guests might not go for this, tell them to 'B(ring) Y(our) O(wn) M(eat),' then let them use the grill when you are finished.

"I do keep plenty of mineral water handy for those who choose not to indulge in alcohol, but I also provide for drinkers with high-quality beers (none that you will see on TV) and 'blush' wines that have been fermented to dryness. These are hard to find in our pseudo-sweet world, but well worth the effort. Chardonnays that are wood aged in oak will raise the event to another level of exquisite as the woody, smoky, toasty flavors of the wine and grilled foods bounce around and off one another in a charming melee.

"By this time, the guests will likewise be bouncing off one another with charm and aplomb, and certainly much good cheer will have been generated by honoring and bringing out the inherent goodness in each and every ingredient, each and every person.

"One final word. Be sure to allow enough time for your charcoal to come to toasty-rosy when you want to begin cooking."

GRILLED EGGPLANT AND RED PEPPER SALAD *serves four to six*

Slice the eggplant crosswise into pieces 1/4 to 3/8 inch thick. Brush each side with olive oil. Grill them over charcoal (are you still using mesquite and deforesting northern Mexico?) until they are well browned on both sides and bend easily when tested with tongs. The eggplant should not be al dente, so if in doubt, take a slice off the grill, cut it open, and try it. Set the eggplant aside.

Cut the red peppers in half, removing the seeds and pith. Cut the halves in half again, toss with olive oil, and grill over charcoal, turning occasionally until the deep red color and the texture have softened and there are spots of black. Set aside.

Rinse and spin dry the basil and arugula. Remove the basil leaves from the stems and cut the arugula into 1-inch lengths. When the eggplant and peppers are cool enough to handle, cut the eggplant rounds into 1-inch strips and the peppers into 1/2-inch pieces. (If you've gotten large sections of black on the pepper skins, remove it before slicing.)

Combine the garlic with the shallots and then with the eggplant and peppers. Then toss with the basil and arugula. Season to taste with balsamic vinegar, salt, and freshly ground pepper.

2 globe eggplants
Olive oil
3 red bell peppers
1/2 bunch basil
1/2 bunch arugula
(if arugula is not available, use whole bunch of basil)
6 cloves garlic, coarsely minced
2 shallots, finely diced
Balsamic vinegar
Salt and black pepper

GRILLED CORN WITH "ANCHO" CHILI BUTTER *serves four to six*

Chili nomenclature leaves something to be desired in terms of clarity. In San Francisco, I get pasilla chilies for my "anchos." It's a brick-red chili, somewhat heart-shaped (fat at the stem end and tapering off to a point), about 3 to 5 inches across and 4 to 6 inches long. Of course, "pasilla" refers to a different chili in other parts of the universe.

8 ears sweet corn
4 "ancho" (pasilla) chilies
1 cup unsalted butter
Zest of 1 lime
Juice of 2 limes
Salt
Cilantro or Italian parsley

The corn is first charcoal-grilled in the husk, then shucked and buttered, turning an appealing and appetite-enhancing brick red. To prepare the corn for grilling, remove the silk and stray flaps of husk. Charcoal-grill over a hot fire for 10 to 12 minutes, turning occasionally, until the husk has turned a rich tan all over with spots of brown and perhaps black. The "burning" husk will give the corn a smoky flavor. Keep warm in a covered baking dish.

This may produce more chili butter than you need, but the leftover can go on omelets, pasta, or vegetables. Roast the chilies for 3 to 4 minutes in a 350° F oven. Remove the seeds and stems, and cut the chili flesh into strips. Grind to a powder in a spice mill or clean coffee grinder. Melt the butter gently and add the chili powder, lime zest, and juice. Salt to taste.

When ready to serve, husk the corn and roll it around in the chili butter. Garnish the serving platter with sprays of fresh cilantro or Italian parsley.

FRESH TOMATOES *serves four to six*

I have become enamored with tomatoes once again. I found a store where the tomatoes actually smell like they've been on a vine, wonder of wonders, as the weather is too foggy to grow them where I live. As other varieties began to come in, it was time for a tomato-eating festival. I could get even more rhapsodical about all these tomatoes, but a tomato in the mouth is worth a good deal more than one on the page. See what you can come up with — or grow for yourself.

The point of this dish is t-o-m-a-t-o-e-s, so the seasoning is meant to be underwhelming. Track down some great, ripe, juicy tomatoes, rinse them, remove the stem, and slice them up. Into halves for the smaller ones, slices or sections for the bigger ones.

Combine the vinegar and olive oil with the herbs, being sure to OMIT the salt and pepper at this point. For 1 to 3 tomatoes, simply toss them together with the dressing. With a greater selection of tomatoes, arrange an attractive platter and pour the dressing over. Grind the pepper over the top. Wait until just before serving to sprinkle on the salt, or the tomatoes will ooze their juices and start to swim. By adding the salt at the very end, the juice stays where it belongs.

2 pounds vine-ripened
  tomatoes, take your pick:
Beefsteak (big and red)
Dry-farmed (big flavor)
Jubilee (rich golden color)
Lemon Boy (pale yellow)
Striped Marvel (red and
  gold, both in one)
Zebra (green with stripes)
Green Grape cherry
  tomato (exquisite
  sweetness)
Peach cherry tomato
  (fuzzy skin, earthy
  flavor)
Yellow Pear cherry tomato
Sweet 100s (smaller and
  sweeter than cherry
  tomatoes)
Yellow Sweet 100s

2 tablespoons champagne
  or white wine vinegar
5/8 cup olive oil
1 tablespoon parsley,
  minced
1 teaspoon fresh
  marjoram, minced
Pepper
Salt

PIZZA BREAD *serves four to six*

Frankly, I'm not into baby-this and special-that or much of any cooking that takes forever. Therefore, this pizza bread. Start to finish, you can make it happen in about two hours, and in keeping with our "light" summer meal, just a modest amount of cheese.

2 tablespoons active dry
  yeast (3 packages)
2 cups warm water
1 teaspoon salt
1/4 cup olive oil
Dollop of honey
2½ cups whole
  wheat flour
2½ cups unbleached
  white flour
Cornmeal (optional)
2 small red onions,
  thinly sliced
3 tablespoons olive oil
Salt and pepper
2 ounces asiago
  (or Parmesan) cheese,
  freshly grated
2 tablespoons thyme,
  minced
Rosemary sprigs for
  garnish

Dissolve the yeast in the warm water (about body temperature). Add the salt, oil, honey, and the whole wheat flour. Beat well with a spoon for a minute or two to develop the elasticity of the dough. Fold in the white flour until the dough comes away from the sides of the bowl. Turn the dough out on a floured board and knead for 5 to 7 minutes, using as much of the remaining flour as necessary to keep the dough from sticking. Oil the bowl lightly and put the dough back in to rise.

Let the dough rise about 40 minutes, then shape into two "loaves." Knead the dough a few times and divide into two halves. Flatten each into a circle or oval about 3/4 inch thick. Sprinkle some cornmeal on two baking sheets and place the four loaves on them. If you don't have cornmeal, just oil the pans. Set them aside to rise.

While the loaves are rising, toss the sliced onions with the olive oil, salt, and pepper. When the loaves have risen (about 25 to 30 minutes), spread the onions on the tops and bake in a preheated 400° F oven about 30 minutes. They should be well browned on the bottom and sides, since the middle of the tops will be moist from the onions. Remove from the oven, sprinkle on the cheese and herbs. Slice and place on a serving platter with the rosemary sprigs for a garnish.

FRESH BERRY COMPOTE *serves four to six*

Once again relying on the magnificence of the ingredients themselves, here's the simplest and the best I can make it. The fruit itself must be very good.

Prep the fruit. I use the end of a vegetable peeler to dig out the hulls of the rinsed strawberries. Then slice them lengthwise into pieces 1/8 inch thick. Rinse the blueberries and pick out the stems, greenies, and moldies. Combine the three kinds of berries with the maple syrup and vinegar. Fold gently with a rubber spatula to mix. Set aside to brew. Stir now and again when you think of it. Taste for seasoning and adjust: more sweet or more sour.

1 pint of strawberries
1 pint of blueberries
1 pint of raspberries
1/4 cup maple syrup
2 teaspoons raspberry
    vinegar

Serve in glass bowls or colored ones that will contrast well with the incredible purples and reds of the fruit.

A LIGHT LUNCH BY THE SEA by Lenee Arlen

Lobster and Ravioli Salad

Crusty French Bread*

Marquise of Chocolate

Raspberry Sauce

serves four

**Recipe not included*

Lenee Arlen has enjoyed careers on the stage, at home, and in the cooking arena. Her pleasures are making people nourished and happy.

"Summer food should be light, fresh, lazy, and fun to prepare. This menu is a pleasure to make and a joy to partake. All that's needed is a small cooler for transport to dock, beach, or boat."

LOBSTER AND RAVIOLI SALAD
serves four

Plunge the live lobsters headfirst into a large pot of rapidly boiling water and cook for 12 to 16 minutes. Remove and drain. When cool, remove the tail and claws of each lobster. For this recipe, use only the tail meat and save the claw meat for garnish.

Pound the basil and salt with a pestle to a fine paste. Add the oil, drop by drop, stirring until well blended. Add a small amount of freshly milled pepper.

Spread out 24 wonton wrappers on a floured board and place a small amount of both cheeses in the center of each wrapper. Brush the edges of the wrapper with warm water and top with another wrapper to form a ravioli. Repeat this process until you have 24 filled ravioli. Crimp the edges or cut into rounds with a cookie cutter (about the size of a half dollar). Transfer to a steamer and steam for 2 minutes. Drain the ravioli and set aside.

Slice the lobster tails into 1/2-inch rounds and combine with 3/4 of the basil dressing in a large bowl. Allow to marinate for 15 minutes.

Divide the lettuces and artichokes among four dinner plates and carefully spoon the rest of the basil dressing on top of each plate. Arrange the lobster rounds on top of the lettuces and surround with ravioli. Sprinkle with cilantro and garnish with the lobster-claw meat that has been carefully removed from the shell.

2 2-pound lobsters
1/2 cup fresh basil
1/2 teaspoon salt
3/4 cup olive oil plus
   a bit more
Pepper
48 Chinese wonton
   wrappers
1/4 cup ricotta cheese
1/4 cup dry goat cheese
3 small heads of lettuces,
   1 Boston, 1 red leaf,
   1 romaine
4 small artichokes,
   steamed
1 bunch cilantro, chopped

MARQUISE OF CHOCOLATE *serves ten*

9 ounces of good bitter-
   sweet chocolate
3/4 cup confectioners'
   sugar
1½ sticks (6 ounces) sweet
   butter, at room
   temperature
5 eggs, separated
Pinch of salt
Raspberry sauce
   (see below)

Melt the chocolate in a small pan over very low heat. Add 1/2 cup sugar and all the butter and the egg yolks, stirring well after each addition. Beat the egg whites in a small bowl with a pinch of salt until stiff and dry. Add remaining 1/4 cup sugar to beaten whites and beat another few strokes until glossy. Remove the chocolate from the heat and fold in 1/3 of the egg white mixture. Gently fold in the rest of the egg whites, being careful not to overmix but making sure all is well blended.

Rinse an 8½-inch springform pan with water. Shake off excess water but do not dry the pan. Fill it with the batter. Refrigerate for 24 hours. Remove the pan from the refrigerator 30 minutes before serving. Release side catch from pan and serve in small slices.

RASPBERRY SAUCE

8 ounces frozen
   raspberries
1 basket fresh raspberries
   for garnish

Defrost and then pass the frozen berries through a sieve. Spoon the resulting sauce over the marquise slices. Top with fresh whole berries.

A MIDDLE EASTERN BARBECUE by Loni Kuhn

Tabbouleh Variation

Pita Burgers with Tatziki

Tchoutchoukaa

Beet Salad

Refreshing Orange Dessert

serves eight

Loni Kuhn has operated her famous *Cook's Tours Cooking School* in San Francisco for the past sixteen years, where many of San Francisco's top chefs have taught classes. Loni is also a passionate gardener and orchid grower.

"The following meal is a casual barbecue for eight friends who love the seasoning of the Middle Eastern countries, all of which use similar ingredients. While there are several recipes, all benefit from being prepared several hours ahead or the day before. It is a marvelous way to entertain, and all recipes may be doubled or tripled for a crowd of hungry consumers! The recipes are healthful and delicious as well as colorful, something I think is very important and which I always stress in my classes. An added plus is that they carry well to a picnic."

TABBOULEH VARIATION
serves eight

2 quarts water
2 beef bouillon cubes
2 bay leaves
6 cloves garlic, chopped
1 pound wehani rice
1/2 pound basmati rice
4 green onions, sliced
    (include the tops)
1 cup chopped red or
    yellow pepper
Salt and pepper
Juice of 3 lemons
3/4 cup of olive oil
2 cups chopped flat-leaf
    parsley
1/2 to 1 cup mint,
    chopped
Fresh dill
Lemon wedges for
    garnish
Tomato wedges for
    garnish

Place water in a large pot, adding bouillon cubes, bay leaf, and garlic. Bring to full boil and stir in wehani rice. Cook for 35 minutes. Place large strainer over a bowl to catch the broth and drain well. Place wehani in a bowl and return broth to the pot and back to boiling. Add the basmati rice, stir well, and cook for 12 minutes. Drain thoroughly. The resulting broth is superb for soup another day. Toss the two varieties of rice with the other ingredients and refrigerate. This salad keeps for several days and is excellent nutritionally. Serve at room temperature, garnished with lemon and tomato wedges.

PITA BURGERS WITH TATZIKI
serves eight

Mix the meat, egg, bread crumbs, 1/2 the cheese, and seasonings together. Form into 8 patties and refrigerate for 2 to 3 hours, or more. Grill over hot fire until rare. Warm the pita breads on the grill, then cut off 1/2 of each pita to make a large open pocket in which to slide the meat. Pass bowls of sliced tomatoes, red onion rings, the remaining crumbled feta, and tatziki (see below) to place in the pitas.

3 pounds lean ground lamb
1 large egg and maybe part of another
1/2 cup fine fresh bread crumbs
1 pound crumbled feta cheese (Bulgarian is best)
6 cloves minced garlic
2 tablespoons fresh oregano, chopped
Cayenne to taste
Salt is doubtful because of the cheese
1 tablespoon cumin
1/4 cup chopped cilantro
1/4 cup chopped mint
8 pita breads
2 tomatoes, thinly sliced
1 red onion, sliced into rings

Tatziki
Combine all ingredients and allow 2 hours for tastes to blend. Pass as a sauce for pita burgers.

1 pint plain yogurt
1 European cucumber, chopped
Chopped garlic
Chopped mint or cilantro
Salt and pepper

TCHOUTCHOUKAA *serves eight*

2 pounds red and yellow
  peppers
2 pounds eggplant
Large bunch of parsley
Large bunch of cilantro
4 to 6 cloves garlic
2 tablespoons paprika
1 to 2 tablespoons cumin
1 teaspoon cayenne
Olive oil
2 pounds really ripe
  tomatoes, peeled
Salt

Broil or grill the peppers until blistered and lightly blackened all over. Place in a paper bag, twist closed, and steam until cool enough to handle. Peel and tear into largish pieces. Slice the eggplant into 1/4-inch-thick rounds and quarter each slice. In a food processor place the parsley, cilantro, garlic, paprika, cumin, and cayenne. Pulse until chopped. Pour 1/4 inch olive oil in a large sauté pan, add all the ingredients, and cook over medium heat, adding more oil as necessary, for 30 to 45 minutes, stirring gently and occasionally. Try not to make it mushy. Place in refrigerator overnight; it is much better the second day. Serve at room temperature.

BEET SALAD *serves eight*

Remove tops from the beets and place beets on a large square of heavy foil. Wrap tightly and bake at 450° F for about 45 to 60 minutes, depending on size. You may test them with a toothpick right through the foil. Peel and cut into small cubes or slices and toss with other ingredients. Marinate overnight. Serve at room temperature.

2 bunches of similarly
   sized beets
1½ teaspoons paprika
2 pinches cinnamon
2 pinches cumin
2 tablespoons orange
   flower water
Salt, pepper, and lemon
   juice to taste
Green onion, chopped

REFRESHING ORANGE DESSERT
serves eight

8 to 10 very large oranges,
   peeled and thinly sliced
Rose or orange flower
   water
Powdered sugar
Cinnamon
Toasted, slivered almonds

Spread the orange slices on a platter and sprinkle with flower water. Cover tightly with plastic and refrigerate overnight. When ready to serve, sprinkle with powdered sugar, cinnamon, and nuts. Almond cookies are nice with this, or you might add melon balls.

AN INDIAN-SUMMER LUNCH ON BOARD
by Arnold Rossman

*Fresh Spot Prawns in Spicy
Peanut Sauce*

*Japanese Soba Noodles with
Toasted Sesame-Ginger
Vinaigrette*

Asian Cabbage Slaw

Marinated Vegetable Julienne

serves four

Arnold Rossman has worked at *Le Cirque, Le Périgord Park,* and *La Tulipe* French restaurants in New York City and at *Campton Place* and *Julie's Supper Club* in San Francisco. He is currently a chef at *Stars* in San Francisco.

"This menu was the result of an invitation to spend the afternoon on a friend's boat on San Francisco Bay on a fine Indian-summer's day. Since no cooking would be done on board, everything was prepared beforehand and simply assembled at the last minute into one terrific dish and dispatched with much gusto and four pairs of chopsticks.

"I can appreciate the special setting of a formal dining room, but my favorite spot for enjoying a wonderful meal is at an informal bistro or trattoria, or in the living room with friends. This is where one can truly relax, and the conversation and wine simply spill forth."

FRESH SPOT PRAWNS IN SPICY PEANUT SAUCE *serves four*

6 cups cold water
2 cups white wine
1/2 cup white wine
    vinegar
Pinch chili flakes
2 stalks lemon grass, sliced
1 small knob ginger,
    sliced
1/2 bunch cilantro,
    chopped
20 medium-large fresh
    prawns or shrimp,
    shelled and deveined
1 bunch cilantro, chopped
    for garnish

Combine all ingredients except prawns and garnish in a stockpot. Bring to a boil and simmer for 20 minutes. Strain, reserving liquid. Discard solids. Bring liquid back to a boil, remove from heat, add prawns, and poach until done, 4 to 7 minutes. Remove from liquid and allow to cool.

1/4 cup creamy peanut
    butter
1/8 cup Japanese rice wine
    vinegar
1 teaspoon Thai chili
    paste
1/2 teaspoon hoisin sauce
1/4 cup pineapple juice
1/8 cup soy sauce
1 teaspoon grated ginger

Spicy Peanut Sauce
Mix all ingredients together and set aside.

JAPANESE SOBA NOODLES WITH TOASTED SESAME-GINGER VINAIGRETTE *serves four*

Cook soba noodles according to directions on package. Drain but do not refresh. Toss with 3/4 cup of the sesame vinaigrette (saving 1/2 cup for vegetables) and reserve.

12-ounce package Japanese buckwheat soba noodles
Toasted sesame-ginger vinaigrette (see below)

Mix black and white sesame seeds together and spread out on a cookie sheet. Toast in a 325° F oven for 15 minutes, stirring occasionally. Allow to cool and set aside for use as garnish just before serving.

1/8 cup black sesame seeds
1/8 cup white sesame seeds

Toasted Sesame-Ginger Vinaigrette
(yields 1¼ cups)
Combine all vinaigrette ingredients and mix well.

1/3 cup toasted Japanese sesame oil
1/8 cup Chinese black vinegar
1/8 cup balsamic vinegar
1/4 cup soy sauce
1/2 teaspoon grated ginger
1 teaspoon finely minced garlic
1 teaspoon Chinese plum sauce
1 teaspoon honey
1 teaspoon Thai chili sauce
3/4 cup pineapple juice
2 tablespoons chopped cilantro

ASIAN CABBAGE SLAW *serves four*

1/3 cup Japanese rice
   wine vinegar
1/4 cup peanut oil
1 teaspoon sugar
Pinch salt and pepper
Large pinch red chili
   flakes
1 small head red cabbage,
   thinly sliced
2 tablespoons chopped
   cilantro
2 tablespoons sliced
   scallions

Combine vinegar, oil, sugar, salt, pepper, and red chili flakes. Toss with cabbage and let stand 1 hour. Then add cilantro and scallions, toss again, and serve.

MARINATED VEGETABLE JULIENNE *serves four*

1 red bell pepper,
   julienned
1 yellow bell pepper,
   julienned
1 green pasilla pepper,
   julienned
2 carrots, julienned
1 green zucchini,
   julienned
1 yellow zucchini,
   julienned
1 bunch scallions, thinly
   sliced
Toasted sesame-ginger
   vinaigrette (see
   preceding page)

Combine all the vegetables and toss with 1/2 cup of sesame vinaigrette.

To Serve
Place marinated soba noodles on a large platter. Arrange red cabbage over the top, leaving a 1½-inch border of noodles exposed. Place marinated vegetable julienne on top of cabbage, and arrange prawns around edge, on top of exposed noodles. Garnish with sesame seeds and chopped cilantro.

A SUMMER DINNER WITH A SOUTHWESTERN TOUCH by Rick Cunningham

Spicy Prawns

Cream Cheese and Chili Dip

Vine-Ripened Tomatoes and Black Beans with Fresh Basil Dressing

Garlic Bread

Pork Chops Smothered in Mushrooms

Mashed Red Potatoes with Green Onions

Sauté of Bok Choy, Carrot, and Red Pepper

Rhubarb-Strawberry Crisp with Vanilla Ice Cream

serves six

A native of the Bay Area, Rick Cunningham studied home economics in college and was regional chef for the *California Cafe* chain prior to his present position as the chef at *Ivy's Restaurant* in San Francisco.

"Everyone seems to have their own special formula for bringing friends together for that 'perfect' dinner. My special occasions have always placed as much importance on the presentation of the food as they do on the execution of the recipes. In planning a special time with good friends I look for a combination of ideas and recipes that will complement each other and my guests."

SPICY PRAWNS *serves six*   *entered*

3 tablespoons sweet butter
2 tablespoons olive oil
2 tablespoons garlic,
  minced
4 tablespoons shallots,
  chopped
2 pounds medium-large
  prawns (16 to 20
  prawns)
1/2 teaspoon red pepper
  flakes
3 tablespoons lemon juice
4 tablespoons fresh dill,
  chopped

Heat the sweet butter and olive oil in a large skillet. Sauté the garlic and shallots for 2 minutes. Add the prawns and red pepper flakes and continue to sauté for 4 minutes or until done. Remove to a glass or earthenware bowl. Add the lemon juice and chopped fresh dill and refrigerate overnight. Peel and devein the prawns to serve.

CREAM CHEESE AND CHILI DIP

Carefully sauté the almonds in vegetable oil over medium heat until lightly browned. Set aside to cool. In a food processor with the metal blade, process the cream cheese, garlic, and almonds. Add milk slowly to desired consistency for dipping. Remove to bowl and fold in the chopped chilies and olives. Can be made a day ahead up to this point and kept covered and chilled. Run the tines of a fork lengthwise down the cucumber to make ridges and slice thinly. Line a serving bowl with cucumber slices and fill with dipping sauce. Serve at room temperature. Place bowl with dip in the center of a platter and surround with the prawns. Garnish with lemon wedges and Italian parsley.

1/2 cup blanched slivered almonds
2 tablespoons vegetable oil
24 ounces cream cheese
2 large cloves garlic, minced
1/2 cup milk (to thin)
8 ounces mild green chilies, chopped
4 ounces chopped olives
1 cucumber
Lemon wedges for garnish
Italian parsley for garnish

VINE-RIPENED TOMATOES AND BLACK BEANS WITH FRESH BASIL DRESSING *serves six*

Black beans (see below)
Fresh basil dressing
  (see below)
6 leaves of red or green
  garden lettuce
3 large, ripe tomatoes

Black Beans:
2 cups black beans
1 teaspoon ground cumin
1 tablespoon brown sugar
4 cups chicken stock
Salt
Freshly ground pepper
1/2 cup fruity olive oil
1/2 cup chopped parsley

Cover 2 cups black beans with 4 cups water and let soak overnight. Drain, place in kettle, and add the cumin, sugar, and chicken stock. Bring to a boil and simmer until beans are tender yet firm, about 2 hours. Add more chicken stock or water if necessary. Remove to strainer and rinse under cold water. Place in a large bowl and toss gently with salt and pepper to taste and the olive oil and chopped parsley. Can be prepared one day ahead and kept covered and chilled.

Fresh Basil Dressing:
1 cup mayonnaise
1 clove garlic, minced
1 teaspoon Worcestershire
  sauce
1 tablespoon green onion,
  finely sliced
1/2 teaspoon powdered
  mustard
1/2 teaspoon sugar
3 tablespoons freshly
  chopped basil
3/4 cup beef broth or
  bouillon
Salt and pepper to taste

In a food processor with metal blade, process the first seven ingredients until smooth. Add beef broth or bouillon a little at a time until proper consistency for dressing is achieved. Add salt and pepper. Can be prepared one day ahead, covered, and chilled.

To serve, line each plate with a lettuce leaf and top with slices of ripe tomato. Spoon over the basil dressing and sprinkle generously with black beans.

GARLIC BREAD

Melt butter with garlic, paprika, and salt and pepper to taste. Simmer 5 minutes, stirring often. Slice bread lengthwise in half and cover each side with the butter mixture. Top with the chopped cilantro and Parmesan cheese and bake at 350° F for 10 minutes or until the cheese melts. Slice and serve with the tomato salad.

1/4 pound unsalted butter
2 tablespoons minced garlic
1 tablespoon paprika
Pinch of salt
Freshly ground pepper
1 loaf extra sourdough bread
1 cup chopped cilantro
1 cup grated Parmesan cheese

PORK CHOPS SMOTHERED IN MUSHROOMS *serves six*

6 tablespoons unsalted
  butter
6 tablespoons flour
1 cup vegetable oil
12 center-cut loin pork
  chops, 1/2 inch thick
1 cup flour
Salt and freshly ground
  white pepper
2 medium onions, diced
2 pounds mushrooms,
  sliced
3/4 cup rich chicken stock
2 cups milk
1 tablespoon dried leaf
  thyme

Make a roux by melting the butter in a saucepan and adding the 6 tablespoons flour. Simmer for 5 minutes, stirring constantly. Remove from heat and set aside. Heat vegetable oil until hot. Dredge chops in a mixture of 1 cup flour with salt and pepper. Fry in hot oil, in batches, until golden brown. Remove chops to a large casserole dish. Pour off the excess oil, turn down heat, and sauté the onions and mushrooms until wilted. Add the chicken stock to deglaze, scraping the bottom of the pan while stirring, and bring to a boil. Return to simmer and whisk in roux, milk, and thyme. Continue whisking until a gravy has formed. Pour over the chops and bake at 350° F for 40 minutes or until tender.

MASHED RED POTATOES WITH GREEN ONIONS *serves six*

Boil the potatoes until tender. Use mixer (or hand masher), adding butter, salt, pepper, and enough milk to whip smoothly. Sprinkle on green onion and fold into potatoes.

4 pounds red potatoes, peeled and cubed
1/2 pound unsalted butter
Salt and pepper to taste
Milk
1 cup green onion, minced

SAUTÉ OF BOK CHOY, CARROT, AND RED PEPPER *serves six*

Blanch the carrots in salted water and then chill. Melt the butter over medium heat, add the shallots, and sauté until tender. Then add bok choy, bell pepper, and carrots. Sauté until tender, yet crispy. Add salt and pepper to taste.

2 pounds carrots, thinly sliced
2 tablespoons unsalted butter
1 tablespoon shallots, chopped
2 pounds bok choy, chopped
1 red bell pepper, julienned
Salt and pepper

RHUBARB-STRAWBERRY CRISP WITH VANILLA ICE CREAM *serves six*

1 cup pecans
2 pounds rhubarb
2 pints fresh ripe
  strawberries
1 cup sugar
1¼ cups flour
1/3 cup light brown sugar
1 tablespoon granulated
  sugar
1/4 tablespoon cinnamon
1/2 cup cold unsalted
  butter (cut into
  small pieces)
Your favorite vanilla ice
  cream

Toast the pecans at 350° F for 5 minutes and let cool. Rinse the rhubarb, trim the ends and any brown spots, and cut into 1/2-inch-thick pieces. Rinse, hull, and slice the strawberries and add to the rhubarb. Toss the fruit with 1 cup sugar and 1/4 cup flour. Let stand while making the topping.

Mix the pecans, remaining flour, light brown sugar, tablespoon sugar, cinnamon, and butter in the bowl of a food processor and process until crumbly. Put the rhubarb-strawberry mixture into a casserole dish, smooth the top, and sprinkle topping evenly over fruit. Bake at 350° F for 45 minutes. This may be made a few hours in advance, then warmed while eating dinner. Serve with vanilla ice cream.

END-OF-SUMMER GRILL
by Jay Harlow

Tapenade with Croutons

Spaghettini with Grilled Tomato Sauce

Grilled Albacore with Oregano Pesto and Grilled Golden Zucchini

Mixed Greens Vinaigrette*

Bartlett Pears and Fontina*

serves six

*Recipes not included

Jay Harlow is author or coauthor of six cookbooks, including The *California Seafood Cookbook* (Aris Books, 1983), *The Grilling Book* (Aris Books, 1987) with A. Cort Sinnes, and books on wine and Asian cooking in the California Culinary Academy cookbook series. His column on seafood, "The Fishmonger," appears weekly in the *San Francisco Chronicle*. Before turning to writing, he was a cook and chef in several Bay Area restaurants, including the *Hayes Street Grill*, the *Fourth Street Grill,* and the *Santa Fe Bar*

and Grill. Since 1983, he has been teaching seafood and grill cookery to home cooks and aspir-
ing chefs throughout California and from Seattle
to New Orleans. He lives in Oakland, California, with his wife, writer Elaine Ratner, and
their two-year-old daughter.

*"Here is a menu for the waning days of summer, when the last vine-ripened tomatoes
and the first of the fall fruits sit side by side in the produce markets and the evenings are
still warm enough for outdoor dining. It's my favorite time of the year to have a few
friends over for a casual backyard meal. With a little advance preparation, this meal can
be cooked entirely on the grill, making it also suitable for a picnic. Be sure to start with
a bigger fire than you think you will need; a good five pounds of mesquite charcoal is
about right for a full-sized kettle grill. By the time you have finished the pasta course,
the fire will have settled down to the ideal cooking stage for the fish. With the robust
garlic, olive oil, and herb flavors of this menu, choose a gutsy Sauvignon Blanc, or
better still a California Pinot Noir Vin Gris or a Bandol Rosé. As the evening cools
and the guests start reaching for their sweaters, switch to a well-aged Cabernet or Merlot
with the cheese and fruit."*

TAPENADE WITH CROUTONS
serves six

In a mortar or blender, combine the olives, anchovies, and garlic and mash to a paste. Gradually add the olive oil, blend until smooth, and add lemon juice to taste. Serve with a knife for spreading on thin croutons (see page 163).

3/4 cup pitted Kalamata or Niçoise olives
2 to 3 canned anchovy fillets, rinsed
3 cloves garlic
1/2 cup olive oil
Lemon juice to taste
Croutons

SPAGHETTINI WITH GRILLED TOMATO SAUCE *serves six*

Cook the pasta in ample boiling water until quite al dente. It will cook further in the sauce. Drain, rinse with cold water to stop the cooking, and moisten with vegetable oil to prevent it from sticking together. This may be done up to a day ahead of time and the pasta refrigerated.

Build a hot charcoal fire in an open or covered grill. While the fire is still at the flaming stage, grill the tomatoes around the edge of the fire until the skins burst and begin to blacken. Remove the tomatoes to a shallow dish, and when cool enough to handle, remove the skins and chop the tomatoes as finely as possible with a knife and fork or metal spoon. Discard the hard cores and any large clumps of seeds.

Set a wok or deep skillet on the grill and add the olive oil and garlic. Cook until fragrant, then add the chopped tomatoes with their juices and the herbs. Cook, stirring, until sauce is well reduced. Season sauce to taste, add pasta, and cook until pasta is heated through. Serve immediately.

1 pound spaghettini or vermicelli
1 tablespoon vegetable oil
2½ pounds small ripe tomatoes
3 tablespoons olive oil
2 cloves garlic, sliced
2 teaspoons fresh oregano or marjoram leaves, or a handful of chopped basil
Salt and pepper

GRILLED ALBACORE WITH OREGANO PESTO AND GRILLED GOLDEN ZUCCHINI *serves six*

6 albacore tuna steaks,
   about 6 ounces each
1/4 cup olive oil
1 teaspoon dried oregano
   leaves, or
2 teaspoons fresh oregano
   leaves, bruised
Salt and pepper
6 golden zucchini or
   crookneck squash, split
   lengthwise
Oregano pesto (see below)

Place the albacore steaks in a roasting pan or plastic bag and add the oil, oregano, salt and pepper. Marinate 1 hour, turning occasionally. Meanwhile, prepare the oregano pesto as directed below.

Remove the fish from the marinade and grill over a medium-hot to hot charcoal fire, 2 minutes per side for a center that is still quite rare, longer for medium or well-done. Baste lightly with the marinade during cooking. Grill the squash halves alongside the fish until lightly browned on both sides. Spoon pesto over each serving of fish.

1 peeled garlic clove
1 tablespoon fresh
   oregano leaves
Salt
5 to 6 tablespoons olive oil

Oregano Pesto
Combine the garlic, oregano, and a pinch of salt in a mortar and pound to a paste. Add 1 tablespoon of the oil and continue pounding and stirring until oil is stained green. Stir in the remaining oil and let stand 30 minutes.

A SUMMER MENU FOR FRIENDS by Rachel Gardner and Catherine Pantsios

Fresh Tomato Tart with Basil

Roast Duck Breast with Herb-Buttered Noodles

Bread Pudding with Fresh Fruit Sauce

serves four

Six years ago, Catherine Pantsios opened *Zola's* restaurant in San Francisco and hired Rachel Gardner as her assistant. Since that time their roles in the kitchen have merged to the point where trust, responsibility, and work are shared equally because the work itself gives them great pleasure and fulfillment and, they hope, is pleasing to others.

"This menu was not devised to overwhelm or astonish, but to be one element contributing to an occasion, an excuse really for friends to enjoy each other, above all. If the setting is in an airy dining room, or overlooking the Bay, if the food is served on earthenware or painted Italian pottery, on a scrubbed plank table or heavy linen cloth, so much the better, but first, let there be something more lasting and profound to be shared among the diners than just food."

FRESH TOMATO TART WITH BASIL
serves four

3 tablespoons butter
1 cup all-purpose flour
1/2 teaspoon salt
2 teaspoons yeast
3 tablespoons warm water
1 egg
1½ pounds fresh toma-
    toes, red, yellow, and
    green-ruffled
Handful of basil leaves
Freshly ground black
    pepper
Coarse salt
4 tablespoons full-
    flavored, green
    olive oil

Make a dough by cutting the butter into the flour, which has been mixed with the salt. Proof the yeast in the warm water and add to the dough together with an egg that has been well beaten. Knead well, until the dough becomes smooth and elastic. Divide the dough into 4 balls and allow it to rise at room temperature until it has doubled, then roll each piece into a circle about 5 inches in diameter. Slice the nicest, ripest tomatoes you can find into thin slices and arrange them on top of the dough. A combination of red and yellow and green-ruffled tomatoes looks especially nice. Sprinkle a fine chiffonade of basil leaves, then grind black pepper over each tart, sprinkle with coarse salt, and drizzle with olive oil. Slide the tarts onto a baking sheet or stone that has been heating in a 500° F oven. When the edges are brown and puffy (in about 10 minutes), remove the tarts with a spatula and serve immediately.

ROAST DUCK BREAST WITH HERB-BUTTERED NOODLES *serves four*

Cut a 1-inch crosshatch through the skin and fat layer of the duck breasts without penetrating into the meat. Place the breasts skin-side down in a skillet and add water to just above the level of the fat. Cook over a high flame until all the water has evaporated and the skin is golden brown. A great deal of duck fat will have been rendered off. (Pour this grease off and save for later sautéing.) Turn the breasts over and finish cooking them in a 500° F oven until the meat is medium rare, which will take from 5 to 10 minutes depending on the size of the duck breasts. Remove the breasts from the skillet and pour off any additional fat that has been rendered. Then add the duck or chicken stock and allow it to boil until reduced by half. Whisk in the butter, continuing to boil until sauce is slightly syrupy. Then whisk in the chopped herbs.

Cook the fettuccine until al dente. Toss the well-drained pasta with the sauce and arrange on four plates. Slice each duck breast on the bias and arrange one breast over each plate of noodles.

4 duck breasts, boned, not skinned
1 cup duck or chicken stock
4 tablespoons butter
Handful of mixed herbs, chopped (tarragon, chives, cilantro, and/or chervil)
1 pound fresh fettuccine (or 1/2 pound dry)

BREAD PUDDING WITH FRESH FRUIT SAUCE *serves four*

2 cups 1/2-inch bread
  cubes
2 tablespoons butter
1 cup milk
1 cup heavy cream
1-inch cinnamon stick
1/2 vanilla bean
4 egg yolks
4 tablespoons sugar
Pinch of powdered
  cinnamon
1 pint ripe berries (blackberries, raspberries,
  and/or boysenberries)
Sugar to taste

Cut day-old bread, such as sweet baguettes, into cubes, after removing the crusts. Sauté them in the butter until golden and crisp, and divide them among four oven-proof ramekins. Scald the milk and cream with the cinnamon stick and vanilla. Beat the eggs yolks with 4 tablespoons sugar and the powdered cinnamon. Remove the stick cinnamon and vanilla bean and whisk the scalded milk into the egg yolks. Scrape the seeds from the vanilla bean and add them to the custard. Strain the custard before dividing it equally among the four ramekins. Allow the bread cubes to soak up the custard for five minutes. Place the ramekins in a larger baking dish filled with hot water halfway up their sides. Bake in a 300° F oven until the custard is set but still creamy. Serve warm or cold with a sauce made from the freshest, ripest berries you can find, cooked slowly with as much sugar as you and the berries require. When the fruit is soft, puree half in a blender and add it back to the whole berries before pouring it over the bread pudding.

SUMMER DINNER MENU
by Peggy Knickerbocker

Warm Figs with Prosciutto*

Soft Polenta Baked with Gorgonzola, Pine Nuts, and Green Onions

Barbecued Orange-Rum Chicken

Barbecued Red Torpedo Onions

Coffee Ice Cream with Praline Sauce

serves four to six

*Recipe on page 194

Peggy Knickerbocker was born and raised in San Francisco, studied in France, and was taught to cook by her mother. With her partner, Flicka McGurrin, she opened her first restaurant at *Mooney's Irish Pub* in North Beach. That venture evolved into the *Cooking Company*. They now own *Pier 23 Cafe* in San Francisco where Peggy is the chef. When she gets the opportunity, Peggy likes to travel the world in search of food and romance.

"I love to cook for my friends, and usually I fret for days over a fancy menu and then come up with something that is easy, colorful, and voluptuous. I like the oohs and aahs when my guests are excited about what is to come. I like to have flavors that are daring and not at all hesitant. I choose dishes that provide a full range of color and tastes.

"I like to get most of the work done ahead of time, arranging the ingredients artistically in bowls and platters, so that there is kitchen art going on as friends arrive. It's fun to barbecue because you have company while you cook, and you can laugh because you always get lots of opinions."

SOFT POLENTA BAKED WITH GORGONZOLA, PINE NUTS, AND GREEN ONIONS *serves four to six*

3 cups chicken broth
6 cloves of garlic, minced
1 cup polenta
1/2 cup heavy cream
1/4 pound butter
1/2 teaspoon white pepper
1/4 cup grated Parmesan
  cheese
1/4 cup Gorgonzola
  cheese, crumbled
4 green onions, chopped
1/4 cup toasted pine nuts

Boil the broth with the garlic and add polenta. After polenta begins to thicken, add cream, stir, and transfer to the top of a double boiler. Cover and cook for 45 minutes to 1 hour. Halfway through, add butter, white pepper, and Parmesan. When finished cooking, pour into a shallow serving bowl and sprinkle with Gorgonzola, chopped green onion, and toasted pine nuts. Bake in preheated 325° F oven for 10 minutes.

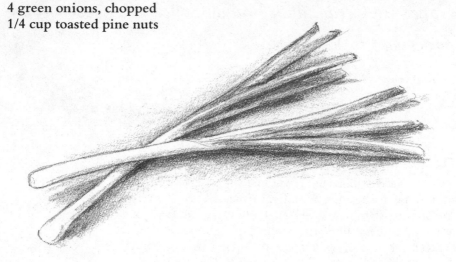

BARBECUED ORANGE-RUM CHICKEN *serves six to eight*

Remove skin and cut chickens in half. Place in flat dish. Combine marinade ingredients and pour enough over chicken to cover, reserving about 1/4 cup. Marinate overnight in the refrigerator. Grill chickens on hot mesquite fire until leg joints move freely (approximately 25 minutes), turning several times and controlling draft to fire so flames do not burn chicken. Place chicken halves on clean platter and bring to the kitchen. Cut each half into four pieces. Serve over a bed of watercress and red and gold cherry tomatoes tossed with remaining marinade or your favorite vinaigrette.

3 broiler chickens
2 bunches watercress
1 pint each red and gold
  cherry tomatoes

Marinade:
2 cups fresh orange juice
Zest of 2 oranges
2 tablespoons mint,
  chopped
2 tablespoons cilantro,
  chopped
2 tablespoons curry
  powder
2 tablespoons chopped
  garlic
1/4 cup soy sauce
1/2 cup Meyers rum

BARBECUED RED TORPEDO ONIONS *serves six to eight*

Peel and score onions, put butter into scores, and salt and pepper to taste. Wrap in foil. Place onions around outside of charcoal fire and cook while chickens are on the grill. Turn once or twice and remove from fire when chicken is done. Serve one onion per person.

6 to 8 small red torpedo
  onions
6 tablespoons butter
Salt and pepper

COFFEE ICE CREAM WITH PRALINE SAUCE

1 cup heavy cream
1 cup dark brown sugar
2 tablespoons sweet butter
2 tablespoons Meyers dark
　　rum
1 cup shelled pecan halves
Pinch of salt
Coffee ice cream

In a heavy saucepan combine all ingredients and cook the mixture over low heat until sugar has dissolved and the texture is somewhat silky, about 12 to 16 minutes. Pour warm sauce over coffee ice cream.

A SUMMER CHINESE DINNER
by Harry and Eloise Lee

Chinese Shredded-Chicken Salad

Steamed Catfish in Black Bean Sauce

Royal Chicken

Chinese Broccoli in Oyster Sauce

serves four

Harry and Eloise Lee and family are the proprietors of the *Royal Kitchen* in San Francisco, an establishment held in high regard for its pesto pizza as well as for its superb Chinese cuisine.

"This dinner is ideally suited for those hot summer evenings where a light but tasty repast is needed. A refreshing chicken salad with the distinctive flavor of hoisin sauce and lemons makes a nice beginning. Succulent catfish steamed in an aromatic black bean paste infused with garlic, ginger, and green onions can be absolute heaven. Very crispy marinated chicken wings, cooked for the briefest time in a sweet, tangy, and pungent sauce lives up to its name, Royal Chicken. Chinese broccoli (gai lon) is an amazingly flavorful vegetable. There is really no similarity between gai lon and plain old generic broccoli, except that they are both green. The gai lon is steamed or boiled just to the point of tenderness. Ribbons of oyster sauce are then poured over the succulent stalks. The preparation is simple and very rewarding.

"Needless to say, rice is a necessity. We could not dream of letting the black-bean-flavored juice of the catfish just sit in its dish. That juice is meant to be spooned onto the fish and the rice."

CHINESE SHREDDED-CHICKEN SALAD *serves four*

1/2 head iceberg lettuce,
   cut into 1/4-inch
   ribbons
3/4 cup cooked chicken
   meat, julienned
4 cloves-pickled shallots,
   finely slivered
8 sprigs cilantro, chopped

Dressing:
3 tablespoons hoisin sauce*
1/4 teaspoon sesame oil
1 teaspoon sugar
2 teaspoons lemon juice

Garnish:
1/4 cup crushed peanuts
8 sprigs cilantro

Combine first 4 ingredients in a mixing bowl. Mix together dressing and add the salad, toss well to mix thoroughly, and put onto individual plates. Top with peanuts and serve, garnishing with whole sprigs of cilantro.

*Available in Asian groceries and in the international section of many supermarkets.

STEAMED CATFISH IN BLACK BEAN SAUCE *serves four*

The whole catfish must first be cut into 1-inch lateral pieces with a very heavy meat cleaver. The easiest way is to let the fish market do it for you. Lay the catfish pieces in a single layer in a rimmed dish suitable for steaming. Prepare the black bean sauce by first mashing the preserved black beans into a paste. Next, separate the green and white parts of the green onion. Mince the green part and add to the black bean paste. Sliver the white part very finely and set aside. Add all other sauce ingredients and mix well. Top the catfish pieces evenly with the sauce and steam the dish for 17 minutes. Sprinkle with the slivered onions and serve immediately.

*Available in Asian groceries and in the international section of many supermarkets.

1½ pounds fresh catfish, cleaned and cut into 1-inch-thick pieces

Black Bean Sauce:
1½ tablespoons preserved black beans*
1 green onion
1/2 teaspoon sesame oil
1 tablespoon thin soy sauce
1 tablespoon dry sherry (not cooking sherry)
2 cloves garlic
1 teaspoon cooking oil
Dash of white pepper
Pinch of salt
1/2 teaspoon fresh ginger, minced

ROYAL CHICKEN *serves four*

2 pounds chicken
  drumettes

Marinade:
4 cloves garlic, finely
  minced
1 green onion, chopped
1 teaspoon fresh ginger,
  minced
1 tablespoon thin soy
  sauce
2 tablespoons dry sherry

Sauce:
1/2 cup pineapple juice
Juice of 1/2 lemon
1 tablespoon thin soy
  sauce
1 clove garlic, mashed
2 tablespoons distilled
  white vinegar
2 tablespoons sugar
4 tablespoons honey
1/2 tablespoon peanut
  butter
2 tablespoons hoisin
  sauce*
1 tablespoon plum sauce*

Batter:
1/2 cup cornstarch
1½ cups flour
1½ cups water
1/4 teaspoon baking
  powder

Combine marinade ingredients and spread over chicken. Allow to sit overnight in refrigerator. Prepare sauce, pouring pineapple and lemon juice into a saucepan over medium heat. Add remaining sauce ingredients in the order given, stirring constantly. Wait for each ingredient to dissolve fully before adding the next. Maintain heat such that the edges just bubble very lightly. Cook for 5 minutes, reduce heat, and keep warm.

Mix together batter ingredients with your hands. Make sure there are no lumps. Batter the marinated chicken and deep-fry in oil at 350° F for 9 minutes or until golden brown. Drain chicken on absorbent paper.

Transfer sauce to large skillet and heat until edges begin to boil. Add chicken and mix quickly to ensure that the chicken remains crispy but is coated with sauce. When the chicken is well coated (about 30 seconds), remove and serve immediately. This should be the final step in the preparation of dinner.

*Available in Asian groceries and in the international section of many supermarkets.

A SIMPLE SOUTHWESTERN DINNER FOR A SUMMER'S EVE by Deborah Madison

Stewed Pinto Beans and Herbs

Wild-Green Salad

Glazed Piñon Bread

Plum Crisp

serves four

Deborah Madison was the founding chef of *Greens Restaurant* in San Francisco and the coauthor of *The Greens Cookbook* (Bantam Books, 1987). She now makes her home in northern Arizona, where she is working on a second book.

"Some friends came to visit this summer from Manhattan, which is very far, in more ways than miles, from northern Arizona. We wanted to see the crater field at the edge of the Painted Desert so we took supper out there one evening and after a long walk, ate as the light left the sky and the stars came out. What we ate wasn't exactly picnic food as people talk about it these days, but it was the kind of food that seemed to go with a spare but dramatic landscape: very simple food with strong, clear flavors.

"To me this is the kind of food that brings one back to basics and underscores the heartfelt feelings among friends. It isn't fancy, it isn't pulling out all the stops and going for the best bottle of wine or the truffle, which, of course, has its place too. It's more the kind of food that stays quietly and deliciously in the background, nourishing life and love. As for ease of preparation and all that, nothing here is particularly hard or time-consuming to make."

STEWED PINTO BEANS AND HERBS
serves four

Straightforward, satisfying, and cheap. I've used wild oregano, bought at the Albuquerque farmer's market, which goes really well with beans, but the Mexican and Greek varieties, both of which are filled with strong flavor, work well too.

1½ cups dried pinto beans
1 tablespoon oil
   (sunflower seed,
   corn, or olive)
1 small onion, finely
   chopped
6 coriander seeds,
   crushed, or
large pinch ground
   coriander
4 juniper berries
1 teaspoon New Mexican
   ground chili
1 teaspoon dried Mexican
   or Greek oregano
Salt

Sort through the beans, rinse them well, then cover with cold water and allow to stand for 6 hours or overnight. Next day, pour off the soaking water and set beans aside.

Heat the oil in a wide-bottomed soup pot, add the onion, coriander, juniper, chili, and oregano. Cook together over a medium heat for 3 to 4 minutes, giving an occasional stir, then add the beans and 8 cups water. Gradually bring to a boil, then lower the heat and cook at just a simmer for 1 hour. Add 1/2 to 1 teaspoon salt and continue the slow cooking until the beans are as tender as you like them, probably another 1/2 hour or so.

Serve in a bowl with the broth. There are lots of tasty additions you can make, such as fresh coriander, mint, scallions, and spoonfuls of thick cream, but try them plain, first. They should have a wonderfully clean, uncluttered taste.

WILD-GREEN SALAD *serves four*

Every area has its offering of wild, edible greens, and in early summer this salad could include wild celery, mustard greens, purslane, dandelion, lamb's-quarters, the tender leaves of small bee plants, tart curly dock, and sweeter mint. Using these greens makes a rugged salad with strong, complex flavors. In this meal it provides just the right counterpoint to the more delicate beans and the tender bread. As wild greens aren't always available, here's an approximate version, drawing heavily upon supermarket resources and your own planter box or garden. But if you have even one or two wild greens, add them to the others; they will change the whole quality of your salad.

Rinse and dry all the greens, then tear or cut them into whatever size you like. Put them in a large bowl with the scallions and toasted sunflower seeds, pour on the dressing, and toss well. Pepper isn't really needed as the greens themselves have plenty of strong, hot flavors.

4 cups escarole or curly endive leaves (the inner, white ones), or small spinach leaves, romaine hearts, or a mixture of all

4 cups mixed greens, such as:
Tender mustard greens or turnip greens
Radish leaves
Rocket or arugula
Watercress, rock cress, or field cress
Nasturtium leaves
Tender leaves of dandelion
Dill or fennel greens
Hyssop leaves and blossoms, and
Any wild greens available

20 mint leaves
12 sorrel leaves
4 scallions, white and firm green parts, chopped, or handful Chinese chives
4 tablespoons sunflower seeds, toasted
The dressing (see below)

The Dressing
Whisk everything together, taste, and adjust with more vinegar or oil, as needed.

2 tablespoons herbal vinegar, such as tarragon vinegar
1/2 teaspoon salt
4 to 5 tablespoons sunflower seed or light olive oil

GLAZED PIÑON BREAD *for one large loaf*

A generous cupful of toasted, ground pine nuts insures the presence of that nutty-pine flavor. Red chili powder, mixed with water and brushed over the dough before baking, gives a beautiful, warm red-orange color to the bread, and where the vent lines have been cut, the dough bakes golden brown. The whole thing may remind you of a big gourd or pumpkin. Baking this on a pizza stone or oven tile will give the best texture.

1 cup pine nuts
1½ packages yeast
   (3¾ teaspoons)
1/2 teaspoon sugar
1 cup warm water
1/2 teaspoon salt
1 cup whole-wheat
   pastry flour
2 or more cups, as needed,
   white bread flour
1 teaspoon chili powder

Toast the pine nuts in a dry skillet until they begin to color, shaking the pan occasionally, then remove from the heat and allow the nuts to cool. Once cool, chop them finely or work in a food processor to make a fine meal. Be careful not to overwork or you will have a nut butter, as there is lots of oil in the seeds.

Stir the yeast and sugar into the warm water and set it aside until bubbles form over the surface, 5 to 10 minutes. Stir in the salt, the pine nuts, whole-wheat flour, and as much bread flour as you can, using a spoon, then turn the dough out on the counter and knead for at least 5 minutes, incorporating extra flour as needed.

Brush a film of oil in a bowl and set the dough in to rise, covered with a damp towel or piece of plastic wrap. Let it double in bulk, then turn it out on the counter, knead briefly, shape into a round ball, and set it aside to rise again on a peel or counter dusted with cornmeal or flour.

While the dough is rising, preheat the oven to 375° F. If you are using a baking tile, heat it at the same time. When the bread has again doubled in size, cut four or five deep slashes across the top with a razor blade or sharp knife. Mix the chili powder with a few spoonfuls of water and paint it over the surface of the bread. Slide the risen bread onto the baking stone and bake until firm on top and lightly browned where there is no chili glaze, about 40 minutes. Set the bread on a rack to cool.

PLUM CRISP *serves six*

A sweet dessert with a tart edge, this crisp can be made in the morning and eaten at night. You can serve it with cream, sweetened with honey or sugar, or a little lighter, with vanilla yogurt. (The latter combination makes a good breakfast too.) This is a good dish for using firm plums. If they're really ripe, mix a teaspoon of tapioca into the fruit to draw up and thicken the juices.

Preheat the oven to 375° F. Rinse the fruit, cut it into sixths, and toss with the sugar and spices. Let it stand while you make the topping, below. When ready, put the fruit into a glass pie plate or other glass or ceramic baking dish, cover with the crisp topping, and bake until the top is lightly browned and the fruit is tender, about 30 minutes. Serve warm or at room temperature.

Combine all the ingredients in a bowl and work them together with your fingers until you have an even-textured meal. Press lightly over the fruit.

2 pounds plums (black plums or a mixture of varieties)
1/2 cup light brown sugar
1/8 teaspoon powdered cloves
1 teaspoon cinnamon
Grated peel of one orange

Topping:
3/4 cup flour
1/2 cup sugar
4 tablespoons butter
1/8 teaspoon salt
1 teaspoon cinnamon

MENU FOR FRIENDS
by Jeremiah Tower

Cornmeal Blinis with Smoked Sturgeon and Caviar

Tarpon Springs Soup

Saddle of Rabbit with Black and Rose Peppercorns

Plum Napoleon with Sabayon Mousseline Sauce

serves four to eight

Jeremiah Tower is the chef/owner of *Stars Restaurant* in San Francisco, and author of *Jeremiah Tower's New American Classics* (Harper and Row, 1986).

"This menu is one I would cook for good friends: ones who would understand that a glass of frozen vodka would have to be downed in a gulp with the blini; that the soup refreshed the palate and re-excited the senses already lagging after the blini; that the rabbit saddle needed an old Cabernet Sauvignon; and that a middle-aged Barsac or Sauternes with the dessert probably matched the company."

CORNMEAL BLINIS WITH SMOKED STURGEON AND CAVIAR *serves eight*

Mix the cornmeal and salt and stir in the boiling water. Cover and let stand for 10 minutes. Beat in the eggs one at a time; then slowly stir in the milk. Mix in the flour and 2 tablespoons melted butter. Beat until the mixture is smooth. The batter should be the consistency of heavy cream. If it is too thick, thin with a little more milk.

Brush a well-seasoned crepe pan with clarified butter and heat. When the pan is hot, pour in about 3 tablespoons batter and tilt the pan to distribute the batter evenly. Cook until the underside is lightly browned, 2 to 3 minutes. Turn and cook the other side another 1 to 2 minutes.

Put each blini on a hot plate and pour 3 teaspoons clarified butter over the blini. Put 1 tablespoon sour cream in the center of each blini, then 1 tablespoon salmon caviar in the center of the sour cream, then 1 teaspoon (or more) black caviar in the center of that. Place 3 slices sturgeon around each blini and serve immediately.

1 cup yellow cornmeal
1/2 teaspoon salt
1½ cups boiling water
2 eggs
1 cup milk
1/2 cup sifted all-purpose flour
2 tablespoons melted butter
3/4 cup warm clarified butter
8 tablespoons sour cream
8 tablespoons salmon caviar
8 teaspoons black caviar
24 thin slices smoked sturgeon

TARPON SPRINGS SOUP
serves four

2 pounds red snapper
   fillets, skinned, cut
   into 1/2-inch cubes
1 large red onion, peeled,
   finely chopped
2 stalks celery, finely
   chopped
2 bay leaves
1 teaspoon fresh oregano
   or marjoram leaves,
   chopped
3 sprigs parsley, stemmed
   and chopped
1 teaspoon fresh thyme
   leaves, chopped
1/4 cup olive oil
3 cups fish stock
1 teaspoon salt
3 egg yolks
1 lemon, juiced
2 cloves garlic, peeled,
   very finely chopped
Freshly ground pepper

Mix the fish, onion, celery, and herbs together and let marinate for 1 hour. Then separate the vegetables from the fish and put them in a pot. Add the oil, 1/4 cup of the fish stock, bay leaves, and other herbs from the marinade. Cover and sweat over low heat for 15 minutes.

Add the fish, remaining fish stock, and 1 teaspoon salt to the pot. Poach gently until the fish is opaque throughout and just cooked, about 7 minutes. Remove the fish, leaving the soup in the pot. Beat the egg yolks, lemon juice, and garlic together. Bring the soup to a boil, turn off the heat, and add the egg mixture. Stir until the soup thickens a bit. Check the seasoning and return the fish to the soup. Serve immediately.

SADDLE OF RABBIT WITH BLACK AND ROSE PEPPERCORNS *serves four*

Unless you make the old-fashioned type of country rabbit stew, cooking the rabbit for a couple of hours until all the meat turns very tender and falls off the bone, the same problem exists with rabbit as with poultry: namely, the breast meat, in this case the saddle, cooks faster than the legs and thighs. In order not to overcook the saddle, I have separated it from the rest of the rabbit.

Rub the rabbit pieces and livers all over with a mixture of the oil, thyme, and tarragon. Let marinate for 2 hours.

Cut the carrots, celery, and onions into 1/8-inch dice. Heat the oven to 375° F. Coarsely crush the black and pink peppercorns. Rub over the tops of the saddles.

Put the onion, celery, carrots, 2 tablespoons butter, and the chicken stock in a pot. Cover and sweat the vegetables for 15 minutes over low heat, taking the cover off for the last 5 minutes. Put the rabbit pieces on a sheet pan in the oven and bake for 15 minutes. Add the livers to the pan for the last 5 minutes. Let rest for 5 minutes in a warm place.

Stir the remaining butter into the vegetable mixture and spoon it onto warm plates. Put the rabbit saddles on the vegetables; slice the livers and put those around the rabbit. Garnish the plates with the chervil sprigs.

4 rabbit loins or saddles
2 rabbit livers
4 tablespoons olive oil
2 sprigs fresh thyme,
    stemmed, chopped
1 sprig fresh tarragon,
    stemmed, chopped
4 medium carrots, peeled
2 stalks celery
1 large onion, peeled
2 tablespoons black
    peppercorns
2 tablespoons rose
    or pink peppercorns
6 tablespoons butter
1/4 cup chicken stock
8 large sprigs fresh chervil

PLUM NAPOLEON WITH SABAYON MOUSSELINE SAUCE *serves six to eight*

The best plums to use are ripe Simka, Santa Rosa, and Queen Anne, but any other combination of cultivated or wild plums will do as long as they are ripe. The Napoleon has to be assembled at the very last moment so that the pastry does not become soggy. It takes only a few minutes to assemble and is an ideal, very easy showstopper.

2 rectangles puff pastry
    12 by 15 by 1/4 inches
12 ripe plums, preferably
    of 3 different varieties,
    pitted
1/4 cup granulated sugar
Pinch salt
1/4 cup water
2 cups sabayon mousseline
    sauce
2 tablespoons confec-
    tioners' sugar

Preheat the oven to 350° F. Put the cold puff pastry pieces on a wet baking sheet and put them in the oven. Cook for 20 minutes. Let cool. When the pastry is cool, slice the pieces horizontally in half, so that you have 4 layers. Scoop any uncooked pastry from the center. Put the pieces on a tray and reserve.

Slice the plums and put them in a sauté pan. Add the granulated sugar, salt, and water and cook over medium heat until the plums are tender and beginning to fall apart. Put in a bowl and cool. When ready to serve, put a bottom pastry layer on a platter, spoon some of the plums over the pastry, then spoon some of the sabayon over that. Put another layer of pastry over the sabayon and continue building the layers, saving the last piece of pastry for the top. Put the top piece on and sprinkle that with the confectioners' sugar.

6 egg yolks
1/2 cup sugar
Pinch of salt
1 cup champagne
    or white wine
1 cup heavy cream

Sabayon Mousseline Sauce (yields 2 to 3 cups)
The secret to holding sabayon (zabaglione) is to keep whisking it over ice without stopping until it is quite cold. Put 2 trays of ice cubes in a container large enough to just hold a wide, rather shallow stainless steel mixing bowl. Half-fill the container with water and keep this ice bath by the stove. Boil a pot of water that is large enough to hold the mixing bowl so that it sits in half its depth of water.

Combine the yolks, sugar, and salt in the mixing bowl. Mix well and add the champagne or wine. Over barely simmering water, whisk the mixture vigorously until it is thick and pale yellow, about 10 minutes. Put the cooking bowl immediately into the ice bath and whisk vigorously again until the sabayon is cold. Keep chilled. When you want to use the sauce, whip the cream and fold it into the sabayon.

MY OWN BIRTHDAY DINNER by Mary Risley

Vegetables à la Grecque

Lobster Risotto

Fresh Berries in Lemon Mousse

serves eight

Mary Risley founded and has been the director of *Tante Marie's Cooking School* in San Francisco since 1973. She began a volunteer organization that distributes excess food from local businesses to neighborhood food programs and to Project Open Hand.

"To me the great pleasure of cooking is having people that I really care for to my house for a meal together. What I really love to do is have five or six people over who sit around my large cooking counter in the kitchen, who chat and sip wine while I cook. Then, we eat right there in the kitchen. The food I like to prepare is invariably comforting – hearty soups, whole-grain breads, salads, fresh vegetables, and grains. More often than not I make a rice dish – maybe country rice with wild mushrooms. The lobster risotto is definitely an extravagance. You see, I was born under the sign of the crab and I changed it to a lobster, so every year on my birthday I have a lobster dinner."

VEGETABLES À LA GRECQUE
serves eight

3 cups chicken stock
1 cup dry white wine
1 cup olive oil
1/2 cup lemon juice
2 large cloves of garlic,
    minced
4 stalks of parsley
1 bay leaf
10 coriander seeds
10 peppercorns
1 tablespoon fresh thyme
2 bunches very small
    carrots
2 bunches miniature
    turnips
4 yellow zucchini
4 green zucchini
2 ears fresh corn
1 pound small green
    beans, tipped
12 small white onions,
    peeled
Minced parsley
Lemon slices

In a nonaluminum saucepan, combine chicken stock, wine, olive oil, lemon juice, garlic, parsley, bay leaf, coriander seeds, peppercorns, and thyme. Bring to a boil and simmer 5 minutes.

Meanwhile, trim and peel the vegetables to cook and marinate in this mixture. Leave a little of the greens on the carrots and turnips, cut the zucchini in sticks, and cut the ears of corn into 1-inch rounds. Cook each vegetable separately in the marinade until almost fully cooked (tender when pierced with a fork). Remove and let cool. When all the vegetables are cooked, taste the marinade, add salt if needed, and spoon some over the vegetables. These can then be stored in the refrigerator overnight. Serve on individual plates as a first course, decorated with minced parsley and lemon slices. Serve with plenty of French or Italian bread.

LOBSTER RISOTTO *serves eight*

To make the lobster stock, kill the lobsters by inserting a sharp knife through the shell directly behind the eyes. Then cut up the lobsters, removing the sacks under the head, and sauté in vegetable oil until pink. Add 1/2 the onion, both carrots, and the celery, all finely chopped, and cook a few minutes longer. Add the tomatoes, roughly seeded, and the bouquet garni. Continue to cook for a few minutes until the vegetables are soft. Add the wine and fish stock and simmer until the lobster pulls away from the shells. (You may substitute 1 cup bottled clam juice and 1 cup water for the fish stock.) Remove the lobster and reserve, returning the shells to the simmering broth. Continue cooking the lobster stock for about 45 minutes. Strain into a saucepan.

To make the risotto, begin about 30 minutes before you want to serve it by placing the remaining 1/2 onion, finely chopped, and 4 tablespoons butter in a medium saucepan and cook until the onion is soft. Add the rice and cook 1 to 2 minutes in the onion mixture. Ladle in plenty of the warm lobster stock. As it is incorporated into the rice, continue adding more stock and cooking the rice, stirring continuously over a medium-high heat. (You may need to add warm water to the stock if you are running out of liquid.) When the rice becomes creamy and each grain is cooked through, add the reserved lobster with 2 tablespoons butter and the Parmesan cheese. Taste and adjust the seasoning. Cover and let rest off the heat for 3 to 5 minutes. Serve immediately on warm plates.

2 live 1¼-pound lobsters
3 tablespoons vegetable oil
1 onion
2 carrots
1 stalk of celery
6 large tomatoes
2 cups dry white wine
2 cups fish stock
6 tablespoons butter
2¼ cups Arborio rice
2 tablespoons freshly grated Parmesan cheese

Bouquet Garni:
4 parsley sprigs
1 bay leaf
1 sprig of thyme

FRESH BERRIES IN LEMON MOUSSE *serves eight*

1 quart mixed fresh berries (small strawberries, raspberries, blueberries, or blackberries)
8 egg yolks
1 cup sugar
3/4 cup lemon juice
1½ tablespoons grated lemon zest
1 cup heavy cream
4 egg whites
Mint leaves for garnish

Sort through the mixed berries, discarding stems, leaves, and undesirables. Do not slice berries or get them too wet by rinsing. Reserve a few berries for garnishing, then divide the rest equally into eight wine glasses or glass bowls.

To make the lemon mousse, in a bowl placed over a saucepan of gently simmering water, whisk together the egg yolks, sugar, lemon juice, and zest. Cook this mixture until thickened. Remove from the heat and let cool. Then fold in the cream, which you have beaten until it forms soft peaks. Then beat the egg whites until stiff but not dry and fold this into the lemon mixture. Pour this over the berries, then garnish with the reserved berries and the mint leaves. Chill until ready to serve.

WEST VIRGINIA SUMMER SUPPER
by Jacquelyn Buchanan-Palmer

Roasted Half-Chicken with Pan Gravy

Mashed Potatoes

Braised Collard Greens

Sliced Tomatoes, Cucumbers, and Red Onions

Berry Pie

serves four

Jacquelyn Buchanan-Palmer grew up in rural West Virginia and Pennsylvania. Formal training began at the California Culinary Academy and her cooking career at the *Union Hotel* in Benicia, California, with Judy Rodgers. She has also been chef at the *Post Street Bar and Cafe* and is currently chef at the *Hayes Street Grill*, both in San Francisco.

"The kitchen table in the house where I grew up was the center of the energy of that house. Aunt Nora sat there to shell beans, jars of crab-apple jelly were left there to cool from the canner, motherly advice was dispensed there, and the kind of home cooking people talk about but few of us eat showed up there on a wonderfully reliable basis.

"I brought from that table and the garden that supported it a love of those pure tastes and a desire to share them with other good people.

"The recipes that follow differ slightly from the way they would be done in West Virginia, but not by much."

ROASTED HALF CHICKEN WITH PAN GRAVY

2½- to 3-pound grain-fed
  chickens (allow 1/2 bird
  per person)
Kosher salt
Freshly ground black
  pepper
Zest of 1 lemon
Rosemary sprigs
Olive oil
Chicken stock
1/2 cup flour

Split the birds down the center of the breastbone and backbone so you have two equal pieces. Place halves in bowl and sprinkle with kosher salt and coarse-ground black pepper, large pieces of lemon zest, rosemary sprigs, and olive oil and toss to coat lightly with oil. This may be done up to two days in advance. Cover and refrigerate. Make a good strong chicken stock with wings or other bones that have been roasted to a light brown. See any general-purpose cookbook for stock procedure.

Bring a cast-iron pan to a medium-high heat and add a very thin layer of olive oil. Put chicken in pan, skin-side down, and shake pan so the pieces don't stick. When the chicken is nicely brown, place pan in a 350° F oven, still skin-side down. After 5 minutes, turn the chicken over. Cook an additional 5 minutes and turn over again. Cook 5 more minutes or until chicken is cooked to your taste. Remove pan from oven and remove chicken from pan to rest and keep warm. Pour out all but 1/2 cup of drippings from the pan and add 1/2 cup flour, stirring constantly with whisk. Cook slowly on top of stove until flour barely browns and seems totally cooked and without lumps. Add chicken stock and stir with a whisk until the gravy is thin and creamy. Add chicken stock as necessary to reach this consistency. Place chicken on a plate or serving dish and either nap with gravy or pass gravy on the side.

MASHED POTATOES

I'll bet everyone knows how to make mashed potatoes. A couple of things I feel strongly about are (1) a ricer, sort of like a large garlic press, that you push the cooked potatoes through, thus ensuring perfect, lumpless mashed potatoes; and (2) lots of good, sweet butter and milk or half-and-half.

BRAISED COLLARD GREENS

Hold the collard leaf and pull it away from the thick stem or rib. Tear the collards into half-dollar-sized pieces. Rinse and let drain in a colander. Put the onion in the bottom of a heavy pot large enough to hold the volume of collards you are cooking. Add to the collards either butter, bacon fat (in this case, reduce salt), or olive oil, salt and pepper, and a little more liquid. Cover and put over low heat. The greens need to cook slowly for half an hour or more depending on how young or old they are. Stir them as they cook and taste for salt, but also taste for when they lose the grassy taste and just when they become unctuous. The butter, bacon grease, or olive oil are necessary to give them richness and smooth their flavor, but individual tastes differ greatly so I leave it to you.

3 bunches collard greens
1 large yellow onion, diced
3 tablespoons butter, bacon fat, or olive oil
Salt and pepper to taste

SLICED FRESH TOMATOES, CUCUMBERS, AND RED ONIONS

You really need to do this with middle-of-the-season fresh tomatoes, cucumbers, and onions. A drizzle of oil and a light splash of vinegar (I like sherry vinegar but grew up with cider vinegar), again a little salt and pepper, and that is it. Basil, when available, is a lovely addition.

BERRY PIE

Pie Crust:
2 cups flour
1/4 teaspoon salt
1/2 cup lard (or 1/4 cup lard and 1/4 cup sweet butter)
6 tablespoons ice water (or more as needed)

Mix flour and salt. Add lard or lard and butter, and mix with pastry blender or rub in with your fingers. Add ice water until it will just come together and form a dough. The essential thing to remember is to have a light hand with the dough. Divide in two, wrap with waxed paper, and refrigerate for 1/2 hour. Roll bottom crust and make a lattice for the top.

Filling:
6 cups berries (choose from blackberries, blueberries, or raspberries)
5 tablespoons flour
3/4 cup sugar (or to taste depending on tartness of berries)
1/2 teaspoon salt
2 tablespoons butter
Grated lemon peel

Mix dry ingredients and sprinkle over berries. Toss gently and add into bottom crust. Dot the top of the filling with chunks of butter and cover with lattice. Bake at 400° F for 1/2 hour and then lower temperature to 350° F and bake for an additional 20 minutes. Serve with cool, un-whipped cream.

SUMMER SUPPER AFTER THEATER OR BALLET
by René Verdon

Cream of Cucumber Soup

Salad with Chicken and Avocado

Strawberries in Rum Cream

serves six

René Verdon was chef to the Kennedy White House in the early sixties, and he has authored four cookbooks: *The White House Chef* (Doubleday, 1967), *French Cooking for the American Table* (Doubleday, 1974), *The Enlightened Cuisine* (Macmillan, 1985), and *Convection Cuisine* (William Morrow, 1988). He founded *Le Trianon* in San Francisco and is currently an independent food consultant.

"Friendship is the art of giving to enhance the art of living."

CREAM OF CUCUMBER SOUP
serves six

3 large cucumbers, peeled, seeded, and minced
3 tablespoons minced onion
3 tablespoons sweet butter
2 tablespoons minced parsley
2 tablespoons flour
2 cups chicken broth
2 cups milk or 1 cup milk and 1 cup cream
1 teaspoon salt
Pinch of cayenne pepper
Pinch of white pepper
Pinch of nutmeg

Simmer minced cucumber and onion in butter until the cucumber begins to soften, about 3 minutes. Add parsley, cover, and braise over low heat for 5 to 7 minutes, stirring often to prevent scorching. Sprinkle with flour and stir until flour is absorbed, about 3 minutes. Add chicken broth and milk and simmer covered for 10 minutes. Season with salt and spices and simmer for 3 minutes longer.

This soup can be prepared in advance and reheated the same day, slowly.

SALAD WITH CHICKEN AND AVOCADO *serves six*

Combine oil, lime juice, and ginger. Sprinkle over cooked chicken. Season with salt, toss to coat, cover, and chill.

Place large lettuce leaf on each of six serving plates. Shred the remaining lettuce. Toss with celery and arrange around large lettuce leaves. Mound the marinated chicken on top of the large lettuce leaves.

Cut avocado into lengthwise slices and arrange 3 slices on top of each mound of chicken. Season with freshly ground pepper. Can be prepared ahead and refrigerated.

6 tablespoons salad oil
3 tablespoons fresh lime juice
1/4 teaspoon freshly grated ginger
6 small chicken breasts, cooked and thinly sliced
Salt to taste
1 large head butter lettuce, rinsed and dried
1 cup sliced celery
2 small or 1 large avocado, peeled, seeded, and brushed with lemon juice
Pepper to taste

STRAWBERRIES IN RUM CREAM *serves six*

3 pints fresh strawberries
1/2 cup sugar
1/3 cup dark rum
2 cups heavy cream
2 dashes vanilla extract

Hull strawberries, cut in half, and sprinkle with 1/3 cup sugar and the dark rum. Marinate in the refrigerator for 1 hour. Whip the cream, sweeten with remaining sugar, flavor with vanilla extract. Fold the marinated strawberries into the whipped cream. Serve very cold.

If desired, raspberries can replace the strawberries.

AN OREGON SUMMER'S MEAL FOR THE BEST OF FRIENDS by Allison Rodman

Grilled Oregon Blackberry Chicken

Oven-Roasted Vegetables with Rosemary and Garlic

Hearts of Romaine with Asiago Dressing

Fresh Baked Bread and Sweet Butter

Peaches, White Wine, and Vanilla Bean Ice Cream

serves six

Food and work have been Allison Rodman's companions all her life, beginning in her parents' wheat fields and kitchen gardens, moving to the yearly harvest of Willamette Valley berries and beans for school money, then unloading trucks full of watermelons and grading eggs in her father's produce market in her teens. During college she baked Viennese pastries from ten P.M. to four A.M., then explored and experienced food with mentors from the Middle East to Baton Rouge. Now in San Francisco, she is part of a culinary community and an ethnic diversity that brings continual pleasure and surprise.

"For many reasons it is an honor to be a part of this book. First of all, my homage to Ruth Brinker and everyone at Open Hand. You have proven you can feed the sick a fresher, healthier diet. Secondly, thanks to Robert Schneider for asking me to participate. He and I began our deep friendship over a broken water pipe one day at Pier 23, and so it has remained despite all the floods we encounter in our life's work. And lastly, because of my friends who have perished in this terrible time – too soon and too hurtful – I dedicate this Oregon summer meal to the best of friends.

"It was a lush green Oregon dusk, my friend Jane was wedded, and the relatives were milling about after the garden wedding and poached-salmon lunch. So the grills were fired, the candles lit, and we finalized the day's vows with a light evening meal full of Willamette Valley succulence."

GRILLED OREGON BLACKBERRY CHICKEN *serves six*

3 whole free-range
  chicken breasts
1/2 cup safflower oil
1/2 cup olive oil
1/2 cup raspberry or
  blackberry vinegar
Kosher salt
Freshly ground pepper
1 teaspoon Dijon-style
  mustard
2 cloves garlic, minced
2 tablespoons minced
  thyme, Italian parsley,
  and marjoram
Zest of 1 orange
2 pints blackberries

Separate chicken breasts into halves, clean off any gristle and extraneous fat, allowing skin to remain, trimming for a neat appearance. Whisk oils into vinegar. Slowly add rest of ingredients to taste, mashing in 1 pint of berries and reserving the remaining pint for garnish. Two hours before grilling, marinate the chicken in 1/2 cup of the marinade, unrefrigerated but in a cool place. Allow enough time for the fire to become very hot when you are ready to grill. Pat the breasts with paper towels so they are moist but not sopping wet and grill to desired doneness. After grilling, arrange on a platter and pour remaining marinade over chicken. Sprinkle last basket of berries on top.

OVEN-ROASTED VEGETABLES WITH ROSEMARY AND GARLIC
serves six

Cut the vegetables into 1½-inch cubes, adding any other vegetables that are in season and look appealing. Toss with olive oil, chopped garlic, and rosemary. Add salt and pepper to taste. Turn the oven to its highest setting and preheat for 15 minutes. Place vegetables one layer deep on a sheet pan and oven-roast for 20 minutes or until almost done. Finish cooking under broiler until edges are blackened and caramelized. Do not stir the vegetables while they are cooking. Remove from pan and serve at room temperature with branches of rosemary for garnish.

2 cups carrots
2 cups eggplant
2 cups squash
2 cups parboiled potatoes
2 cups fresh pimento or
   golden bell pepper
2 cups red onion
1/2 cup fruity olive oil
2 tablespoons chopped
   garlic
2 tablespoons chopped
   rosemary leaves
Kosher salt
Freshly ground pepper
Sprigs of rosemary for
   garnish

HEARTS OF ROMAINE WITH ASIAGO DRESSING *serves six*

2 heads romaine lettuce

Rinse the lettuce, separate out the smallest leaves, and trim the medium leaves to bite size and reserve the larger leaves for seconds or another salad, another time. Roll in towels and crisp in the refrigerator.

Asiago Dressing

2 eggs
1 clove garlic, minced
1 lemon, juiced
Kosher salt
Freshly ground pepper
3/4 cup fruity olive oil
1/4 pound asiago cheese

Place 2 eggs in a small bowl and slowly pour boiling water over the eggs. Let sit 1 minute, no longer. Separate the yolks from the whites. Place the coddled yolks in a medium-sized, steep-sided bowl. Save the whites for some other use, or discard. Add the garlic, lemon juice, salt, and pepper to the egg yolks and whisk while gradually adding olive oil, drop by drop. Taste for balance of acid, pepper, and salt. If too thick, add water 1 tablespoon at a time. This dressing should be used within a few hours, kept cool. To serve, toss lettuce leaves with dressing. Arrange on platter and grate cheese over the top.

611

$\dfrac{8}{9}$

PEACHES, WHITE WINE, AND VANILLA BEAN ICE CREAM *serves six*

One hour before dinner, peel and pit the peaches. If they are difficult to peel, drop them into a pot of boiling water for 30 seconds, remove with a slotted spoon, and refresh in cold water until cool before peeling. Slice the peaches into a ceramic or glass bowl, add the sugar and wine.

One-half hour before dessert, remove the ice cream from the freezer and allow to soften for easy scooping.

When ready to serve, scoop the ice cream into a gorgeous bowl, pour in the peaches and wine, and fold lightly until mixed but not to milkshake consistency. Scoops of ice cream should remain whole. Serve immediately with crisp nut cookies.

6 tender, sweet, ripe
   freestone peaches
6 teaspoons sugar
3 cups dry white wine
3 pints of your favorite
   vanilla bean ice cream
12 crisp nut cookies

F A L L

A BENEVOLENT BREAKFAST MENU
by Marion Cunningham

Applesauce

Shirred Eggs with Ham

Whole Wheat Sponge Roll

Lemon Curd

Marion Cunningham is author of *The Fannie Farmer Baking Book* (Knopf, 1984) and *The Breakfast Book* (Knopf, 1987). She also revised *The Fannie Farmer Cookbook* (Knopf, 1979) and she currently writes a column for the *San Francisco Chronicle* and is consultant to several California restaurants.

"I love the combination of gently baked eggs with little slivers of ham, only enough to give a bit of flavor. Warm applesauce and freshly brewed coffee go together with the egg-and-ham dish. The delicate sponge roll filled with tart lemon curd and perhaps a second or third cup of coffee will be a balm for the day to any cross spirits. A good breakfast is always benevolent."

APPLESAUCE *yields three cups*

4 large, firm green apples, peeled, cored, and cut into eighths
1/2 cup water
Sugar to taste
3 tablespoons lemon juice

Put the apples and water into a sauté pan. Turn heat to medium and cook, stirring often, until the apples become tender, about 5 or 6 minutes. Add sugar and lemon juice and stir to blend well. Cook another 1 or 2 minutes. Remove from heat and mash with a fork.

SHIRRED EGGS WITH HAM

Whole eggs gently baked in buttered ramekins are known as shirred eggs. For each egg, melt 1 teaspoon butter in a ramekin in a 325° F oven. Put 1 tablespoon chopped ham in the bottom of each ramekin. Break an egg into each ramekin, salt and pepper it, and bake for 12 minutes, or until the egg is just set. Serve immediately.

You may pour 1 teaspoon melted butter or 2 teaspoons cream over the egg before baking. Shirred eggs are a convenient dish to serve when you have invited a number of people for breakfast. You might try using well-buttered muffin tins instead of ramekins, when you have a crowd.

WHOLE WHEAT SPONGE ROLL
serves ten

Preheat oven to 350° F. Grease a 15½-by-10½-by-1-inch jelly-roll pan and line with waxed paper. Grease and lightly flour the waxed paper.

Put the eggs and sugar into a mixing bowl and beat for about 4 minutes (an electric mixer is almost a must for this recipe) until pale, fluffy, and light.

Mix the flours, baking powder, and salt in a bowl, stirring with a fork to blend well. Turn the mixer to the lowest speed and sprinkle the flour mixture and the vanilla over the egg mixture, mixing for just a few seconds. Remove the bowl from the mixer, and using a spatula, gently finish folding the flour into the egg mixture until no white streaks show. Spread the batter evenly in the jelly-roll pan. Bake for about 12 minutes, or until the top of the cake is golden.

Spread a tea towel on the counter and sift a little confectioners' sugar evenly over the towel. Invert the cake onto the towel. Remove the waxed paper and roll the cake up lengthwise in the towel. Leave rolled up until you are ready to fill it. Then unroll, spread the lemon curd filling evenly over the cake, reroll, and place on a serving plate. Sprinkle the top with confectioners' sugar, slice, and serve.

Note: This roll can be baked the night before serving, rolled as above, and left at room temperature until morning to fill and serve. If you wish to make this into a dessert roll, use all cake flour.

5 eggs
1/2 cup granulated sugar
1/4 cup whole wheat flour
1/4 cup cake flour
1/2 teaspoon baking powder
1/4 teaspoon salt
1 teaspoon vanilla extract
Confectioners' sugar for sprinkling
Lemon curd (see next page)

LEMON CURD *yields two cups*

Grated zest of 2 large
  lemons
6 to 7 tablespoons fresh
  lemon juice
8 tablespoons (1 stick)
  butter
1 cup sugar
4 eggs

Put the zest, lemon juice, butter, and sugar into the top of a double boiler, or in a metal bowl over simmering water. The water must not boil. Stir occasionally until the butter melts and the sugar dissolves. In a bowl, beat the eggs until thoroughly blended. Stirring constantly, spoon a little of the hot lemon mixture into the eggs. Pour the egg mixture into the bowl or pan, still stirring constantly, and continue to cook over the simmering water until the curd is thick. Remove from the heat and store in the refrigerator until needed.

AN EARLY-FALL LUNCH
by Laurie Schley

Baked Lima Beans

Three-Grain Quick Bread

*Eggplant Sautéed with Scallions
and Red Pepper*

*Endive and Spinach Salad with
Feta Cheese, Cherry Tomatoes,
and Mint*

Deep Dish Pear-Apple Pie

serves four

Laurie Schley was trained as a cook in Boston
and has since worked at the *Timberline Lodge* in
Oregon, *Hayes Street Grill* and *Greens* in San
Francisco, and at *Tassajara Hot Springs*. Currently she is administrative assistant at the San
Francisco Zen Center.

"In restaurant cooking we become overwhelmingly concerned with taste, visual aesthetics, efficiency. When I'm in my kitchen cooking for friends, I like to think about elemental forces: life and death, growth and decay, host and guest, fire, water, time, and nourishment — the mysteries of our ordinary life."

BAKED LIMA BEANS *serves four*

These baked beans are a favorite recipe of my grandmother's; cook them with bacon strips on top for a more authentic version. Like most bean dishes, this tastes even better the next day. You can make it up the night before and let it bake several hours in a slow oven.

2 cups dried lima beans
1 tablespoon oil
2 medium yellow onions, chopped
4 cloves garlic, chopped
1 teaspoon salt
1 to 2 tablespoons light, sweet miso
1 tablespoon dry mustard
1/4 teaspoon cayenne, or
1 teaspoon black pepper
1 sweet cooking apple, peeled whole

Soak the beans 6 hours or overnight. Drain, add water to cover, bring to boil. Drain again, add water to cover (this will de-gas the beans). Cook (or pressure cook) until done, approximately 1½ hours.

Meanwhile, heat 1 tablespoon oil in a sauté pan and add onions, garlic, and salt. Cook at high heat until hot, then reduce heat and cook until well done, slowly, to bring out sweetness. You can add a little bean liquid or water if they dry out. When beans are cooked, drain them in a colander and save the liquid in a bowl or a casserole dish in which you will bake the beans. There should be at least 2 cups of liquid so add water if necessary. Dissolve the miso in a small amount of liquid and add back to liquid with the mustard and pepper. Taste the liquid; it should taste about as salty and peppery as you want the final dish to taste; if not, correct seasoning. Combine beans, liquid, onions, and the apple in baking dish. Cook at 350° F for 2 to 3 hours, covered. Remove cover 1/2 hour before serving if it seems too soupy. The apple will fall apart; remove core and stir before serving. This dish tastes good warmish, not too hot.

THREE-GRAIN QUICK BREAD
yields one loaf

Preheat oven to 375° F. Combine dry ingredients and combine wet ingredients. Add dry to wet, stirring in quickly. Do not overmix; batter will be somewhat wet. Pour into a greased standard bread pan. Reduce heat to 350° F and bake for 1 hour or until toothpick comes out clean. Best served warm out of the oven.

1 cup whole wheat flour
1 cup rye flour, barley
 flour, or oat bran
1/2 cup cornmeal
1 teaspoon baking soda
1 teaspoon salt
2 to 3 tablespoons
 safflower oil
1/4 to 1/3 cup maple
 syrup or molasses
1¾ cups buttermilk

EGGPLANT SAUTÉED WITH SCALLIONS AND RED PEPPER
serves four

Heat the oil in a large frying pan. Add eggplant, garlic, red pepper, and salt and cook at fairly high heat until almost cooked. Add scallions for last few minutes of cooking. Just before done, add vinegar and mirin or sugar.

4 tablespoons olive oil
2 medium American
 eggplants, or
6 Japanese eggplants cut
 into 1/2-inch cubes
4 cloves garlic, crushed
 or chopped
1 tablespoon crushed
 red pepper
2 teaspoons salt
4 to 6 scallions
Splash of balsamic vinegar
Splash of mirin
 (sweet sake), or
1 teaspoon sugar

ENDIVE AND SPINACH SALAD WITH FETA CHEESE, CHERRY TOMATOES, AND MINT *serves four*

8 cups curly endive cut or
   torn into bite-size
   pieces and rinsed
8 cups spinach torn into
   salad size and rinsed
1/2 pound feta cheese
1 basket cherry tomatoes
1 tablespoon chopped
   mint leaves

Dressing:
2 shallots
2 tablespoons sherry
   vinegar, or other
   favorite vinegar
1 teaspoon salt
2/3 to 3/4 cup olive oil
Pepper

To make the dressing, chop the shallots and add to the vinegar, with the salt. Let sit 5 minutes. Whisk in oil. Add pepper to taste.

Combine all other salad ingredients and dress as lightly or heavily as you like.

DEEP DISH PEAR-APPLE PIE *serves four*

This dessert started as an experiment in making an extremely low-fat treat. With the flavorful, perfumy apples of early fall it is scrumptious. This dish is dedicated to all our friends on restricted diets.

Combine oat bran, raisins, and 1 tablespoon syrup. Spread oat-bran mixture in the bottom of a deep dish pie pan or other baking dish. Slice alternating layers of apples and pears into pan. Combine water, 1 tablespoon syrup, and seasonings and pour this over fruit. Sprinkle almonds on top. Bake at 350° F until done, about 1 hour, covered with foil except for the last 15 minutes.

*Butter Buds are available at many supermarkets. In this recipe they provide the flavor of butter without the fat.

1/2 cup oat bran
1/4 cup raisins, chopped
2 tablespoons maple syrup
3 to 5 Gravenstein apples, or other good cooking apples
2 to 3 cooking pears
1 cup water or apple juice
1 tablespoon Butter Buds*
1 teaspoon cinnamon
1/4 teaspoon nutmeg
Pinch of cloves
Dash of salt
1/4 cup chopped almonds (optional)

AN AUTUMN MENU FOR FRIENDS by Paul Bertolli

Fennel, Mushroom, Parmesan, and White Truffle Salad

Duck Legs Braised with Onions and Cabbage

Lettuces Vinaigrette

Seckel Pears Poached in Red Wine with Burnt Caramel

serves four

Paul Bertolli has been chef at *Chez Panisse* in Berkeley since 1982 and is responsible for the creation of the restaurant's changing nightly menu. Previously, he worked in restaurants in Florence, Italy. When not working, he pursues his interests in music and gardening.

"When I think of making any menu, particularly one for friends, I try to imagine a succession of dishes that make me hungry. Good cooking, after all, is about sharing one's hunger and the corresponding need for food's fulfillment. Cooking offers the possibility of making a very fundamental nurturing gesture, a gesture of love, which leaves an unmistakable taste in food. We all remember and crave such cooking. I am privileged to offer the menu following with the hope that it feeds the cause of Project Open Hand, and through them, those unfortunate ones, infirm and without resources, who are most desperately in need of a nurturing meal."

FENNEL, MUSHROOM, PARMESAN, AND WHITE TRUFFLE SALAD
serves four

This is a delicate, pastel-colored salad to make in late autumn when fresh Italian white truffles are available. It is one of the most striking combinations of flavors and textures I know of.

The success of this dish depends upon all the ingredients being very fresh. Shave the truffle, mushroom, and fennel into very thin slices. A mandoline is a very useful tool. If the outer skin of the truffle appears at all tough or dry, peel it. The most flavorful mushroom to use is the fresh bolete, which is deliciously nutty even when raw. Unless the bolete is in absolutely firm, fresh condition, substitute the white-capped button mushrooms commonly available throughout the year. They too should be firm and moist with gill covers that have not yet opened. Dress this salad with a vinaigrette, combining the lemon juice with fine golden extra virgin olive oil that has a buttery smooth character. Avoid green oils, which can be piquant in the finish. Salt and pepper to taste, sprinkle with freshly grated Reggiano Parmesan cheese, and serve immediately.

2 white truffles (about 1 ounce each), brushed clean
2 *Boletus edulis* mushrooms (about 3 ounces each), brushed clean
2 very fresh bulbs Florence fennel
2 teaspoons lemon juice
3 tablespoons extra virgin olive oil
Salt
Pepper
Reggiano Parmigiano cheese

DUCK LEGS BRAISED WITH ONIONS AND CABBAGE *serves four*

4 duck legs (2 pounds)
1 tablespoon additive-free
    kosher salt
3/4 teaspoon freshly
    ground black pepper
1 teaspoon thyme
3 large red onions
    (2 pounds), halved,
    cut into thick slices
1/4 of a savoy or Dutch
    white cabbage
    (12 ounces), roughly
    cut up
Heaping 1/2 teaspoon salt
3 tablespoons balsamic
    vinegar
2 cups full-bodied poultry
    or beef broth
3 tomatoes (12 ounces),
    cored, peeled, and
    quartered

Trim the fat in pockets against the skin around the flesh of the duck legs. Hold the flat end of the knife blade to the fat and scrape it to the side or cut it free. Trim the excess skin so that it extends slightly beyond the flesh of the leg.

Mix together the kosher salt, 1/2 teaspoon freshly ground pepper, and 1/2 teaspoon of the thyme, and sprinkle both sides of the legs with the mixture. Set the legs on a plate at room temperature for 1½ hours to absorb the salt.

Preheat the oven to 350° F. Warm a 12-inch cast-iron pan over the stove. Place the duck legs in the pan, skin-side down (it isn't necessary to add any fat to the pan), and cook them slowly for 20 minutes, or until they achieve an even mahogany color. As the duck legs cook, pour off the fat that collects in the pan and reserve it. The legs should not fry in their fat. When the legs are browned thoroughly on the skin side, remove them from the pan.

Wash out the cast-iron pan and return it to the stove. Measure out 1/4 cup of the rendered duck fat and warm it in the pan. Add the onions and soften them over medium heat, stirring often, for 7 to 8 minutes. Add the cabbage, regular salt, the remaining 1/4 teaspoon pepper, balsamic vinegar, and the remaining 1/2 teaspoon thyme, and cook the mixture for 5 minutes, until the cabbage is wilted. Transfer the cabbage and onions to a ceramic or enamel baking dish and lay the duck legs on top of them. Pour the broth over the legs and set the tomatoes, lightly salted and peppered, around them. Cover the pan tightly and place it in the oven for 1½ hours. When done, the legs should be tender throughout and should yield easily to a toothpick.

Remove the duck legs from the baking dish and pour the braising liquid through a sieve into a wide sauté pan. Arrange the braised vegetables on a serving platter, place the legs on top, and hold the platter in a warm oven while you finish the sauce. Set the pan with the strained braising liquid slightly off the burner and turn the heat to high. Reduce the liquid until it is slightly thick and about 1 cup remains.

Serve the duck legs on warmed plates with a healthy portion of the onions, cabbage, and tomatoes. Spoon some of the sauce over each.

LETTUCES VINAIGRETTE

First-picked tender leaves are perhaps best dressed just with soft extra virgin olive oil, salt, and pepper. At this stage they are most fragile and likely to be overwhelmed by vinegar. Dress sturdier leaves in vinaigrette, or a light, lemony cream dressing. It would be impossible to give precise instructions for a vinaigrette that would ensure consistent results. Both vinegar and olive oil are much too variable. Furthermore, salad lettuces require adjustments of the quantity and character of the vinaigrette according to the stage at which they are picked. Generally speaking, 3 to 4 tablespoons of vinaigrette will dress two large handfuls of mixed lettuces.

To make vinaigrette, begin with finely diced shallots. Pour good vinegar over them and allow them to stand for a half hour or so, if time permits; this draws out the flavor of the shallots. Dissolve a little salt in the vinegar, pepper the mixture, and stir in extra virgin olive oil to your taste. If you like the flavor of garlic, you may wish to smash a piece and let it soak with the shallots. I prefer a vinaigrette on the tart side, but not so much so that it leaves a bite in the back of the throat. Dress the lettuces lightly and immediately before you serve them.

SECKEL PEARS POACHED IN RED WINE WITH BURNT CARAMEL
serves eight

Seckel pears are small, have reddish-brown skin, and appear in the market in the early fall. Like Bosc pears, they are meaty fleshed and quite firm when fully ripe. Seckel pears are ideal for poaching because they resist turning to mush when cooked and their skins do not crack or wrinkle. Although the pears can be peeled for this dish, they seem nude this way, and it is best to present them with their skins on.

Caramelization of sugar occurs at temperatures from 310° to 350° F and is evidenced by a change in color and aroma. As the temperature increases, white sugar transforms to various shades of gold to brown, and the aroma from buttery to nutty. The best indication of the finished stage of the caramel for this recipe is the dark, red-amber color the caramel takes on seconds after it begins to caramelize. The addition of wine at this point will stop the cooking. It is a good idea to have your lower arm and hand covered with a long oven mitt when adding the wine. Caramel burns terribly if it lands on you.

This is not a refined dessert. Because the skins are left on the pears and because of the bitter-sweet sauce, its effect is more rustic. When Seckel pears are cooked, their pale yellow color is transformed to a faded tawny brown; glistening under the wine glaze, they are strongly evocative of autumn.

Put the sugar and water into a deep 3-quart stockpot. Put the pot on the stove over medium-high heat and stir the mixture until the sugar is completely dissolved. With a brush dipped in hot water, wash down the sides of the pan where any

2/3 cup granulated sugar
1 cup water
4 drops lemon juice
2 cups dry red wine
    (preferably Zinfandel)
8 Seckel pears
3/4 teaspoon balsamic
    vinegar
1 tablespoon dark
    molasses

(continued next page)

undissolved sugar crystals may have attached during stirring. Undissolved sugar clinging to the pan can later fall back into the syrup and cause crystallization. Bring to a low boil. Add the lemon juice. At this point, and until the sugar caramelizes, do not stir or move the pot at all. As water evaporates, the solution becomes more sugar saturated, unstable, and prone to recrystallization.

When the water has evaporated, after about 10 minutes, the sugar temperature rises rapidly until it reaches 310° F and begins to take on color. The advanced stage of caramelization, which gives this dessert a desirable bittersweetness, is evidenced by a light smoke rising from the pan, a dark red-amber color, and the aroma of toasted marshmallows. Stand back to add the wine; the pan will sputter violently. The wine will harden some of the caramel. Whisk the mixture until all the caramel is dissolved. Place the whole pears in the pot. Reduce to a simmer and cover. Poach the pears gently for 20 minutes.

Remove the pears and transfer them to a platter. Reduce the wine syrup to a scant cup. Add the vinegar and molasses and stir well. Taste the syrup. If you have taken the caramel too far and it is too bitter, correct it by dissolving more sugar in the hot wine syrup to your taste. Pour the syrup over the pears. The pears should be served at room temperature. As the pears cool, repeatedly spoon the syrup over them. As the syrup cools, it will thicken and form a glaze over and around the pears.

FAVORITE FLAVORS FOR FRIENDS by Amey B. Shaw

Arugula, Pear, and Hazelnut Salad

Cioppino

Butternut Squash-Praline Soufflé with Rum Lemon Sabayon

serves six

Amey B. Shaw has been cooking for twelve years and has been a chef for six. Beginning at Pizza Hut and receiving training in the Contra Costa College Culinary Arts program, Amey went on to be chef at the *Claremont Resort Hotel* and later executive chef of the *Fourth Street Grill*, both in Berkeley, California. She is currently executive chef at *The Maltese Grill* in San Francisco.

"These are three of my favorites. The nuttiness of the arugula in the first course reminds me of hazelnuts and thus the hazelnut oil in the vinaigrette. The cioppino combines the favorite flavors of saffron and Pernod. The dessert is both elegant and simple to prepare, utilizing a staple fall food, butternut squash."

ARUGULA, PEAR, AND HAZELNUT SALAD *serves four to six*

2 ounces raspberry
  vinegar
Kosher salt
Freshly ground black
  pepper
4 ounces neutral salad oil
4 ounces hazelnut oil
6 handfuls arugula, rinsed
  and dried
3 ripe pears (choose best
  in season)
3/4 cup toasted hazelnuts,
  coarsely chopped

To make the vinaigrette, pour the vinegar into a nonreactive bowl, add a pinch of salt and pepper, whisk in the oils in a steady stream, and set aside.

Place the arugula (rocket) in a wooden salad bowl and lightly sprinkle with salt. Thinly slice the pears and add to bowl. Drizzle the dressing over the salad and toss gently. Arrange on chilled salad plates and garnish with toasted nuts and black pepper and serve immediately.

CIOPPINO *serves eight*

For the croutons, first make the garlic oil. Grind the whole head of garlic, including the skins, in a blender or food processor. Strain through a fine sieve and add the oil.

Place the thin slices of baguette in a large mixing bowl and pour in enough garlic oil to coat thoroughly. Toss gently. Arrange on a cookie sheet and bake in a preheated 350° F oven for 10 minutes, or until golden brown. Let cool.

For the rouille, mash the garlic in a mortar with the peppers and the cayenne until they form a paste. Add the egg yolk and keep stirring. Slowly drizzle in the olive oil, drop by drop, until an emulsion begins to form. When all the oil is absorbed, taste and season with lemon juice and salt to taste.

For the cioppino, place the well-drained tomatoes in a layer on a cookie sheet and drizzle with olive oil and sprinkle with black pepper. Roast in a 400° F oven for 30 minutes or until lightly caramelized. Combine the stock, tomatoes, saffron, and orange zest in a large kettle over low heat. Set aside and keep warm.

Put enough olive oil to cover the bottom into a large sauté pan and place over medium heat. Add the fennel, leeks, and carrots and cook about 2 minutes. Add the shallots and cook 1 or 2 minutes longer. Add the garlic, turn the heat to high, and add the Pernod and flame if possible. Add the fish broth, the clams, and the crabs. Cover tightly. After about 2 minutes add the mussels and cover. As soon as the mussels and clams have opened, turn the heat down to simmer.

Croutons:
1 head garlic, broken apart
1 quart light olive oil
40 thin slices baguette

Rouille:
4 garlic cloves
2 red jalapeño peppers, roasted, peeled, and seeded
2 teaspoons cayenne pepper, lightly toasted
1 egg yolk
1 cup extra virgin olive oil
Lemon juice to taste
Salt to taste

Cioppino:
1 cup tomatoes, drained, seeded, and chopped (fresh or canned)
1 tablespoon extra virgin olive oil
Freshly ground black pepper
6 cups rich fish stock
2 tablespoons saffron threads, toasted and pulverized
Zest of 1/2 orange
Light olive oil for sautéing
1/2 cup fresh fennel, julienned
1 cup leeks, julienned
1 cup carrots, julienned

(continued next page)

2 tablespoons minced
  shallots
1 tablespoon minced
  garlic
3 ounces Pernod
24 Manila clams,
  scrubbed
2 freshly killed Dungeness
  crabs, cleaned, quar-
  tered, and lightly
  cracked
32 mussels, scrubbed and
  debearded
2 pounds squid, cleaned
  and cut into 1/2-inch
  rings

Have 8 large soup bowls warmed, and arrange all the shellfish with a quarter crab, 4 mussels, and 3 clams in each bowl.

Add the squid to the broth and let cook for 30 seconds. Arrange the squid in the bowls. Arrange 4 croutons upright in each bowl. Top a fifth crouton with a tablespoon of rouille and place flat in the bowl. Carefully pour in broth and vegetables and serve immediately. Pass additional rouille.

BUTTERNUT SQUASH-PRALINE SOUFFLÉ WITH RUM LEMON SABAYON *serves six*

For the praline, cook sugar and water together until a candy thermometer reaches 310° F. Add nuts and cook to the caramel stage, about 3 more minutes. Spread on a buttered cookie sheet and let cool. Grind and set aside.

Praline:
1 cup sugar
1/3 cup water
1 cup chopped pecans

For the soufflé, butter and sugar a 6-cup soufflé mold. Cook the diced squash in enough water until soft, drain, puree, and strain into a bowl.

Put the cream, flour, and sugar in the top of a double boiler. Cook, stirring, over medium heat until thickened. Whisk in the egg yolks, one by one. Add the rum and 1/2 cup of the praline. Continue to cook until the mixture ribbons. Add to the squash puree. Whisk egg whites until they hold short peaks and gently fold into base. Spoon into the soufflé dish, bake at 325° F for 40 minutes.

Soufflé:
12 ounces butternut
    squash, peeled, and
    diced
2/3 cup heavy cream
5 tablespoons flour
3/4 cup sugar
4 egg yolks
1 teaspoon dark rum
5 egg whites

For the sabayon, place egg yolks and sugar in the top of a double boiler, whisk until thick. Add the cream and rum. Place pan over simmering water and continue whisking until sauce reaches ribbon stage.

Sabayon:
4 egg yolks
1/2 cup sugar
1/2 cup heavy cream
1/4 cup dark rum

Make a simple syrup by combining the sugar and water in saucepan and boil for 5 minutes. Blanch lemon zest in this syrup. To serve, pour sabayon onto 4 plates. Spoon equal portions of the soufflé onto each and garnish with praline crumbs and lemon zest.

Garnish:
1/4 cup sugar
1/2 cup water
Zest of 2 lemons

OUR SUNDAY DINNER MENU
by Donna Grace Nicoletti

Antipasto

Lentil and Chard Soup with Tomato Concasse

Ricotta Gnocchi

Tomato Sauce with Italian Field Mushrooms

Bracciole (Meat Rolls)

Garden Salad with Balsamic Vinaigrette

Honey-Basted Pears with Chocolate Sauce

serves six

Donna Grace Nicoletti was born in Chicago to a traditional Italian family. She worked as an editor in the corporate world until she began attending cooking school in California at the age of thirty. She is currently the chef at the *Atrium* restaurant in San Francisco.

"Sunday dinner in my Italian family was a feasting marathon. The preparations began on Saturday night when the pasta was made. Cooking continued early Sunday morning, briefly interrupted to attend mass, then resumed until the entire family assembled around the table at three in the afternoon. With the clamor of conversation at a high pitch, the food was consumed, and when we were ready for more, my mother, grandmothers, and aunts cleared the dishes and reset the table for the next course. The mid-dinner break came about six and the men and children wandered off for a walk around the neighborhood while the women washed the dishes and once again, set the table in preparation for dessert. When it was finally over six hours after it began, the women still faced washing more dishes, while the men, exhausted (from what?), napped on the couch. I ate this way every Sunday for the first twenty-one years of my life. Now it seems like days gone by in more ways than one. My 'Sunday Dinner' menu is based on all of those Sunday memories but scaled down for the 1990s."

ANTIPASTO

On a platter arrange the cheese, drizzled with olive oil and sprinkled with black pepper. Add to the arrangement the prosciutto, olives, artichoke hearts, and the fennel, which has been tossed with lemon juice, olive oil, parsley, salt, and pepper.

Fresh mozzarella cheese, thinly sliced
Extra virgin olive oil
Freshly ground black pepper
Prosciutto, thinly sliced
California oil-cured olives, or
Kalamata olives, or
Sicilian olives
Marinated artichoke hearts
Florence fennel, thinly sliced
Lemon juice
Parsley, finely chopped
Salt to taste

LENTIL AND CHARD SOUP WITH TOMATO CONCASSE *serves six to eight*

4 cups water
1 tablespoon dried sage
2 bay leaves
1 cup lentils, sorted
Olive oil
4 cups yellow onions, roughly chopped
1 tablespoon pureed garlic
1 teaspoon butter
1 cup white wine
3 large bunches of white-stemmed chard, leaves removed and the ribs and stems roughly sliced into 1/4-inch pieces
8 cups chicken stock, heated
1 teaspoon dried oregano
1 teaspoon dried thyme
Salt and pepper
1/2 teaspoon lemon juice

1 large ripe tomato
Salt

Lentils
Boil water with dried sage and bay leaves. Do not add salt to lentil water. When water boils, add lentils and cook over medium heat stirring occasionally for 8 to 10 minutes or until they are soft but still hold their shape. Strain, lay out on a cookie sheet, toss with a little olive oil, and set aside.

Cook onions in soup pot with the garlic, 1 teaspoon salt, the butter, and 1 tablespoon of olive oil until the onions are soft. Add the wine and cook until the alcohol flavor is gone (just a few minutes). Add the sliced chard stems and cook until soft. Then add chard leaves, the hot stock, the oregano, and thyme. Cook for about 8 minutes until the chard leaves are soft. Be careful not to overcook the leaves or they will turn brown.

When chard is cooked, puree in a blender and pass through a food mill to remove any fibers. Put soup back on the heat and add the lentils. Simmer for about 10 minutes, then season with salt, pepper, and lemon juice if needed.

Tomato Concasse
Peel and seed tomato. Dice evenly into medium-sized pieces. Salt lightly. When the soup has been served into bowls, add about a teaspoon of the tomato as a center garnish in each bowl.

RICOTTA GNOCCHI
serves six to eight

Gnocchi can be made 1 or more days in advance.

Lightly mix the 4 cups of flour and the salt with ricotta cheese. Add beaten eggs and mix together with your hands until just blended. Allow to rest, covered with a damp cloth, for 15 minutes.

During the following process, use more flour as needed. Cut the dough into pieces the size of tennis balls. Roll each ball into strands the diameter of a quarter. Cut the strands into scant 1/2-inch pieces. Roll each piece in the palm of your hand for a few seconds to make them round and smooth. Then lightly press the gnocchi with the tines of a fork. This is a traditional marking. At this point, the gnocchi can be refrigerated overnight or frozen for up to 2 weeks. In either case, toss with a bit of flour, try to keep them separated from each other, and wrap well with plastic wrap.

When ready to cook, remove from refrigerator or freezer (they take only about 10 minutes to defrost). Boil plenty of salted water. Add the gnocchi (about 4 ounces per person) to the water and cook for about 5 to 6 minutes. Drain. Put into a bowl and toss with enough of the tomato mushroom sauce to coat well. Reserve the rest of the sauce for the bracciole (recipe follows). Serve individual portions of the gnocchi on dinner plates. Make sure each plate has some mushrooms topping the portion.

4 cups flour
2 teaspoons salt
2 pounds fresh ricotta cheese (without gelatin)
2 large eggs, beaten
Extra flour for rolling
Tomato sauce with Italian field mushrooms (see next page)

TOMATO SAUCE WITH ITALIAN FIELD MUSHROOMS

6 cups yellow onions,
  finely chopped
Salt
2 tablespoons pureed
  garlic
Olive oil
1/2 cup white wine
2 28-ounce cans of Italian
  whole tomatoes or
10 to 12 large, vine-
  ripened tomatoes
1 teaspoon ground fennel
  seed
1 teaspoon dried oregano

Tomato Sauce

Cook the onions with a few pinches of salt, 1 tablespoon garlic, and 1 tablespoon olive oil until the onions are soft. Add the wine and cook until the alcohol has been cooked off (just a few minutes). Puree the tomatoes and put through a food mill to remove the seeds and skins. Add the tomatoes, fennel seeds, and oregano. If making bracciole, add the meat at this point, also. For canned tomatoes, cook the sauce with the meat for about an hour. For fresh tomatoes, cook for about 1½ hours.

2 pounds Italian field
  mushrooms, or
3 pounds commercial
  mushrooms
2 tablespoons fresh
  chopped parsley with a
  small amount of fresh
  thyme and rosemary
  mixed in
Pepper

Mushrooms

Slice the mushrooms into 1/4-inch thick slices. Heat a sauté pan with a little olive oil covering the bottom. When very hot, add mushrooms and sear them until they are browned. Add a few pinches of salt and more pureed garlic while they are cooking. Depending on the size of your sauté pan, you may have to sear the mushrooms in a few batches. Don't overload the pan or they will not cook properly.

When the sauce is close to finishing its cooking, add the mushrooms and the fresh herbs and pepper to taste.

BRACCIOLE (Meat Rolls)
serves six

Mix the bread crumbs, Parmesan cheese, and oregano with a few pinches of salt. Set aside.

Trim any gristle and fat from the steak and pound it out until it is about 3/8 inch thick. Cut into pieces about 4 inches long (with the grain) and 3 inches wide (across the grain). In the center of each cut piece, sprinkle a generous tablespoon of the breadcrumb mixture. Roll up each piece in the direction of the grain and hold together with cotton twine as you would for a roast. If you do not have twine, a few toothpicks will also work.

In a sauté pan, sear the bracciole until brown on all sides, then add the tomato sauce at the same time as you add the tomatoes. Cook along with the tomatoes for 1 to 1½ hours. The meat should easily be penetrated with a fork when done. Set the bracciole in a serving bowl and cover with some of the tomato sauce. Serve as an accompaniment to the gnocchi.

1½ cups bread crumbs
1½ cups grated Parmesan cheese
1 tablespoon dried oregano
Salt to taste
3 pounds flank steak
Tomato sauce (see preceding page)

GARDEN SALAD WITH BALSAMIC VINAIGRETTE

Mix romaine hearts (the inner leaves of 3 to 4 heads of romaine), escarole (inner leaves of 1 head), and a few torn leaves of radicchio, rinsed, dried, and tossed in balsamic vinaigrette.

Balsamic Vinaigrette
Slowly whisk olive oil into the vinegars to emulsify. Add salt and garlic.

2/3 cup extra virgin olive oil
1/3 cup balsamic vinegar
Dash of champagne or white wine vinegar
1/2 teaspoon salt
1/2 teaspoon pureed garlic

HONEY-BASTED PEARS WITH CHOCOLATE SAUCE *serves six*

For Chocolate Sauce:
6 ounces semisweet
　　chocolate
2 ounces unsalted butter

6 firm, ripe pears
1/4 cup pear liqueur
1/3 cup honey
1 cup whipped cream
　　(optional)

In the top of a double boiler, melt the chocolate and the butter. While you are preparing the pears as below, occasionally whisk the chocolate mixture. When fully melted, turn the heat to very low and keep warm.

Preheat oven to 350° F. Cut pears in half lengthwise and carefully seed and core them without damaging the flesh. Butter a baking dish and lay them in the dish, cut side down. Add just enough water to the dish to barely cover the bottom and put in the oven. In a small saucepan on the stove, immediately reduce the pear liqueur just to cook off the alcohol, then add the warm reduction to the honey. After the pears have cooked for about 10 minutes, baste them with the honey. Repeat this every 5 or 6 minutes until they begin to soften. The cooking time will vary depending on the size, ripeness, and firmness of the pears – roughly 20 to 30 minutes. The pears should be softened yet still firm.

Remove from the oven and baste once more with the honey. Put two halves in each serving dish and drizzle warmed chocolate over them. If you like, nestle a small dollop of whipped cream on the side of each dish. Serve immediately.

AN EARLY-FALL SUPPER
by David Zafferelli

Camarones al Queso di Punta

Roast Pork

Chili and Tequila Sauce

Salsa Fresca

Lemon Buttermilk Pie with Strawberries

serves six

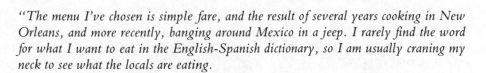

David Zafferelli spent many years cooking on Cape Cod and in New Orleans before finally coming to San Francisco. Although he loves all styles of food, Italian and Southern and Coastal Mexican cuisines are his passion. He is currently the chef/owner of *David Zafferelli Catering* in San Francisco.

"The menu I've chosen is simple fare, and the result of several years cooking in New Orleans, and more recently, banging around Mexico in a jeep. I rarely find the word for what I want to eat in the English-Spanish dictionary, so I am usually craning my neck to see what the locals are eating.

"The first course is a mildly spicy shrimp and pepper pan roast from a little beach town north of Puerto Vallarta. We devoured this dish for lunch in an open-air restaurant one afternoon. It was served with hot tortillas and cold beer. Feel free to use hotter chilies if you like your food lively.

"The second course is a dressed-up version of a dish I enjoyed in a small family-run restaurant on the road to Guadalajara. I've also simmered chunks of grilled lamb in this sauce with wonderful results.

"Dessert is from an old friend who learned to cook as the oldest child in a family of twelve from Thibodaux, Louisiana. I've added the strawberries and port."

CAMARONES AL QUESO DI PUNTA
serves six as an appetizer

This dish may seem like a bit of work for an appetizer, but the preparation can all be done in advance. It's a quick pan roast that's ready in minutes.

1 jalapeño pepper
1 small red bell pepper
1 large pasilla chili, or
1 small green pepper
2 tablespoons olive oil
2 tablespoons butter
1 medium onion, halved
    and sliced vertically
3 large cloves garlic,
    chopped coarsely
1 large tomato, seeded and
    chopped
2 tablespoons fresh lime
    juice
1 teaspoon salt
1 pound large shrimp,
    peeled, deveined, and
    halved
1/2 cup cilantro leaves
1 large ripe avocado, diced
4 ounces jack cheese,
    sliced 1/4 inch thick
2 ounces crumbled feta or
    mild goat cheese

Roast peppers over an open flame or under your broiler until blackened. Place in a plastic bag or a bowl covered with plastic wrap until cool enough to handle. Peel and seed the peppers and then cut them into strips. Use gloves with the jalapeño.

In a hot skillet, heat the olive oil and butter until the butter foams. Add the onions, garlic, tomatoes, lime juice, and salt in that order, sautéing briefly after each addition. When the onions have become translucent and soft, add the cleaned and halved shrimp. When the shrimp are pink but still a bit glassy, add the pepper strips, cilantro leaves, and the avocado. Transfer to a heat-proof serving dish, top with the cheeses, and cover or set under the broiler until the cheese just begins to melt. Pass Tabasco or Mexican hot sauce at the table.

ROAST PORK *serves six*

Salt the roast evenly and place in a deep, non-reactive pan. Cover with marinade ingredients. Cover tightly with plastic wrap and refrigerate. Turn occasionally. This step should be done at least 8 hours before you plan to cook the roast, and it would actually benefit from a longer marinating time, up to 4 days. Remove the roast from its marinade and pat dry. Tie the meat with kitchen twine, rolling and pressing it to make the shape regular. I like to cook this roast over a medium-hot fruitwood or mesquite fire. Turn the roast frequently to sear for about 10 minutes before cutting into 1-inch slices. Grill the slices 4 or 5 minutes per side, brushing with a little marinade. Arrange on a serving platter, and drizzle the warm chili sauce around the edge. Serve with black beans, salsa fresca, warm tortillas, and the remaining sauce on the side. You may also oven roast the pork for 10 minutes in a 400° F oven, before lowering the heat to 325° F. Continue cooking the pork for approximately 30 minutes per pound until the internal temperature reaches 165° F. Baste with the chili sauce for the last 20 minutes. Again, be sure to let the roast rest for 10 minutes or so before slicing so that the meat will retain all of its juices.

2 pounds boned pork loin roast (trim all but a thin sheet of surface fat)
2 tablespoons coarse salt

Marinade:
1 large onion, thinly sliced
2 bay leaves
3 cloves crushed garlic
8 to 10 black peppercorns
Enough dark beer to cover roast

Chili and tequila sauce (see next page)

CHILI AND TEQUILA SAUCE
serves six

After several attempts to duplicate this sauce, I still felt something was missing. Finally I remembered that the town in which I enjoyed this dish was near the town of Tequila. Remembering the habit of using whatever local spirits are at hand, I tried tequila, and it worked.

16 to 18 dried ancho chilies
1 large chili chipotle (canned in *adobo* is okay)
1/2 cup chopped onions
2 tablespoons olive oil or lard
1/2 cup gold tequila
1 cup tomato sauce
1/2 teaspoon oregano
1 cup stock (chicken or beef)
4 large cloves garlic
2 tablespoons fresh lime juice
1 teaspoon sugar
Salt to taste

Soak the ancho chilies and the chili chipotle, if dried, in lukewarm water until they are soft. You may need to weight them with a plate to keep them submerged. In a sauté pan, cook the onions in the olive oil until limp. Deglaze with the tequila, add the tomato sauce, oregano, and stock, and simmer for about 10 minutes.

In a food processor or blender, puree the softened chilies. Add the chipotle now if using one canned in adobo sauce. Add the raw garlic, the lime juice, the sugar, and enough of the chili soaking liquid to process until smooth. Add the tomato mixture and continue processing until smooth enough to pass through a sieve, then return the mixture to the pan. Simmer until the sauce thickens slightly. The consistency should be similar to a marinara sauce. Salt to taste. This sauce may be made ahead and reheated. It keeps very well refrigerated and is excellent as a base for an authentic *carne con chiles*.

SALSA FRESCA

Combine ingredients and let stand together for at least 1 hour. For hotter salsa, add more chilies. Any small, hot chilies may be used. A canned chipotle will add plenty of fire.

2 large tomatoes, seeded and diced
2 to 3 serrano chilies, seeded and finely chopped
5 teaspoons fresh lime juice
1/2 cup chopped cilantro
1/2 cup finely chopped red onions or scallions
1 small red or yellow bell pepper, chopped fine
Salt to taste

LEMON BUTTERMILK PIE WITH STRAWBERRIES

This pie is best if served the same day it's prepared. As is true of so many Southern desserts, it is quite simple to prepare. It is one of the most popular desserts I've served both in New Orleans and here in San Francisco.

1½ pints fresh
   strawberries
1 tablespoon sugar
2 tablespoons port wine

Rinse, drain, and slice the berries. Toss with sugar and wine and let stand 1 to 2 hours.

It is very important to have all your ingredients at room temperature for this pie to prevent the filling from separating.

3 eggs
1 cup sugar
1/2 teaspoon salt
1 tablespoon flour
Zest of 2 lemons
3 tablespoons fresh
   lemon juice
1 teaspoon vanilla
1 cup buttermilk
6 tablespoons melted
   butter, cooled
1 9-inch pie crust, pre-
   baked and cooled

Beat the eggs by hand until light and gradually beat in the sugar until you reach the ribbon stage. If you use an electric mixer, the end result will be too foamy. Add the salt, flour, lemon zest, lemon juice, and vanilla in that order, beating continuously. Carefully stir in first the buttermilk and then the melted butter. Make sure the butter has cooled. Pour the mixture into your prebaked shell and bake 10 minutes at 400° F, and then at 350° F for 20 to 25 minutes. The center of the filling should still be loose, as it will continue cooking as it cools. The pie will slice best if allowed to cool completely. Serve with a spoonful of strawberries on the side.

AN AMBITIOUS DINNER FOR FOUR by Judy Rodgers

Grilled Fresh Anchovies with Mint

Grilled Salmon and Radicchio

Black Risotto with Squid

Puff Pastry Barquettes with Pastry Cream and Wild Strawberries

Judy Rodgers is a native of St. Louis. She studied cooking in France and made a name for herself as the chef of the *Union Hotel* in Benicia, California, where her regional fare was widely acclaimed. Currently she is the chef at *Zuni Cafe* in San Francisco.

"This is a curious menu, and an ambitious one. It has delighted a group of my closest friends."

GRILLED FRESH ANCHOVIES WITH MINT *serves four*

20 fresh whole anchovies
Extra virgin olive oil
Kosher salt
Fresh mint
10 bamboo skewers
Lemon wedges

The anchovies should be glistening silvery-blue and firm. Rinse, scale, and gut them quickly. Pat them dry and marinate in extra virgin olive oil, kosher salt, and lots of fresh, roughly chopped mint. Carefully skewer 4 or 5 fish at a time, "ladderlike," passing a bamboo skewer through the collars and a second skewer near the tails. Grill over hot coals until the fish are golden and crispy, turning once. Serve immediately, on the skewers, with lemon and a cruet of oil. Eat the anchovies with your fingers.

GRILLED SALMON AND RADICCHIO *serves four*

1 pound filleted salmon
Extra virgin olive oil
Kosher salt
2 heads of radicchio
Salt and pepper to taste
Balsamic vinegar

Prepare the salmon by rubbing it with liberal amounts of olive oil and kosher salt. Cut the radicchio heads into quarters and season them with salt, pepper, olive oil, and a sprinkling of balsamic vinegar.

Grill the fish and the radicchio over hot coals until the fish is medium rare and the radicchio is slightly charred on the outside.

Serve with cruets of the best extra virgin olive oil and balsamic vinegar available, allowing each diner to dress his or her plate to taste.

BLACK RISOTTO WITH SQUID
serves four to six

Clean the squid, taking care to remove the silvery ink sacs from the jellylike mass inside the bodies. Crush the ink sacs in a mortar and then scrape them into a fine sieve. Ladle broth over them to extract their ink, which you should recuperate in a bowl. Continue adding broth, scraping and pressing the sacs to extract every bit of ink. Make an infusion with this broth, the chili, and the basil stems. Bring to a simmer and strain after 15 minutes or so. The broth should be black and spicy.

Slice the squid bodies into 1/3-inch rings. Do not bother to skin them. Rinse and drain the bodies and tentacles.

To make the risotto, sweat the onion until soft and translucent in the butter in a wide sauté pan. Add the rice and stir over a low flame until well coated. Add the simmering broth in 6- to 8-ounce increments, never flooding the rice, but never allowing it to dry out. Stir occasionally, not constantly, always maintaining a gentle simmer. After about 20 minutes the rice should be just al dente. Add the squid and a palmful of kosher salt. Cook until the rice and squid are just done. Stir in the fresh basil leaves. Spill onto a wide, deep platter and serve immediately.

2 to 3 pounds fresh squid
8 to 10 cups lightly salted fresh chicken broth
A few dried chili pods
1 bunch basil
1 yellow onion, freshly diced
3 ounces unsalted butter
1 pound Arborio rice
Kosher salt

PUFF PASTRY BARQUETTES WITH PASTRY CREAM AND WILD STRAWBERRIES

1½ cups all-purpose flour
1½ cups salted butter, softened
6 tablespoons ice water

Make a rough puff pastry combining flour and butter. Add ice water. Give the pastry 3 to 4 simple turns, then roll 1/8 inch thick. Cut into small diamond shapes and fold in the edges. Bake in a 450° F oven until golden, 10 to 15 minutes. Cool on a rack.

1 vanilla bean, split and scraped
1 cup whipping cream (unpasteurized preferred)
2 tablespoons sugar
Pinch of salt
2 egg yolks

Beth's Pastry Cream
Steep the vanilla in the cream over a very low flame. Add the sugar and salt and stir to dissolve. Stir a bit of the cream into the yolks, then stir the yolks into the warm cream. Cook until thickened. Pass through a strainer into a deep bowl and stir occasionally as it cools. Refrigerate. The flourless pastry cream will thicken as it chills.

To serve: Set out a plate of pastry shells, a bowl of the cream, and baskets of wild strawberries (or the best berries you can find). Do not assemble these tartlets ahead of time. Part of the pleasure of this is in piling on the custard and berries.

A WINNING COMBINATION
by Bradley M. Ogden

Roasted Baby Artichokes

*Grilled Quail with Mustard Glaze
and Braised Swiss Chard*

Creamy Cepe Polenta

Tomato Coulis

Buckwheat Dill Muffins

Chocolate Decadence Cake

serves four

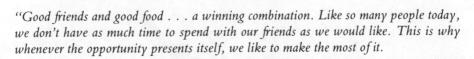

Bradley M. Ogden graduated from the Culinary Institute of America in Hyde Park, New York, where he received the prestigious Richard Keating award for "the student most likely to succeed." In 1983 Brad left the *American Restaurant* in Kansas City, Missouri, to join the *Campton Place Hotel*. In May 1989, he became the chef/owner of the *Lark Creek Inn* in Larkspur, California. His first book will be published by Random House in December 1989. He frequently participates in charity fundraisers and appears in videos and on television.

"Good friends and good food . . . a winning combination. Like so many people today, we don't have as much time to spend with our friends as we would like. This is why whenever the opportunity presents itself, we like to make the most of it.

"I like to keep food preparation simple with the emphasis on the natural flavors. Chilled champagne, sliced sun-ripened tomatoes with basil vinaigrette, barbecued oysters, grilled soft-shell crabs, corn on the cob dripping with butter, skewers of small red new potatoes with artichokes, and freshly baked shortcake with wild berries describe only a few. The simplicity of these delicacies will leave us plenty of time to enjoy the company of our friends . . . and possibly a quick game of basketball."

ROASTED BABY ARTICHOKES
serves four

2 lemons
8 baby artichokes
Pinch of salt
2 garlic cloves
1/4 teaspoon kosher salt
1/8 teaspoon cracked
    black pepper
1/2 cup diced fresh
    tomatoes
3 ounces Pinot Noir
5 fresh thyme sprigs
3 fresh rosemary sprigs
8 fresh parsley stems
2 tablespoons balsamic
    vinegar
3 tablespoons olive oil
1/3 cup chicken stock

Squeeze the juice from 1 lemon into 4 cups water. Cut the remaining lemon in half. Wash the artichokes and remove the tough or discolored outer leaves. Cut off the stem close to the base. Chop about 1/2 inch off the top center leaves; then snip the remaining thorny tips. Squeeze lemon juice immediately on each artichoke and place them in the water mixed with lemon juice. Drain before cooking.

Place all of the ingredients in the baking dish with the artichokes. Bake uncovered for 20 minutes in a preheated 375° F oven. Baste occasionally with the juices from the pan. Test for doneness by piercing the bottom of an artichoke with a paring knife. If it is tender, it is done. Let cool in dish. Cut in half and remove the thistles. Sauté until lightly brown in olive oil and serve 4 halves per person as an appetizer.

GRILLED QUAIL WITH MUSTARD GLAZE AND BRAISED SWISS CHARD *serves four*

Bone the quail with a small, sharp paring knife by cutting down the breastbone and carefully cutting away the carcass, keeping the blade of the knife toward the carcass so that is does not puncture the meat. Cut through the wing and leg joints and free the carcass. Lay the quail out flat, rub with mustard, and marinate with the rest of the ingredients. Place the quail in the refrigerator, covered with plastic wrap, for 24 to 48 hours, turning occasionally.

For the mustard glaze, combine vermouth, vinegar, lemon juice, bay leaf, mustard seeds, peppercorns, coriander seeds, parsley stems, and quail stock. Over high heat, reduce mixture to 1/4 cup. Strain and blend with softened butter and Dijon mustard.

Light a charcoal or gas grill. While the grill is heating, remove quail from marinade, brush off the herbs, rub with olive oil, and season lightly. Grill for 3 minutes, basting occasionally with the mustard glaze. Turn the quail over and grill for another 3 minutes, but still keeping the quail pink.

Place the chard in a covered pan with the butter and water. Bring to a boil. Reduce to a simmer and cook for 5 minutes. Season with salt and pepper to taste and set aside.

To serve, lay the chard down in equal portions on the plate. Place the grilled quail on the chard and drizzle with a little of the mustard glaze. Surround with the roasted new potatoes and garlic and serve with polenta (see next page).

8 quail, whole

Marinade:
4 tablespoons Dijon mustard
2 teaspoons cracked black pepper
3 tablespoons olive oil
1/4 cup Madeira
1/2 teaspoon kosher salt
12 sage leaves
8 rosemary sprigs
12 thyme sprigs
8 winter savory sprigs

Mustard Glaze:
1 cup dry vermouth
1/2 cup white chardonnay vinegar
2 tablespoons lemon juice
1/2 bay leaf
1 teaspoon mustard seeds
1 tablespoon whole black peppercorns
1/2 teaspoon coriander seeds
6 parsley stems
1 cup quail stock
4 tablespoons unsalted butter
1 tablespoon Dijon mustard

Braised Swiss Chard:
2 bunches Swiss chard, cleaned, stems removed, and broken into 2-inch pieces
3 tablespoons unsalted butter
1/2 cup water

CREAMY CEPE POLENTA
serves six to eight

2 cups water
2 cups chicken stock
1 3-inch sprig of rosemary
4 teaspoons garlic, minced
1 cup polenta (germinated cornmeal)
1/4 pound butter, unsalted
1/2 pound cepes (wild mushrooms), cleaned, trimmed, and sliced 1/4 inch thick
1 tablespoon kosher salt
1 teaspoon ground white pepper
3 tablespoons chopped parsley, sage, and marjoram
2/3 to 1 cup sour cream or mascarpone

Preheat oven to 350° F. Bring the water and stock to a rolling boil in oven-proof pot. Add the rosemary sprig, 2 teaspoons garlic, and polenta, stirring with a wooden spoon continuously, to ensure there are no lumps, for 5 to 10 minutes.

Cover pot and place in preheated oven, baking for 45 minutes, stirring occasionally. Remove from oven and add half the butter. Hold on a double boiler to keep warm.

Melt the remaining half of the butter in a sauté pan. Put the cepes in the skillet, sautéing in the butter for 2 minutes. Add remaining 2 teaspoons garlic and season with salt and pepper to taste. Sauté for another 2 to 3 minutes or until mushrooms are soft. Add mushrooms to the polenta with the herbs and sour cream. Season to taste if necessary and serve immediately.

TOMATO COULIS *yields 1½ cups*

Start a charcoal fire or heat the grill or broiler. Season and lightly coat the tomatoes with part of the olive oil, place on grill, and cook until almost soft but still capable of being picked up with a pair of tongs. Remove the seeds from the tomatoes and strain to reserve juice, then chop the pulp coarsely.

Add 2 tablespoons of olive oil to a heavy-bottomed saucepan and heat over a moderate fire. Add the shallots and garlic and sauté for a few minutes. Add the tomato pulp, tomato juice, and the rest of the ingredients except the herbs, salt, and pepper. Simmer for 30 minutes. Strain coulis and discard tomato pulp. Place coulis back on the fire and reduce if necessary to 1½ cups. Cool coulis slightly, add the herbs, and season to taste. Serve with polenta.

4 large tomatoes, grilled, or 1 28-ounce can Progresso tomatoes
4 tablespoons olive oil
1/2 cup shallots, sliced
5 garlic cloves, slivered
2 serrano chilies
1/2 cup light chicken stock or duck stock
1/2 bay leaf
1/2 cup Pinot Noir or Zinfandel
1/4 cup balsamic vinegar
3 tablespoons chopped herbs: basil, parsley, cilantro
Kosher salt to taste
Cracked black pepper to taste

BUCKWHEAT DILL MUFFINS
makes 12 muffins

Preheat oven to 375° F. Butter muffin cups. Mix dry ingredients in a bowl. Add the fresh dill. In a separate bowl, mix the remaining ingredients. Carefully combine all ingredients, taking caution not to overmix. Fill muffin cups 2/3 full and bake until done, approximately 10 to 15 minutes.

1 cup all-purpose flour
1 cup buckwheat flour
1 teaspoon salt
1/2 teaspoon baking soda
1½ tablespoons baking powder
4 tablespoons granulated sugar
4 tablespoons fresh dill, chopped fine
2 eggs
1¼ cups buttermilk
4 ounces sweet butter, melted

CHOCOLATE DECADENCE CAKE
makes 1 10-inch cake

12 ounces semisweet
  chocolate
4 ounces unsweetened
  chocolate
12 ounces unsalted butter
1¾ cups sugar
1/2 cup water
7 eggs
1 cup heavy cream,
  whipped
Extra chocolate to grate
  for garnish

Cut chocolates and butter into small pieces. Put in a bowl.

Mix 1½ cups sugar with water in a saucepan and bring to a boil. Pour over chocolate and butter. Stir until melted.

Whip eggs and 1/4 cup sugar in mixer until double in volume. Stir into chocolate mixture until no white streaks appear.

Pour batter into greased and paper-lined 10-inch cake pan. Bake at 350° F on a sheet pan with 1 inch of water in it (as you would a cheesecake) for approximately 40 to 50 minutes until it is set. Cool cake and put in refrigerator overnight.

To release cake, dip pan in hot water and run knife carefully around the edge. Frost with whipped cream and decorate with grated chocolate.

Recipe by Joann Vasquez.

A FALL AFTERNOON GARDEN REVERIE
by Ina Chun and Doug Gosling

*Lillet with Leaf of Rose Geranium**

Hopi Blue-Corn French Bread

Herb Flower Butter

Shiso-Wrapped Scallop Kabobs

Grilled Radicchio and Pancetta

Salad Confetti

Warm Figs and Prosciutto

Fresh Lemon Verbena Ice Cream

Dark Roast Squash Pie with Hazelnut Crust

*Fresh Orange Bergamot and Anise Hyssop Tea**

serves four to six

Recipes not included

Ina Chun has spent the last nine years growing specialty cut flowers and produce at her farm, Ohana Ranch in Sebastopol, California. Convinced that a "right livelihood" can be an everyday reality and not just an ideal to dream about, Ohana Ranch distributes its products to Bay Area establishments with the idea of bringing the special vitality of garden-grown goods to more urban environs.

Doug Gosling first heard stories from his mother about her Norwegian grandmother who tended hollyhocks, roses, and peonies among the vegetables she grew on the family farm in Saskatchewan. He still holds that image dear as he gardens in the foggy coastal mountains of western Sonoma County at the Farallones Institute. Manager of the gardens since 1982, he sees gardening as a practice that cultivates a partnership with nature to create beauty and sustenance for the body and spirit. His special intent at the Farallones is to rediscover "heirloom" and little-known varieties of Asian, European, and Native American vegetables and work with local restaurants and distributors such as Ohana Ranch to introduce them into the marketplace and ensure their preservation.

"A beautiful, productive, and diverse garden is a cook's best friend in creating an inspired meal, and no one better honors the hard work of a vegetable gardener than a creative, appreciative chef. A 'cook's garden' is a wellspring of bounty, nourishment, comfort, and healing for the body and soul.

"Over the years we have delighted in watching our gardens work their magic when friends join in the process of discovering and gathering the ingredients for a meal, preparing the food with us, and even picking and arranging the flowers for the table. There is a special communion among friends and the food they share when the meal is experienced in the garden from which it sprang. When we sit long enough to appreciate it, we are gently reminded that life is a garden which abounds with all that is essential for us to be sustained and fulfilled."

HOPI BLUE-CORN FRENCH BREAD
makes three loaves

This is a hearty, coarse-textured sweet bread with a crunchy, thick crust. The ground Hopi blue-corn flour imparts a lavender hue that contrasts beautifully with the golden exterior.

In a large mixing bowl combine the butter, salt, honey, and boiling water. Stir to mix. In another, smaller bowl, sprinkle the yeast over the lukewarm water and stir until dissolved. When the butter mixture cools to lukewarm, add the yeast water and mix well. Add the cornmeal a little at a time to the wet mixture. Then start adding the white flour until you have added about 2 cups. The dough will be quite thick, but not too thick to stir with a wooden spoon. Beat this "sponge" quite vigorously for about 10 minutes. Then add flour until the dough is a kneading consistency. It should feel like an earlobe. Turn the dough out onto a floured bread board and knead for 10 minutes, adding flour as necessary. Form into a ball and let rise in a warm place for about 1½ hours. The dough should double in size. Punch it down and let it rise again about an hour or until it doubles. Divide the dough into three parts and shape each part into a long, slender loaf. Cover them with a tea towel and let them rise until they are almost double in size. Spritz the tops of the loaves with cold water, and with a sharp knife make diagonal slashes across the top of each one. Boil the whole corn kernels until they have a chewy consistency. When the kernels cool, decorate the loaves by pushing the cooked whole corn kernels into their surface.

Bake in a preheated 400° F oven for almost an hour. Every 15 minutes or so, spritz the tops of the loaves with more cold water. This helps make the crusts crunchy.

1 tablespoon sweet butter
1 tablespoon sea salt
1 tablespoon honey
2 cups boiling water
1 tablespoon yeast
2/3 cup lukewarm water
2 cups coarsely ground Hopi blue-corn meal (available in natural food stores)
4 to 5 cups unbleached white flour
A handful of whole blue-corn kernels

HERB FLOWER BUTTER

Soften a stick of sweet butter at room temperature so that it can be pushed into a decorative butter mold. Unmold onto a plate. Pick herb flowers such as hyssop, lemon thyme, or red marjoram and push into the surface of the molded butter until it is completely covered.

SHISO-WRAPPED SCALLOP KABOBS

4 to 6 large sea scallops
   per person
Equal number of large
   shiso leaves (green
   perilla)
Virgin olive oil
Lemon juice
Freshly ground pepper

Wrap each scallop in a shiso leaf and thread 4 on a skewer. Baste thoroughly with olive oil. Grill very lightly, about 3 minutes. Remove from heat, sprinkle with lemon juice and freshly ground pepper. Serve warm.

GRILLED RADICCHIO AND PANCETTA

3 to 4 pancetta (Italian
   bacon) slices
   per person
Equal number of
   radicchio wedges
Good olive oil
Lemon juice
Italian flat-leafed parsley

Wind pancetta carefully around each wedge of radicchio and pin in place with toothpicks. Baste liberally with olive oil. Grill until pancetta is cooked through and radicchio is soft and collapsed. Remove from grill and remove toothpicks. Squeeze fresh lemon juice liberally over all and sprinkle with chopped parsley.

SALAD CONFETTI

With the incredible abundance of beautiful lettuces and salad green varieties for growers and chefs to choose from, a salad can easily become the centerpiece rather than simply a prelude to a meal or a palette cleanser at the end of it. Such an enormous variety of texture, color, and tastes exists that eating a salad can be an adventure, even a revelatory experience to those unaware of all these possibilities. We like to preserve the integrity of taste and appearance of each salad ingredient by leaving it as whole as possible and picking leaves that are no larger than a single-bite size. It is also important that the dressing be light and not overpower the ingredients. Start with a foundation of sweet crisp lettuces such as the Crimson Bronze Arrowhead or Marvel of Four Seasons and the lime-green succulence of Little Gem romaine. A confetti salad is a study in contrasts: the fuchsia graininess of Red Orach with the pale blanched spears of Belgian endive; the sweetness of Italian flat-leafed parsley or Russian red kale with the bitterness of radicchio or the sourness of French sorrel; the succulence of purslane or MacGregor's Favorite beet green with the filigree of chervil; the mildness of mizuna or chickweed with the surprising bite of arugula, Osaka purple mustard, or nasturtium leaves, or the mustiness of amaranth or quinoa leaves. Toss these ingredients with the dressing. Garnish the salad with pea blossoms, clove pinks, or violets, shoestring slices of ruby chard, thin slices of red or yellow sweet pepper, or wedges of yellow, orange, or red tomatoes.

**2 or 3 varieties of leaf
 lettuce
Different varieties
 of greens
Leaves and flowers
 of herbs**

Garnish:
**Edible flowers
Thin strips of sweet red
 pepper
Wedges of tomatoes**

Dressing:
**2 to 3 tablespoons
 raspberry vinegar
1/2 cup virgin olive oil
Minced zest of 1/2 lemon
Salt and pepper**

WARM FIGS AND PROSCIUTTO

2 to 3 Black Mission or
  Adriatic figs per person
Equal number of thin
  prosciutto slices
Good olive oil
Lime juice
Toasted pine nuts

Halve figs. Wrap each half with a slice of prosciutto and secure with a toothpick. Merely warm figs on the grill; don't cook the prosciutto. Remove quickly, drizzle liberally with olive oil and lime juice. Sprinkle with toasted pine nuts.

FRESH LEMON VERBENA ICE CREAM *yields one quart*

Several handfuls of fresh
  lemon verbena
2-inch piece of vanilla
  bean
2 cups heavy cream
2 cups half-and-half
3/4 cups sugar
Pinch of salt

Place lemon verbena and vanilla bean in a stainless steel pan with cream and half-and-half. Warm over medium heat to extract aromatic oils from the herbs without boiling the cream. Add more herbs, if necessary, until the flavor is to your liking. Remove the verbena and vanilla bean. Split the bean lengthwise and scrape seeds into the cream. Add sugar and salt and heat gently until dissolved. Cool mixture and freeze in ice cream maker according to manufacturer's instructions.

Verbena

DARK ROAST WINTER SQUASH PIE WITH HAZELNUT CRUST

This is a spicy, rich, harvest-season pie that can be made with any orange sweet-meated winter squash such as Red Kuri, sugar pumpkin, or Sweetmeat.

Mix ingredients in the order given. Pour into the hazelnut pie shell and bake in a preheated oven at 450° F for 10 minutes and 40 more minutes at 350° F or until set.

3 cups freshly steamed
  and pureed winter
  squash
3/4 cup maple syrup
2 tablespoons molasses
1/4 teaspoon ground
  cloves
1 tablespoon freshly
  ground cinnamon stick
  (a coffee grinder works
  well for this)
1 teaspoon salt
1 tablespoon vanilla
1 tablespoon finely
  ground dark roast
  coffee
4 eggs slightly beaten
1/2 pint heavy cream

Hazelnut Crust
Mix the dry ingredients together first and then mix with the other ingredients. Mix until the pastry just sticks together. Let rest in the refrigerator for 20 to 30 minutes. Press into a pie pan.

1¼ cups unbleached white
  flour
1/4 pound finely ground
  toasted hazelnuts
1/4 cup brown sugar
1/2 teaspoon freshly
  ground cinnamon
Pinch of nutmeg
4 ounces unsalted soft-
  ened butter
1 large egg yolk
1 teaspoon vanilla
Zest of one lemon,
  minced

A MENU FOR FAMILY AND FRIENDS by Rick O'Connell

*Roast Chicken with Rosemary
and Lemon Under Skin*

Gratin of Potatoes

Corn Pudding

*Hearts of Romaine
with Oil and Vinegar**

Raspberry Tart

serves six

**Recipe not included*

Rick O'Connell was formerly the executive chef at *Rosalie's* and *RAF*, both in San Francisco, and is presently consultant to the *Emery Pub* in Emeryville, California.

"This is really a family-and-friends dinner. I have three grown children, and they now have their own families and busy lives, so our times together are very simple. Nancy, my youngest daughter, always takes care of the baking of the biscuits and pies and cakes. We all pace ourselves so we can have some of everything. The menu is enlarged sometimes and fancied-up, but this is really what we enjoy the most."

ROAST CHICKEN WITH ROSEMARY AND LEMON UNDER SKIN *serves six*

Preheat oven to 475° F. Split the bird down the back and flatten. Gently slip fingers under skin to partially separate it from the flesh. Do not remove skin; leave it attached to create pockets for lemon slices and rosemary. Remove seeds from lemon rounds and sprinkle with rosemary leaves. Slip the lemon slices under the skin on both the breast and thigh. Brush the chicken with olive oil and sprinkle with salt and pepper to taste. Place in a baking pan that is only slightly larger than the chicken, skin side up. Roast for 25 to 30 minutes, or until done.

3½- to 4-pound chicken
1 lemon, cut into very
    thin slices
1/4 cup rosemary leaves
Olive oil
Salt and pepper

GRATIN OF POTATOES *serves six to eight*

Preheat oven to 350° F. In a large skillet, heat the olive oil and gently cook the onion and garlic until soft. Add the chard and heat, then add the basil and parsley and heat until all the greens are wilted. Butter a baking pan. Spread half of the potato slices in the bottom of the pan. Sprinkle with salt and pepper. Spread chard mix over potato. Add remaining potatoes, and season with salt and pepper. Dot with butter and top it all with cream. Cover the pan with foil and bake for 45 to 60 minutes.

4 tablespoons olive oil
1½ cups chopped onion
2 tablespoons minced
    garlic
2 cups blanched, chopped
    Swiss chard
1 cup chopped basil
1/2 cup chopped Italian
    parsley
8 cups thinly sliced
    potatoes
Salt and pepper
6 tablespoons sweet butter
3 cups heavy cream

CORN PUDDING *serves six*

Kernels and cream
   scraped from 6 ears
   of corn
1 onion, minced
6 cups warm milk
   (or cream)
6 eggs

Combine all ingredients, salt and pepper to taste, and pour into a buttered baking dish. Bake at 325° to 350° F for 1 hour or until set.

RASPBERRY TART *serves six to eight*

4 half-pint baskets of
   raspberries
1 cup sugar
Juice of 1/2 lemon
Baked tart shell
   (see below)

Combine half of raspberries with sugar and lemon juice and bring to a full boil and cook for 4 to 5 minutes. Allow to cool completely. Spread filling in a baked tart shell. Arrange remaining berries in circles over filling. Serve with mascarpone or softly whipped and sweetened cream.

Note: An equal amount of peeled and pitted apricots could replace raspberries.

3 cups flour
2/3 cup sugar
Pinch of salt
2/3 cup unsalted butter
Grated rind of 1 lemon
1 egg, beaten

Pastry for Tart Shell (yields two 9-inch crusts)
Combine flour, sugar, and salt. Cut in butter and lemon rind with pastry cutter or 2 knives. Pull together with beaten egg. Roll out dough on a floured board to fit a 9- or 10-inch pie pan. Fit into pan, laying foil directly over the dough. Fill with beans or rice or anything to prevent the dough from puffing up while baking. Bake tart shell blind at 375° F for 15 minutes. Remove foil and continue to bake until golden brown.

GOING WILD FOR DINNER
by Sammie Daniels

*Bisque of Drakes Bay Oysters
and Wild Watercress*

*Roasted Loin of Reindeer
or Roebuck*

Wild Mushroom Tart

*Grilled Peaches with
Wild Blackberries*

serves eight

Sammie Daniels continues to delight her bed-and-breakfast guests in both Inverness, California, and Tuscany, Italy, with lively, imaginative, and memorable meals.

"This 'Going Wild' dinner was prepared for a small group of friends in the late autumn as I began to shift my thoughts toward winter foods. Serve this dinner on a simple table. It is a country dinner, and the point is to enjoy it, not to make it complicated."

BISQUE OF DRAKES BAY OYSTERS AND WILD WATERCRESS *serves eight*

8 to 10 shallots, peeled
  and halved
3 large new potatoes,
  peeled and sliced
2 cloves garlic, pressed
1 tablespoon butter
1 tablespoon olive oil
1½ quarts whole milk or
  cream (or a mixture
  of both)
1 quart freshly shucked
  oysters
Salt and pepper to taste
Pinch of cayenne
2 cups wild watercress,
  cleaned and stemmed
3 tablespoons butter for
  garnish
Paprika for garnish

In a large heavy-bottomed saucepan, slowly
sauté the shallots, potatoes, and garlic in the butter and olive oil. Do not let the mixture burn,
but for wonderful flavor the vegetables must be
cooked very slowly for about 20 minutes or until
fork-tender. Add the milk mixture, then the oysters, poaching slowly until they are plumped.
Season with salt, pepper, and cayenne and add
the cress. Heat until barely wilted. Serve in large
bowls with a knob of butter and some paprika
to color.

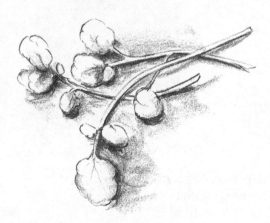

ROASTED LOIN OF REINDEER OR ROEBUCK *serves eight*

Preheat oven to 375° F. Sprinkle the meat with some cognac and salt and pepper and some pats of butter on top. Roast for 6 to 7 minutes per pound until it is just rare (about 15 minutes). Do not overcook. During the cooking, if it appears dry, then add a little broth to the pan. Take it from the oven and let the juices ooze. Carve into eight round slices.

1¾ pound loin of reindeer or roebuck
Cognac
Salt and pepper to taste
Butter
Beef or veal broth

WILD MUSHROOM TART *serves eight*

Clean the mushrooms with a damp towel. Peel the shallots. Peel the apples and quarter them. Put the garlic through a press. Heat the goose fat, if available, and add the shallots with the sugar and salt and pepper to taste, and cook over low heat for 30 minutes. Now add the mushrooms, cloves, and pressed garlic and cook another 10 minutes. From time to time add a little broth if necessary. Now add the apples and cook another 10 minutes. Add thyme and marjoram to taste. This should now have the consistency of a thick stew. Spread the mixture in the pre-baked tart shell and heat the whole tart for 20 to 30 minutes at 350° F until it is very hot. Serve hot or at room temperature.

16 ounces porcini mushrooms or other wild mushrooms
8 shallots
2 apples
2 cloves garlic
2 tablespoons goose fat or vegetable oil
1 tablespoon sugar
Salt and pepper
2 cloves
1 cup chicken broth, more or less
Small bunch of thyme
Marjoram to taste
12-inch round puff pastry tart shell

GRILLED PEACHES WITH
WILD BLACKBERRIES *serves eight*

4 freestone peaches
1/4 cup cognac or vin
   Santo
2 tablespoons sugar
1 quart wild blackberries
3 tablespoons sweet butter
3 tablespoons brown sugar
1/2 cup crème fraîche

Before dinner, halve and pit the peaches. Put them cut-side down in one layer in a flat dish with the cognac or vin Santo mixed with the sugar as a marinade. Butter and sugar a large oven-proof dish. Spread the berries, which have been picked clean, but not rinsed, in the bottom of the dish in one layer. Dot with butter and sprinkle with brown sugar. After dinner, put the berries under the broiler until they start to bubble and brown on top. Remove the peaches from the marinade and grill them skin side away from flame, or put them under the broiler when the berries are done. When the peaches are warmed and tender (5 to 10 minutes, depending on the heat of the grill), serve them with the wild berries, remaining marinade, and crème fraîche spooned over, in that order.

A glass of Sauterne would provide the perfect finish.

FALL MENU FOR FRIENDS SERVED AT HOME
by Todd Muir

Thai Soup with Salmon

Sun-Dried Tomato Pasta

Fall Vegetables

Spit-Roasted Cornish Game Hens

Mixed Berry Cobbler

Cinnamon Ice Cream*

serves six

*Recipe not included

Todd Muir is a graduate of the California Culinary Academy in San Francisco. He worked at *Chez Panisse* in Berkeley before opening *Madrona Manor Restaurant* in Healdsburg, California, in 1983. He was recently named one of the "Rising Star" chefs in America by *Hospitality* magazine.

"Fall is the perfect time for gatherings at home. The season's vegetable harvest is bountiful, and the feel of winter is in the air. On cool evenings a cozy fire, an apéritif, and relaxed conversation precede dinner."

THAI SOUP WITH SALMON
serves six as a first course

1 pound fresh salmon
1 yellow onion, sliced
Peanut oil
2 cups bok choy, chopped
4 cloves garlic, minced
1 tablespoon julienned
    ginger
1 quart fish stock
    (or clam juice)
1 12-ounce can coconut
    milk
2 stalks lemon grass, cut
    lengthwise into
    2-inch lengths
1 tablespoon sugar
1/4 cup rice wine vinegar
2 tablespoons Szechuan
    pepper oil (see below)

Bone, skin, and cut salmon into cubes. In a stockpot, sweat onions in peanut oil. Add bok choy, garlic, and ginger and cook until soft. Remove from pot and reserve. Put salmon in stockpot and cook briefly. Remove salmon and reserve. Combine stock, coconut milk, and lemon grass in pot, and simmer for 20 minutes. Return salmon, bok choy, garlic, onions, and ginger to pot and add remaining ingredients. Serve hot.

2 cups peanut oil
1/4 cup paprika
1/4 cup chili pepper flakes
1 head garlic, peeled
1/4 cup minced ginger
1 tablespoon toasted
    sesame oil

Szechuan Pepper Oil (yields 2½ cups)
Place all ingredients in a small saucepan over medium heat. Bring to a boil, reduce heat to simmer, and cook for 1/2 hour. Remove oil from heat, filter into a pouring container, and allow to cool. Store pepper oil in a cool, dark place.

SUN-DRIED TOMATO PASTA
yields 2 pounds

Place all ingredients into a mixer bowl. Using the paddle attachment, with mixer on #2 speed, beat the ingredients for 3 to 5 minutes to form a dough, stopping the mixer to scrape the sides of the bowl as necessary. Turn the dough onto a worktable and knead for 1 to 2 minutes.

Allow the dough to rest for approximately 1 hour before making it into pasta or wrap and refrigerate or freeze.

See page 211 for directions on rolling and cutting pasta dough.

8 tablespoons sun-dried tomato paste
4 cups flour (all-purpose or semolina)
6 eggs, beaten
1/4 cup olive oil
1/4 teaspoon salt

FALL VEGETABLES *serves six*

2 bunches baby carrots
1 green and 1 yellow
    squash, cut in 1½-inch
    pieces
1 red and 1 yellow bell
    pepper, cut in 1½-inch
    pieces
1 basket cherry tomatoes
2 small Japanese eggplants,
    cut in 1½-inch pieces
12 pearl onions
Basil leaves
2 tablespoons olive oil
2 cloves garlic, minced
Salt and pepper to taste
Freshly grated Parmesan
    cheese

Blanch vegetables until al dente. Toss vegetables with olive oil, garlic, salt and pepper, and Parmesan.

SPIT-ROASTED CORNISH GAME HENS *serves six*

Fresh thyme, marjoram,
    sage
1/3 cup honey
3 tablespoons vinegar
Salt and pepper to taste
3 tablespoons minced
    garlic
3 Cornish game hens

Mix together first five ingredients and marinate game hens for four hours.

Spit roast for 1 hour over low fire.

Arrange 1/2 game hen per person on nest of cooked pasta and surround with vegetables.

MIXED BERRY COBBLER

Toss together ingredients for filling and set aside.

Mix together dry ingredients for biscuit and cut in butter with a pastry cutter until a coarse-meal texture has been achieved. Blend together vanilla, yogurt, and milk, then add to flour/butter mixture and mix briefly until just combined. Place dough on floured surface and press out to 3/4-inch thickness. Cut into circles with 2¼-inch cutter. Brush with milk and sprinkle with granulated sugar. Bake at 400° F until golden.

To assemble, heat the berries and juice in a pan until thick and bubbly. Pour into serving bowls, top with a biscuit and a scoop of cinnamon ice cream.

Filling:
1/2 cup plum juice
1 tablespoon cornstarch
1 teaspoon cinnamon
1/2 teaspoon grated
    nutmeg
1 tablespoon fresh ginger,
    minced
2⅓ pounds fresh berries
    (raspberries, blackber-
    ries, or boysenberries)
1/4 cup amaretto
2/3 cup brown sugar

Biscuit:
9½ ounces all-purpose
    flour
1⅓ ounces ground pecans
3¾ ounces brown sugar
2/3 teaspoon salt
2/3 teaspoon baking soda
2⅔ teaspoons baking
    powder
2⅔ ounces butter
1/2 teaspoon vanilla
4 ounces yogurt
2⅔ ounces milk
Additional milk to
    brush over
Granulated sugar

A HALLOWEEN DINNER
by David Pellerito

Arugula and Orange Salad

Fresh Pumpkin-Stuffed Pasta

Walnut Sauce

serves six

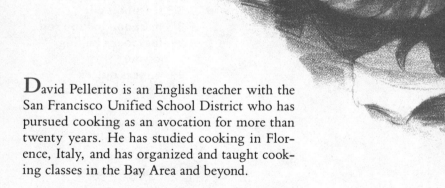

David Pellerito is an English teacher with the San Francisco Unified School District who has pursued cooking as an avocation for more than twenty years. He has studied cooking in Florence, Italy, and has organized and taught cooking classes in the Bay Area and beyond.

"I began collecting pumpkin recipes over twenty years ago when I decided to host a Halloween party for my new-found friends in San Francisco. Back then we were all new to the city and without family. We established our own traditions, which included a 'pumpkin feast.' Over the years we have added new dishes and omitted others. Our meals often included a dozen or more items and ranged from pumpkin soup and bread made with and shaped like a pumpkin, to various stews made with pumpkin, to a variety of desserts with pumpkin.

"The recipes that follow are favorites and have been served to many loved and loving friends."

ARUGULA AND ORANGE SALAD
serves six

Rinse and dry the arugula well. Remove the stems and tear into smaller pieces if the leaves are large. Arrange them in a wide bowl or serving dish.

With a sharp knife slice the peels, pith, and outer membrane from the oranges. Slice them into 1/8-inch rounds. Arrange the rounds on the arugula.

Remove the roots and most of the green tops from the green onions. Slice the onions into 1/8-inch rounds and sprinkle them over the orange slices.

Remove the pits from the olives and cut them into slivers. Sprinkle these on the orange slices as well.

To serve, thoroughly combine the lemon juice, olive oil, and the salt and pepper with a whisk or a fork until the mixture is homogeneous and the salt is dissolved. Taste for salt and pepper. Pour the dressing over the oranges and toss them well with the arugula. Sprinkle with the pumpkin seeds. Serve immediately.

1 large bunch arugula (rocket)
3 large seedless oranges
1 bunch green onions
6 oil-cured black olives
Juice of 1 lemon
6 tablespoons extra virgin olive oil
Salt and freshly ground black pepper to taste
2 tablespoons roasted pumpkin seeds

FRESH PUMPKIN-STUFFED PASTA
serves six

1 cup pumpkin pulp,
  pureed (see note)
1/4 cup toasted home-
  made bread crumbs
6 Italian amaretti cookies,
  crushed (about
  1 ounce)
1 egg, beaten
1/2 cup freshly grated
  Parmesan cheese
Grated zest of 1/2 lemon
  (optional)
1/8 teaspoon freshly
  grated nutmeg
1/2 teaspoon salt or to
  taste
1 recipe egg pasta (see
  below)
Walnut sauce (see next
  page)
1/2 cup additional freshly
  grated Parmesan cheese

Place pumpkin in a large bowl. Add the bread crumbs, the amaretti cookies, the egg, 1/2 cup Parmesan, the lemon zest, nutmeg, and salt. Mix very well and reserve. Prepare the pasta and roll it into thin sheets. Do not allow to dry.

Place 1/2 teaspoon mounds of the stuffing mixture in rows on a sheet of pasta. Each mound should be 1 inch from the edge and 2 inches from its neighbor. Slightly moisten between the rows of stuffing with a finger or pastry brush dipped in water. Cover the mounds with another of the sheets of pasta. Press pasta with fingers around each mound to seal and to remove trapped air. Using a 2-inch round scalloped pasta cutter, cut out circles around each mound. Seal edges of tortelli by squeezing gently with fingers all around. Let tortelli dry on a floured cloth for at least 1 hour before cooking.

To cook tortelli, place them in 6 quarts of boiling salted water. Stir gently. When the tortelli float to the surface, they are done. Taste one to be sure. Remove and serve immediately with walnut sauce and additional Parmesan cheese.

Note: Choose a small pumpkin that is heavy for its size. Japanese pumpkins with green skins and orange flesh are excellent. Bake whole pumpkin in a 375° F oven until it is tender. Remove skin and seeds. Puree the flesh in a food mill. If the puree seems too liquid, heat it in a saucepan to evaporate some moisture. Measure out 1 cup. Reserve remaining pumpkin for another use.

Fresh Egg Pasta (yields 1 pound)

3 cups unbleached white
  flour (or substitute
  semolina for half
  of this)
3 extra large eggs plus
  1 egg yolk
1 tablespoon olive oil
  (optional)
1/2 teaspoon salt

Place the flour on a flat surface or in a large bowl and make a well in the center of it. Put the remaining ingredients in the well and mix them well with a fork. After they are well mixed begin incorporating the flour until all the liquid is absorbed and you have a soft but not sticky dough. You may have to add more flour or perhaps a little more liquid to achieve this consistency. This entire procedure can easily be done in a food processor. The key is balancing the liquid with the dry ingredients. The dough will probably form a ball or mass on top of the steel blade, and it will be kneaded by the machine.

If you have not used a food processor, you will have to knead the dough either with your hands or with a pasta machine. With your hands, knead the dough on a lightly floured surface for about 10 minutes or until the ball is smooth and shiny. With a pasta machine, put lemon-sized pieces of dough through the widest setting on the machine, being sure to fold the dough into thirds after each pass through the rollers. If you are going to roll the dough with a rolling pin, let the dough rest, covered, for 20 to 30 minutes before rolling it out. This rest is not necessary if you are using a pasta machine.

With a rolling pin, roll the pasta out on a large lightly floured surface, stretching it as you roll. Rotate the dough a quarter turn each time you roll. The finished dough should be less than 1/16 inch thick. If using a pasta machine pass the pieces of kneaded dough through the rollers, decreasing the distance between the rollers with each run through. Do not fold it during this process. Continue to stretch it until you have reached the desired thickness. Flour the dough as necessary to keep it from sticking.

Allow the pasta to dry slightly before cutting it. To do this, arrange it on a suitable drying rack or spread it out on lightly floured towels. Let it dry until it no longer feels cold and wet, but do not let it become brittle. This could take 5 minutes or much longer. The time varies considerably, so feel it frequently as it dries.

Cut as desired using a knife, pasta cutter, or a machine. Use as directed.

WALNUT SAUCE *yields enough for*
1 pound of pasta

2 tablespoons olive oil
1 dozen walnuts, shelled
  and finely minced
1 teaspoon salt
1/2 teaspoon freshly
  ground black pepper
1/2 cup sweet butter
1/4 cup fresh tomato
  puree
1/2 cup chicken or meat
  broth
1 cup freshly grated
  Parmesan cheese

Heat olive oil in a saucepan and add minced walnuts, salt, and pepper. Sauté over low heat for 2 minutes.

Add butter and tomato puree. Cook another minute. Add broth and cook, stirring often, over low heat for about 10 minutes, until sauce reduces and thickens. Add to drained pasta along with the Parmesan cheese and mix well.

A COLD-WEATHER DINNER by Carol Brendlinger

Salad of Bitter Greens with Pomegranate and Cucumber

Clay-Pot Roast Duck with Olives and Garlic

Deep-Dish Quince Pie

serves four

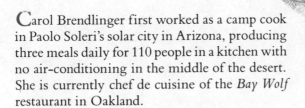

Carol Brendlinger first worked as a camp cook in Paolo Soleri's solar city in Arizona, producing three meals daily for 110 people in a kitchen with no air-conditioning in the middle of the desert. She is currently chef de cuisine of the *Bay Wolf* restaurant in Oakland.

"I tend to take a scholarly but improvisational approach to cooking. I love to go back to the roots of a cuisine, study the historical and social influences on the culture, and pick out the basic forms and essences. Then I put them back together again in a more modern style. In short, I create something.

"I envision serving this autumn menu when it is chilly outside, with a nice fire crackling inside."

SALAD OF BITTER GREENS WITH POMEGRANATE AND CUCUMBER *serves four*

For the salad greens I recommend a mixture of any of these: frisée, rocket, Belgian endive, baby kale, watercress, or baby red mustard.

1/2 hothouse cucumber
1 fuyu (Japanese)
   persimmon
2 quarts salad greens,
   rinsed and dried
2 pomegranates
2 tablespoons fresh
   lemon juice
1/3 cup olive oil
1 shallot, minced
Salt and pepper to taste

Peel, seed, and julienne the cucumber and persimmon. Add to the greens in a large salad bowl. Juice one pomegranate with a lemon juicer and remove the seeds from the other one. Make the dressing by whisking together the pomegranate juice, lemon juice, olive oil, shallot, salt and pepper. Toss with the greens. Sprinkle the salad with the pomegranate seeds and serve immediately.

CLAY-POT ROAST DUCK WITH OLIVES AND GARLIC *serves three to four*

Soak a clay pot with its lid for 15 minutes in warm water. Put the potatoes, olives, and garlic cloves in the bottom of the pot. Put the seasonings inside the duck and place it on top of the potatoes. Pour the wine over all. Put the lid on the pot and bake at 350° F for 1½ hours. Remove from the oven and let rest for 15 minutes. Carve the duck and arrange on a platter with the potatoes, olives, and garlic. Degrease the cooking juices, add some chopped fresh herbs, and pour over the duck. You can also serve it with a roasted tomato puree heated with a dash of Pernod.

You can substitute boned duck legs for the whole duck if you need to expand the recipe.

1 pound baby potatoes
1 cup olives (black, green, or mixture)
2 heads garlic, separated into cloves but not peeled
1/2 lemon
1/2 onion
1 teaspoon salt
1 teaspoon pepper
2 bay leaves
1 duck, fresh Petaluma Long Island variety, trimmed
2 cups white wine
Large handful of fresh herbs (parsley, thyme, mint, cilantro, or fennel weed)

DEEP-DISH QUINCE PIE *serves four to six*

4 quinces
1/4 cup lemon juice
1 cup sugar
1 cup water
1 sheet puff pastry, 1/4
  inch thick, cut to fit a
  2-quart baking dish,
  chilled
1 egg

Peel and core the quinces. Slice thinly and mix with the lemon juice, sugar, and water. Put in a 2-quart baking dish and bake at 350° F for 3/4 hour or until tender. The quince cooking can be done ahead of time. Put the chilled puff pastry on top of the quinces. Beat the egg with a little bit of water and brush over the puff pastry. Cut a decorative pattern in the pastry to make steam vents. Bake at 450° F for 1/2 hour or until the pastry is a rich brown and cooked through. Serve hot or at room temperature. Ginger crème fraîche or ice cream would be a wonderful accompaniment.

Note: You can bake the quinces at the same time as the duck if your oven is large enough. Then you finish baking the pie while you are eating the rest of the meal.

Also note: You can substitute your favorite pie crust for the puff pastry.

A DINNER AT HOME WITH FRIENDS by Fred Halpert

*Salad of Roasted Squab with
Mixed Greens*

*Lasagne with Lobster and
Chervil*

*Sautéed Norwegian Salmon with
a Tomato Coulis and Tarragon*

*Fresh Fruit with English Cream
and Mint*

serves four

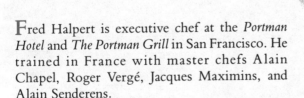

Fred Halpert is executive chef at the *Portman
Hotel* and *The Portman Grill* in San Francisco. He
trained in France with master chefs Alain
Chapel, Roger Vergé, Jacques Maximins, and
Alain Senderens.

*"When cooking for friends, I'm usually at home and do not have access to all the
equipment normally at my disposal. So with this in mind, I've created a menu based on
simpler items and equipment that is now commonly found in households.*

*"The menu illustrates my fondness for fresh herbs, which I feel give each dish an aromatic
enhancement. These recipes are based on items that are found throughout the entire year
and are fairly simple to follow."*

SALAD OF ROASTED SQUAB WITH MIXED GREENS *serves four*

2 whole squab
   (1 pound each)
4 handfuls assorted lettuce
   (red leaf, green leaf,
   or Boston)
2 shallots
3 tablespoons walnut oil
1/2 tablespoon sherry
   vinegar
1/2 tablespoon balsamic
   vinegar
Salt and pepper to taste
4 ounces baby green beans
2 tablespoons unsalted
   butter
1 bunch chives

Bone squab, retaining only the legs and breasts. Rinse the lettuce and tear into bite-size pieces. Spin dry and set aside. Finely chop the shallots. Add the shallots to the walnut oil and slowly whisk in both vinegars. Season to taste with salt and pepper.

Clean and tip the green beans and blanch briefly in boiling water. Drain and set aside.

Season the squab and sauté in butter over a high flame. Remove the breast meat when it is medium rare; continue cooking the legs until done.

Toss the lettuce with 1/2 the vinaigrette and arrange on four plates. Thinly slice the squab breasts and arrange as fans over salads. Toss beans and chives with remaining vinaigrette and arrange beside the salads. Place one squab leg on top of beans.

LASAGNE WITH LOBSTER AND CHERVIL *serves four*

Plunge the lobster headfirst and upside down into boiling water, cover kettle, and weight down if necessary. When water comes back to a boil, remove the cover and continue to boil slowly for 15 to 18 minutes. Drain the lobster and allow to cool. Remove the tail meat and slice into 4 medallions. Cover and reserve. Remove the rest of the lobster meat and refrigerate for later use. Save all the shells for the lobster stock.

For the stock, finely chop the onion, carrots, and celery and sauté in olive oil for 3 to 5 minutes. Add the roughly chopped and seeded tomatoes, bay leaf, and fresh tarragon and continue to cook for another 3 to 5 minutes. Add the lobster shells, wine, and water and simmer until reduced by half. Strain stock into saucepan and reserve.

Run the sheets of pasta through the successive thicknesses of a pasta machine until the thinnest setting has been used. Set aside on the countertop. Rinse chervil and shake dry. Chop chervil coarsely. Moisten pasta very lightly with water using a small brush. Sprinkle chervil, reserving a small amount for garnish, on one sheet of pasta. Place the second sheet of pasta directly over the first sheet and roll with a rolling pin. On the next-to-thinnest setting, run the pasta through the machine once again. Punch out eight medallions of pasta with the cookie cutter, allowing two pieces per person.

Seed the red peppers and julienne into thin strips. Reduce the lobster stock by 2/3 (to yield 2/3 to 1 cup) and add the lobster, peppers, butter, and lemon juice. Season and set aside.

Boil pasta for 2 to 3 minutes and drain. Return sauce to the heat. Place one medallion of pasta on a plate, arrange one medallion of lobster and peppers on top, then add a second medallion of pasta on top of lobster. Pour sauce around the lasagne and garnish with remaining chervil.

1½-pound live lobster
2 cups lobster stock (see below)
2 sheets fresh pasta
1 bunch chervil
Cookie cutter (2½-inch diameter)
Hand pasta machine
Rolling pin
2 red bell peppers
2 tablespoons butter
1 teaspoon lemon juice

Lobster Stock:
1 onion
2 carrots
1 stalk celery
3 tablespoons olive oil
3 large tomatoes
1 bay leaf
3 sprigs fresh tarragon
Lobster shells
2 cups dry white wine
2 cups water

SAUTÉED NORWEGIAN SALMON WITH A TOMATO COULIS AND TARRAGON *serves four*

16 ounces Norwegian
  salmon
1/4 cup olive oil
Salt and pepper to taste
4 tomatoes
1/2 teaspoon lemon juice
1 bunch tarragon,
  chopped, reserving a
  few leaves for garnish

Cut the salmon into four equal portions. Place on a sheet pan, coat with olive oil, and season to taste. Remove cores from tomatoes, and squeeze out excess water before pureeing in a food processor. Strain to remove seeds. Add 2 tablespoons olive oil, lemon juice, and chopped tarragon to tomato puree. Season to taste.

Sauté salmon in a hot pan until medium rare. Place coulis on a warm plate, arrange salmon, and top with reserved tarragon leaves.

FRESH FRUIT WITH ENGLISH CREAM AND MINT *serves four*

Split vanilla bean in half, scrape out the seeds, and add to milk. Heat milk to boiling over medium heat. Combine the egg yolks and sugar and beat until the mixture lightens in color. Add 1/3 of the boiled milk to the yolks and sugar, whisking thoroughly. Add the remaining milk and return to the heat. Continue cooking over medium heat, stirring with a wooden spoon until the mixture has thickened and coats the spoon with a thick creamy layer. Do not overcook or the eggs will scramble. Remove from heat and strain through a fine sieve into a cold bowl. Cool, stirring now and then. Refrigerate until ready to serve. Cut the fruits – which might include various pears and apples, berries, or tropical exotics such as mango, papaya, or starfruit – according to their shapes and mix together. Place fruit in a serving bowl, cover with custard sauce, and sprinkle with mint leaves.

1 vanilla bean
2 cups milk
4 egg yolks
3¼ ounces sugar
Assorted fresh fruit
   (in season)
Mint leaves, julienned

WINTER

A HOLIDAY BREAKFAST
by Phillip Quattrociocchi and Roberta Klugman

Champagne and Fresh Orange Juice

Holiday Eggs with White Truffles

Black Forest Ham

Potatoes with Fontina Cheese

Walnut Bread

Fresh Fruit and Coffee

serves four

Phillip Quattrociocchi is president and cofounder of *San Francisco International Cheese, Inc.,* a full-service specialty food import and distribution company. Phil is internationally respected as a businessman, cheese expert, and fine-food connoisseur.

Roberta Klugman is a North Dakota native now living in San Francisco and is an executive for *San Francisco International Cheese*. She is on the board of the San Francisco Professional Food Society. Having been a cook for 150 geologists in Montana, she now only cooks for friends.

"Christmas morning is a grand time to spend with dear friends. A special brunch or breakfast featuring scrambled eggs with white truffles, Black Forest ham, prosciutto, or bacon, walnut bread, champagne, fresh orange juice, potatoes with fontina cheese, fresh fruit, and coffee is our usual menu, but please feel free to complement the egg dish with your own good ideas, remembering to use foods that do not distract from the delicate nature of the white truffle. Everyone has their own favorite way of making scrambled eggs — here is ours."

HOLIDAY EGGS WITH WHITE TRUFFLES *serves four*

2 tablespoons butter
6 eggs
1/2 to 1 teaspoon crème
   fraîche (optional)
Salt and pepper to taste
1/4 cup grated Gruyère
   cheese, or more to
   taste (optional)
1 small white truffle
   (about 3/4 ounce)

Melt butter in heavy skillet and break eggs into pan. Stirring with fork or whisk, add crème fraîche and salt and pepper, mixing until light and fluffy, then add the optional grated Gruyère. At the very last minute add the thinly sliced white truffle and serve immediately.

Note on white truffles: These jewels are available in the United States usually November through December. They arrive with good Italian dirt. Do not be surprised if a truffle has a little worm; it is harmless. White truffles are fragile and should be packed in rice and used within 24 hours after purchasing for best flavor. Keep fresh eggs in the rice with the truffles. Make certain the white truffles are covered by the rice, cover, and keep refrigerated. The heavenly aroma of the white truffle will permeate the eggs. To clean the truffle, brush gently with a toothbrush and a little water. Pat dry and slice with a truffle slicer, very sharp knife, or even a sharp potato peeler. Slice the truffle just prior to adding it to the eggs.

Note on Gruyère: This is our first choice for the cheese in this dish as its nutty, earthy flavor complements the truffles and it melts nicely.

POTATOES WITH FONTINA CHEESE
serves four

Boil potatoes in salted water for 15 to 20 minutes, or until just done. Allow to cool until you can handle them, then slice potatoes and place in a shallow pie pan. Grate or slice fontina over potatoes and place in a hot oven or under broiler until cheese melts.

4 medium red potatoes
1/4 pound fontina cheese

WALNUT BREAD *makes 2 loaves*

3¾ cups whole wheat
  flour
1 cup all-purpose flour
2 cups lukewarm water
1 tablespoon honey
1 cake fresh (wet) yeast, or
1 package dry yeast
2½ teaspoons salt
1/4 cup walnut oil
1¼ cups walnuts, coarsely
  chopped
1 egg, beaten (for glaze)

Put both flours in a bowl, make a well in the center, and add 1/2 cup of the water. Add the honey and crumble the yeast over the water in well. Stir to dissolve. Add remaining water and salt and stir gently until a smooth dough is formed. Add more flour if necessary. Knead dough on floured surface for about 8 minutes or until smooth and elastic. Add more flour if dough sticks to board. Place dough in oiled bowl and turn so top is oiled. Cover with damp cloth and allow to rise in a warm place until doubled in bulk, approximately 1½ hours.

Butter two 7- or 8-inch round cake pans. Knock the air out of the risen dough and knead in the walnut oil and walnuts. Keep working until oil and nuts are fully incorporated. Shape into 2 round loaves and set in cake pans. Once again, cover with a damp cloth and set in a warm place to double in bulk, about 45 minutes. Set oven to 425° F.

Make 3 or 4 slashes in the top of each loaf and brush with beaten egg. Bake for 15 minutes, then lower heat to 375° F. Continue baking for another 30 to 35 minutes or until loaves sound hollow when tapped. Allow to cool on rack.

A SIMPLE MENU OF FAVORITE TASTES
by John Schmidt

Grilled Marinated Shrimp

Polenta

Spicy Pork Stew

Lime Sour Cream

Apple-Walnut Kuchen

Hot Cream Sauce

serves four to six

John Schmidt is chef/co-owner of the *New Boonville Hotel* in rural Mendocino County, California.

"These are some of the most popular dishes at the restaurant, and they still remain our favorites as well. The pork stew began as a traditional chile verde, one of the first things I learned to make. Served on the polenta it makes for a complete meal in itself. The grilled shrimp are so easy to prepare, yet they make the meal that much more special. Our apple-walnut kuchen began as a family breakfast cake, but served with the cream sauce, it always seems to be a favorite any time of day."

GRILLED MARINATED SHRIMP *serves four to six*

1/2 cup orange juice
1/2 cup olive oil
1 tablespoon balsamic
  vinegar
1 chopped jalapeño
  pepper
2 cilantro sprigs
Salt and pepper
1 pound large shrimp,
  peeled, with tails on
Juice of 1 orange
2 tablespoons virgin
  olive oil
Cilantro for garnish

Combine first six ingredients and marinate shrimp for 1 to 2 hours. Grill over hot fire for 1 to 2 minutes per side. When tails curl inward, remove from grill and place in bowl. Toss with juice of 1 orange and virgin olive oil. Serve with cilantro-and-garlic mayonnaise or salsa.

POLENTA *serves six*

6 cups chicken stock
1 small onion, minced
Zest of 1 orange, chopped
1/2 red bell pepper,
  minced
1 jalapeño or Thai chili
  pepper, chopped
  (optional)
Salt and pepper to taste
1½ cups polenta
1/2 cup butter
1/2 cup chopped parsley

Bring stock to a boil. Add onion, orange zest, and peppers. Season to taste. Whisk in polenta, reduce heat to medium, and continue stirring for 5 to 8 minutes. Add butter and parsley, reduce heat to low, and keep tightly covered until served.

SPICY PORK STEW *serves four to six*

Heat peanut oil on high in a heavy sauté pan. Add garlic cloves, and when hot, brown the pork in small batches, removing to large casserole dish. Season meat well with coarse salt. Remove all but 1/4 cup oil from pan and slowly brown onions, deglazing pan. Season onions and add to casserole dish. Cook tomatillos and tomatoes with beer and orange juice, season, and add to casserole. Combine the fresh and dried chilies and cilantro, check for salt, and add to stew. Cook for 1½ to 2 hours in a 350° F oven. Pork should be tender but not falling apart. Skim off any fat and stir to release color from the dried chilies. Serve over polenta, and garnish with cilantro sprigs and lime sour cream.

1 cup peanut oil
1 head whole garlic cloves, peeled
2 pounds pork stew meat, cut into large cubes
Coarse salt
1 large yellow onion, halved and matchsticked
1 pound tomatillos, peeled and quartered
1 pound ripe tomatoes, cut into large chunks
1 cup dark beer
1 cup orange juice
1 to 2 jalapeño peppers, sliced into rounds
2 to 3 dried pasilla chilies, rinsed
1/2 bunch cilantro, roughly chopped
Polenta (see preceding page)
Cilantro sprigs for garnish
Lime sour cream (see below)

LIME SOUR CREAM

Stir sour cream till smooth, add chopped lime zest and juice. Let sit for 1 hour before using.

1 cup sour cream
2 limes, zest and juice

APPLE-WALNUT KUCHEN

9-inch pie plate
3 to 4 tart, green apples
1/3 cup shortening
3/4 cup sugar
1 egg
3/4 cup light cream
1¾ cups flour
2 teaspoons baking
  powder
1/2 teaspoon salt
1/2 teaspoon nutmeg
1/4 teaspoon vanilla
Zest of 1 lemon, chopped
1/2 cup walnuts, chopped
Additional granulated
  sugar to sprinkle
Cinnamon
Hot cream sauce
  (see below)

Grease the pie plate. Peel, core, and slice the apples. Preheat the oven to 375° F. Cream shortening and sugar together till smooth, add egg, and beat 2 to 3 minutes more. Add cream and continue beating until smooth.

With an electric mixer on low speed, add next four dry ingredients to wet mixture and mix until smooth. Add vanilla and zest, stir, and turn into pie plate. Arrange apple slices around edge, add walnuts in the center. Sprinkle generously with sugar and cinnamon. Bake for 25 to 35 minutes or until done. Serve with hot cream sauce.

HOT CREAM SAUCE

2 cups heavy cream
1/2 cup sugar
1/4 cup butter
Zest of 1 lemon, chopped
1/4 teaspoon fresh nutmeg

Combine ingredients in heavy saucepan and cook over medium heat until boiling. Immediately reduce heat and cook for 5 to 10 minutes, watching carefully so it doesn't boil over. Heat and whisk just before serving over kuchen slices. Keeps well.

A WINTER LUNCHEON FOR GOOD FRIENDS
by Stanley Eichelbaum

Wild Mushroom Soup

Braised Rabbit with Thyme and Mustard Seeds

Green Salad with Lime-Ginger Vinaigrette

Lemon Mousse with Cassis Sauce

serves six

Stanley Eichelbaum writes a food column for the *San Francisco Chronicle* and is chef/owner of *Café Majestic* in San Francisco.

"What are friends for, if not to be scrupulously honest with you on all matters, from your vices to your cooking? I can't say that this dictum always works, but I've long felt that friends were the best source for opinions on new recipes. So when I want to try out a new dish, I feed it first to friends and solicit their comments afterward. I like to experiment with food, as any chef does, and I take great pleasure in preparing something wild and fanciful for a group of friends, praying that they won't be too harsh with me. And most often, their criticism will be very beneficial. That's the way I cook for friends, and there's really nothing more satisfying than to watch them eat, and know that my efforts are being appreciated."

WILD MUSHROOM SOUP
serves six to eight

1 pound mixed
    mushrooms
2 or 3 shallots
1 onion
2 carrots
2 cloves garlic
3 stalks celery
2 tablespoons tomato
    paste, or
1/3 cup sun-dried
    tomatoes
2 potatoes
Bouquet garni (see below)
Butter
Olive oil
1/2 cup sweet vermouth
    or Madeira
1 or 2 tablespoons cognac
6 to 8 cups chicken stock
1/2 cup heavy cream
Salt and pepper
White wine

Bouquet Garni:
6 parsley stems
2 bay leaves
1 tablespoon thyme
3 whole cloves
1 teaspoon white
    peppercorns

If using dried mushrooms, soak for 20 minutes in warm water. Wipe fresh mushrooms clean with damp cloth. Slice 5 or 6 mushroom caps into julienne pieces and set aside for garnish. Remaining mushrooms should be chopped coarsely in food processor. Also chop shallots, onion, carrots, garlic, celery, and tomatoes, if using sun-dried tomatoes. Slice potatoes. Tie bouquet garni in cheesecloth.

Heat some butter and olive oil in a soup pot and sweat shallots, onion, mushrooms, and other vegetables for 10 minutes. Add vermouth (or Madeira) and cognac. Cover with chicken stock. Add bouquet garni and tomato paste (or tomatoes). Bring to boil. Reduce heat and simmer 45 minutes. Remove bouquet garni and allow to cool somewhat. Puree in blender. Stir in cream. Salt and pepper to taste. Sauté mushroom garnish in butter with a dash of wine. Add to soup. May be made a day ahead and reheated without boiling.

BRAISED RABBIT WITH THYME AND MUSTARD SEEDS *serves six*

Dredge the rabbit pieces in flour, salt, and pepper. Brown the pieces in hot oil and butter in a large sauté pan, 5 or 10 minutes. Transfer to an oven-proof casserole. Add garlic, thyme, wine, tomato, chicken stock, and mustard seeds. Cover and place in 375° oven for 45 minutes. Remove rabbit and keep warm. Degrease and strain sauce. Reduce to desired thickness. Serve with potatoes or noodles. Garnish pieces of rabbit with more of the thyme and mustard seeds.

1 3- to 3½-pound rabbit, cut up
1/2 cup flour
Salt and pepper
1/2 cup olive oil
2 ounces butter
3 cloves garlic, finely minced
4 to 6 tablespoons fresh thyme leaves (or 3 tablespoons dried thyme)
1½ cups dry white wine
5 ounces tomatoes, peeled, seeded, and chopped
1 to 2 cups chicken stock, or rabbit stock
4 tablespoons mustard seeds

GREEN SALAD WITH LIME-GINGER VINAIGRETTE *serves six*

Juice of 2 limes
2 tablespoons good wine
  vinegar
1/3 cup olive oil
1/3 cup vegetable oil
1 tablespoon sugar
1 tablespoon fresh
  chopped ginger
1 tablespoon dill
Salt and pepper to taste
2 small heads green-leaf
  or red-leaf lettuce

Combine all ingredients except lettuce and emulsify well, using a blender or a wire whisk. Separate lettuce leaves, rinse and spin dry, tear leaves into bite-sized pieces, and place in large salad bowl. Pour dressing over lettuce and toss well. Serve immediately.

LEMON MOUSSE WITH CASSIS SAUCE *serves six*

Start by making a lemon curd. Chop the lemon zest. Place zest and lemon juice in the top of a double boiler with 1 cup sugar and the egg yolks. Stir with a whisk. Gradually stir in butter. Let thicken over gently boiling water, stirring constantly; this should take about 20 minutes. Set aside to cool.

To make the mousse, place 1½ cups of the lemon curd in a mixing bowl with stiffly whipped cream and the rum. Whisk till blended. Beat the egg whites until they hold stiff peaks and gently fold into mixture. Spoon mousse into serving ramekins or glasses. Chill.

To make the sauce, cook half of the black currants or blueberries with 1/2 cup sugar and the water. Simmer 10 minutes and add crème de cassis. Simmer 15 more minutes.

Sauce should be syrupy. When done, add remaining currants or blueberries. Set aside to cool. Before serving, spoon sauce over mousse.

Mousse
Zest and juice of 4 lemons
1 cup sugar
10 eggs, separated
4 ounces butter
1/2 cup heavy cream
1/4 cup dark rum

Cassis Sauce
2 cups black currants (available frozen or canned), or
2 cups blueberries
1/2 cup sugar
1 cup water
1/2 cup crème-de-cassis liqueur

A HEARTY WINTER LUNCH by Ron Clark

Winter-Harvest Pie

*Tossed Green Salad**

serves six

*Recipe not included

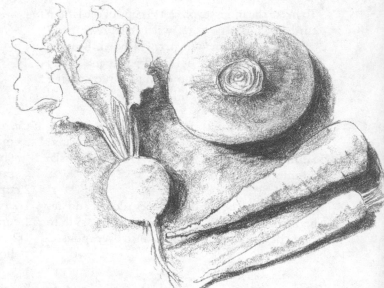

Ron Clark is a classically trained chef, journeyman butcher, and cookbook writer for Ortho Books. He currently manages a specialty foods distribution company in San Francisco.

"My passion will always be cooking for close friends and family.

"The cold winter months of January and February present a special challenge of finding creative ways to use vegetables. Root vegetables dominate the produce shelves and provide a delightful opportunity to prepare hearty midwinter meals. This winter-harvest pie showcases a beautiful mélange of meaty, full-bodied vegetables lightly flavored by three cheeses and encased in a flaky pastry. Served at the table in a cast-iron skillet, this is a delicious meal in itself. If desired, a light tossed salad will complete this cold-weather feast."

WINTER-HARVEST PIE *serves six*

Prepare the pâte brisé in a food processor using steel blade. Put flour and salt in food processor. Cut butter into 1/2-inch pieces and add to bowl. Process until butter is fully incorporated into flour. Mixture will resemble cornmeal in texture. Add water all at once, and process until dough first forms a single ball. Stop immediately and empty contents onto work surface. Lightly dust with flour and knead several times to finish mixing. (If made by hand, chill for several hours before rolling out.) Divide dough into two equal parts. Roll each half into rounds 1/4 inch thick. Place the bottom half into an ungreased 10-inch cast-iron skillet, carefully pressing the dough into place. Trim excess dough, leaving a 1-inch lip beyond the edge of the skillet. Place the other half of the dough on a sheet pan lined with waxed paper or parchment. Place sheet pan and skillet in refrigerator to rest.

Preheat oven to 500° F. Cut tops off of red and gold peppers, rinse and remove seeds. Lightly oil outside with olive oil, and place stem-side down on sheet pan. Place in hot oven until peppers lightly blacken, in about 10 to 15 minutes. Be sure to have a good exhaust fan for this one. Immediately remove from oven and place peppers in a paper bag and close. In 10 minutes, remove from bag. The blackened skin of the peppers will steam loose while cooling in the bag. Scrape and peel skin from peppers, reserving the sweet meat. Cut peppers into 1-inch strips.

Poach slices of beets, turnips, carrots, and parsnips until vegetables are just al dente. Remove and stop further cooking by plunging into cold water. When cool, drain and set aside.

Sauté onions and garlic in olive oil and butter until golden brown, about 10 to 15 minutes over low to medium heat. Reserve.

(continued next page)

Pâte Brisé:
3½ cups flour
2 teaspoons salt
12 ounces butter
2/3 to 1 cup ice water
1 egg for egg wash

1 medium red pepper
1 medium gold pepper
Olive oil for sautéing
2/3 cup each, 1/4 inch
   thick: beets, turnips,
   carrots, and parsnips
1 medium onion,
   in 1/4-inch rounds
1 tablespoon minced
   garlic
1 tablespoon butter
1/2 bunch red chard
1/2 bunch mustard greens
1/2 cup zucchini
   in 1/4-inch slices
1/2 cup fresh bread
   crumbs
Salt and pepper to taste
1 pint ricotta cheese
1 cup grated dry
   Monterey Jack cheese
1 cup grated Jarlsberg
   cheese

Remove and discard stems from chard and mustard greens, and cut leaves into 1/2-inch-wide strips. Lightly sauté in olive oil until greens wilt, about 5 minutes. Reserve.

Sauté zucchini over high heat until al dente, about 5 to 10 minutes. Reserve.

Remove pie crusts from refrigerator. Lightly poke bottom pie crust every inch or so with a fork. Dust bottom of pie with bread crumbs. Salt and pepper vegetables to taste. Layer ingredients in following order: Ricotta, grated cheese, onions and garlic, beets, parsnips, red and gold peppers, ricotta, carrots, turnips, chard and mustard greens, onions and garlic, grated cheese, zucchini, red and gold peppers, ricotta, and grated cheese. Filling should form a dome several inches higher than the skillet. Be careful to keep edge of pie dough clean and free of filling. Brush edge of pie dough with egg wash. Cover pie with top layer of dough. Close side by firmly crimping top and bottom together in a fluted pattern. Use extra dough to make decorations for top of pie. Leaves and stems make an attractive top. Cut 3 slashes 2 inches long in the center of the pie for venting. Lightly brush crust with egg wash, and poke more vent holes with a fork. Place in preheated 425° F oven. After 15 minutes, turn oven down to 350° F and continue to cook until golden to dark brown, about another 20 minutes. Serve immediately.

A SAVORY WINTER MENU
by Nancy Jenniss Oakes

Corn Blinis with Smoked Salmon, Crème Fraîche, Tobiko (Flying-Fish Roe), and Chives

Roasted Young Chicken with Sage Butter and Grilled Shiitake Mushrooms

Leek and Potato Timbale

Butternut Squash Puree*

Green Salad*

Cheese Croutons

Pumpkin Bread Pudding with Whiskey Crème Anglaise and Cranberry Syrup

serves eight

*Recipes not included

Nancy Jenniss Oakes has been involved with the restaurant business for eighteen years. For the first eight years she worked in the dining rooms until, with the help of Pat O'Shea and friends, she ventured into the kitchen of the *Mad Hatter,* where her lunches became legendary. She has recently launched the already highly acclaimed *L'Avenue* in San Francisco.

"It's ironic that the theme of this book is cooking for friends. That's how I initially became interested in the restaurant trade. Years later, cooking for my friends has become a refuge from an often demanding business. I still find it rewarding to transform a physical necessity into one of life's pleasures.

"Cooking for friends should not be difficult. Many of my best meals have been simple and satisfying. I do like to add a few special touches to show some effort, but I know that a pleasant meal doesn't hinge upon elaborate preparations. I try not to let the menu come between me and my guests. I like to plan some items that can be made in advance so that my guests can engage me in conversation over a glass of wine, not a cutting board. And those are the best memories."

CORN BLINIS WITH SMOKED SALMON, CRÈME FRAÎCHE, TOBIKO, AND CHIVES *yields sixteen blinis*

5 medium-sized ears
  white corn (frozen
  white corn is okay)
6 tablespoons flour
4 whole large eggs
1 teaspoon kosher salt
1/4 teaspoon freshly
  ground black pepper
1/2 cup heavy cream
1/4 cup melted butter
Peanut oil for cooking
8 ounces crème fraîche,
  whipped until it forms
  soft peaks
16 thin slices smoked
  salmon (or smoked
  trout)
1 bunch chives, finely
  chopped
4 ounces tobiko or any
  fine-textured caviar

Remove corn from cob and put kernels into a medium-sized bowl. Sprinkle with flour and mix well. In another bowl combine eggs, salt, pepper, and cream and beat lightly. Add to the corn and mix well. Stir in melted butter. Can be made several hours in advance.

To cook, in a well-seasoned or nonstick sauté pan heat peanut oil (batter should sizzle when dropped into the pan). Make blinis about 2 to 3 inches in diameter in the hot oil. Bubbles will form on top of the pancake. When they start to break around the edges, turn the blinis over. They should have nice golden brown markings. Cook until the center is firm, remove from the pan, and keep warm until all blinis are cooked. This should be close to serving time.

To assemble, warm 8 plates, place 2 blinis on each plate with 1 heaping tablespoon of crème fraîche. Arrange 2 slices of salmon near the crème fraîche, sprinkle with chives, and top off with 1 heaping teaspoon of caviar.

Great with champagne!

ROASTED YOUNG CHICKEN WITH SAGE BUTTER AND GRILLED SHIITAKE MUSHROOMS *serves eight*

For this recipe the mushrooms and sage butter are worked under the skin to cover the breast meat. The birds are cooked at a very high temperature so that the skin will achieve good color and be very crispy. At the same time, the butter protects and flavors the meat.

Rinse chickens inside and out, pat dry, and place birds on their backs, breast side up. Starting at the top (wing end), loosen the skin that covers the breast, being very gentle; do not tear the skin. Work sage butter and mushroom strips under the skin so that the mixture covers the breast meat. Pat the skin back in place.

Preheat oven to 500° F. Place birds in roasting pan, on a rack if you like, brush with olive oil, and sprinkle with salt and pepper. Cook for 20 to 30 minutes. Test for doneness by shaking leg. If leg is loose in the socket, then the bird is done.

8 1-pound poussins (young chickens)
1 recipe sage butter (see below)
Grilled shiitake mushrooms (see below)
Olive oil to brush over birds
Salt and coarse-ground black pepper

Sage Butter
Put all ingredients into a food processor and process until well combined or mix by hand until smooth.

1/2 pound unsalted butter, softened
1 bunch fresh sage (about 20 leaves), cut into chiffonade
Grated peel of 1 lemon
2 cloves of garlic, chopped
1/4 teaspoon coarse-ground pepper
1 tablespoon Dijon-style mustard
1 tablespoon sherry vinegar
1/2 teaspoon kosher salt

Grilled Shiitake Mushrooms
Brush mushrooms with olive oil and sprinkle with salt and pepper. Grill mushrooms on a char-grill or broil them close to the flame or heating element in the oven. When mushrooms become tender and a little crispy, remove from the heat and allow to cool. Julienne them and combine with sage butter.

16 large shiitake mushrooms
Olive oil to brush on mushrooms
Salt and coarse-ground black pepper

LEEK AND POTATO TIMBALE
serves eight

2 large leeks
1/2 cup butter
1 large potato, peeled
1 cup grated asiago cheese
3 tablespoons champagne
   vinegar
3/4 cup panko (Japanese
   bread crumbs), or
3/4 cup light bread
   crumbs (not too
   finely ground)
3 eggs
1½ cups heavy cream
1 teaspoon kosher salt
1/4 teaspoon freshly
   ground black pepper
1 tablespoon fresh thyme
   leaves
1 clove garlic, finely
   chopped
1 tablespoon olive oil

Preheat oven to 350° F. Butter timbale molds, ramekins, or little soufflé dishes. Rinse leeks and cut white part into thin slices. Rinse leeks again and pat dry. Melt butter in sauté pan and cook leeks until soft. Set aside. Grate potato and cheese into a mixing bowl and add champagne vinegar and toss. Add 1/2 cup bread crumbs, eggs, cream, leeks, and salt and pepper. Mix well and divide equally into buttered molds.

In a small bowl, combine remaining bread crumbs, thyme, garlic, and olive oil. Mix with fingers until oil is incorporated into bread crumbs. Sprinkle on top of timbales. Place molds on a baking sheet and bake at 350° F for 20 to 30 minutes until mixture is set. May be made in advance, turned out of molds, and reheated under broiler or in oven.

CHEESE CROUTONS *serves eight*

Preheat oven to 375° F. In a food processor using the steel blade, or by hand using a fork, blend the Roquefort and mascarpone and sprinkle with black pepper to taste.

Slice 16 1/4-inch-thick slices from the baguette. Place slices on baking sheet and toast until bread begins to brown. Turn over and toast the other side. Spread some of the cheese on each crouton and set aside.

Just as you are about to serve the salad, return the croutons to the broiler long enough to melt the cheese. Serve warm as a garnish to the salad.

4 ounces Roquefort cheese
4 ounces mascarpone cheese (or Brie)
Freshly ground black pepper
Baguette of French bread

PUMPKIN BREAD PUDDING WITH WHISKEY CRÈME ANGLAISE AND CRANBERRY SYRUP *serves eight*

2-quart casserole dish (and another pan large enough to contain it)
1½ loaves homestyle white bread, unsliced
1 cup canned pumpkin puree
1 cup milk
1 cup heavy cream
1/2 cup unsulphured molasses
1/2 cup lightly packed brown sugar
3 eggs
1 teaspoon cinnamon
2 teaspoons vanilla extract
Pinch of salt
Pinch of nutmeg

Garnish:
1/2 cup granulated sugar
2 tablespoons water
18 pecan halves

4 egg yolks (at room temperature)
1/2 cup white sugar
2 cups milk, scalding hot
1 teaspoon vanilla extract
2 to 4 tablespoons whiskey (or your choice of liquor)

8 cups cranberries, sorted and rinsed
1½ cups sugar
4 cups water

Butter casserole. Cut crust off bread and cut to fit in casserole in two layers. Whisk together remaining ingredients. Place one layer of bread in casserole and pour half of custard mixture over the bread. Arrange the next layer of bread, then pour remaining custard over it. Press bread down gently, allowing bread to soak up liquid for 60 minutes, or overnight would be better.

Place casserole in a larger pan and add enough hot water to come halfway up the sides of the casserole. Cover with aluminum foil and bake at 350° F for 45 minutes. If a crusty top is desired, remove foil and bake 10 more minutes.

For pecan garnish, combine sugar with water in a saucepan. Bring mixture to a boil, stirring occasionally until sugar is dissolved. Cook syrup uncovered and undisturbed over a moderately high heat. Swirl the pan until the syrup is a deep caramel. Remove pan from heat and quickly stir in pecans. Transfer pecans individually onto an oiled baking dish to cool. Serve with whiskey crème anglaise and cranberry syrup.

Whiskey Crème Anglaise
Beat egg yolks and sugar until pale in color and thick. Whisk in hot milk gradually. Heat in a heavy saucepan over low heat. Stir constantly until the custard coats the spoon, 10 to 15 minutes. Do not boil. Allow to cool to room temperature, add vanilla and liquor, and chill in refrigerator.

Cranberry Syrup
In a saucepan, combine cranberries, sugar, and water. Bring mixture to a boil and simmer for 45 minutes, stirring occasionally. Pour mixture through a sieve. If mixture is too thin, reduce to syrup consistency.

A LIVELY-FLAVORED MENU FOR FRIENDS
by Karen A. Lucas

Scallops with Leek Sauce

Fennel and Citrus Salad

Rabbit with Pancetta and Mushrooms

Pasta or Couscous*

Green Vegetable*

Papaya-Lime Granita

serves four

*Recipes not included

Karen A. Lucas is presently chef/owner of *Blue Heron* catering company. She has been a chef in Bay Area restaurants for ten years, among them *The Broadway Terrace Cafe* and *Rapallo Restaurant*. Karen has traveled extensively in Asia and Europe and has contributed articles and recipes to many magazines and cookbooks. She is the coauthor of *Antipasto Feasts: Variations on a Theme with Aperitivi and Sweets* (Aris Books, 1988).

"When I invite good friends to dinner, I choose a menu that's not fussy but has lively flavors and uses interesting products. I like to serve four leisurely courses centering the evening around the table. I'm careful to choose dishes that can be prepared partially or completely in advance so I can join the fun and not be buried in the kitchen."

SCALLOPS WITH LEEK SAUCE
serves four

1 pound (5 medium) leeks
1/2 cup white wine
1 cup water
4 tablespoons butter, cut
    into 1/2-inch cubes
1 pound sea scallops
1/2 teaspoon salt
1/4 cup flour
1 tablespoon butter
1 tablespoon vegetable oil

Fish is a natural first course and can appear elegant but be quite easy to finish at the last minute. The leek sauce for this scallop dish is prepared ahead, and the scallops are quickly sautéed and served.

Trim the root end and green stalks (except for 1 inch) from the leeks and discard. Slice leeks crosswise into 3/4-inch pieces and rinse well. Place in a small saucepan with the wine and water. Bring to a boil, reduce heat, and simmer covered over medium-low heat for 30 minutes or until leeks are tender. Puree the leeks and 1/4 cup of the liquid (discard the remaining liquid) in a food processor until very smooth. Pass puree through a strainer and set aside. Can be prepared up to one day ahead.

Gently reheat puree to a simmer. Stirring constantly, add 4 tablespoons butter a few pieces at a time. As soon as the last cubes are added, remove saucepan from heat and let sauce stand in a warm place until needed. Do not reheat sauce.

Dry scallops well between paper towels. Sprinkle with salt, dust with flour, and pat off excess. Heat a large skillet over medium-high heat. When hot, add 1 tablespoon butter, the oil, and scallops in a single layer. Without moving them about, let the scallops brown on one side, about 3 minutes. Turn scallops over and brown on the other side, about 1 minute. Remove from heat.

Spoon leek sauce onto 4 plates. Set the scallops on the sauce and serve at once.

FENNEL AND CITRUS SALAD
serves four

A crisp, interesting salad is always a refreshing second course, and this fennel-and-citrus combination is one of my favorites.

Trim the stalks and feathery tops from the fennel. Cut the bulb in half from top to root. Slice in very thin slices and place in a medium bowl. Cut all peel and white pith from oranges and grapefruit. Divide citrus into sections and add to fennel.

In small bowl whisk together the vinegar, oil, salt, and pepper. Toss the dressing with the fennel and citrus. Can be prepared up to 1 hour ahead and held covered and refrigerated.

1 large, fresh fennel bulb
   (sweet anise), about
   1 pound
2 oranges
1 pink grapefruit
1 tablespoon raspberry
   vinegar
3 tablespoons extra
   virgin olive oil
1/2 teaspoon salt
Freshly ground black
   pepper

RABBIT WITH PANCETTA AND MUSHROOMS *serves four*

1/2 pound pancetta
   (Italian bacon), cut
   into 1/2-inch cubes
1 onion, cut into
   large dice
1/2 pound mushrooms,
   sliced
1 cup beef stock
1 cup red wine
Salt and pepper to taste
2 fryer rabbits, cut into
   serving pieces
4 tablespoons oil
1/2 cup flour
1/2 teaspoon ground
   cinnamon

In a large sauté pan over medium-high heat, fry the pancetta until lightly browned (about 5 minutes). Add the onion and sauté until tender (about 4 minutes). Reduce heat to medium-low, add mushrooms, and sauté 4 minutes. Add the stock and wine and simmer for 5 minutes. Set aside.

Salt and pepper the rabbit pieces. Heat a large sauté pan over medium heat. Add 2 tablespoons oil. Dust the rabbit pieces with flour. Shake off excess and place half of the pieces in sauté pan. Brown each piece (about 4 minutes per side) and set aside. Add the remaining 2 tablespoons oil and rabbit pieces to the pan and brown in the same way. Toss the browned pieces with 2 tablespoons of the flour and the cinnamon and place in a large oven-proof casserole. Can be prepared several hours ahead to this point.

Heat oven to 375° F. Bring pancetta-stock mixture to a boil and pour over the rabbit. Cover casserole and bake 50 minutes. Serve rabbit and sauce over pasta or couscous.

PAPAYA-LIME GRANITA *serves four*

Granita is a coarse-textured shaved ice that is both very refreshing and easy to make. Be sure to begin the granita earlier in the day or make it several days ahead.

Combine water and sugar in a small saucepan and heat until the sugar is dissolved. Let cool. Peel, seed, and in a food processor, puree the papaya. Pass the puree through a strainer and add to the cooled sugar water. Juice the limes and add the juice to the papaya mixture.

1 cup water
1/2 cup sugar
1 large, very soft papaya
8 fresh limes

Pour mixture into a shallow pan or ice cube tray and put into freezer. When ice crystals start to form (usually in a couple of hours), stir the mixture from side to side every 20 minutes. When thoroughly frozen, cover and hold for up to one week. To serve, mound granita in dessert glasses and serve at once.

DINNER FOR A LOVED ONE
by Joyce Goldstein

Sauerbraten

Potato Pancakes

Red Cabbage

Sacher Torte

serves four to six

J oyce Goldstein, chef/owner of *Square One Restaurant* and *Caffè Quadro* in San Francisco, has been active as a cooking teacher and food writer since 1965. She is currently a columnist for the *San Francisco Chronicle* and is writing a cookbook, *Tastes of the Mediterranean* (William Morrow, 1989). Joyce has been active in raising funds for AIDS causes and the United Way.

"This dinner for a loved one and good friends is for Peter Seigler. When he was working as a waiter at Square One, Peter used to be the taster for the sauerbraten. Every time we make sauerbraten, I try to make it just the way Peter liked it. It reminded him of home, but now it always reminds me of him. And that makes it special."

SAUERBRATEN *serves four to six*

Combine all ingredients except beef to form marinade. Marinate beef for 2 to 3 days. Cook meat in marinade on top of stove over low heat in a heavy, covered pot, about 2 to 2½ hours or until tender.

3 pounds round roast of beef
2 cups red wine
2 to 3 tablespoons red wine vinegar
3 tablespoons brown sugar
1/4 cup tomato puree
3 cloves garlic, minced
1 teaspoon salt
1/2 teaspoon pepper
1 teaspoon Worcestershire sauce
2 teaspoons dry mustard
2 teaspoons soy sauce
1 teaspoon ground cloves
8 crushed gingersnaps
2 cups beef broth
2 onions, thinly sliced

POTATO PANCAKES *serves four to six*

1 medium yellow onion,
   diced small (about
   1¼ cups)
1 egg
3 large russet baking
   potatoes, peeled, diced
   small (about 4 cups)
5 to 7 tablespoons flour,
   depending on wetness
   of potatoes
Salt and pepper to taste
Vegetable shortening for
   frying

Blend the onion and egg in a blender until they are liquefied. Add about a third of the potato cubes and blend very quickly, just until the lumps disappear. Add the rest of the potato cubes and stir them into the puree. Blend quickly to eliminate all lumps but do not puree for more than a minute. If you have to do this blending in batches, remove half of the potato batter, add the rest of the cubes and puree quickly, and combine with the rest of the batter. Pour all into a bowl and add the flour and salt and pepper. If the batter is very wet, blot the top with a towel until most of the water is eliminated.

To fry the pancakes, heat a heavy, deep pan and melt the shortening to about 1/2 inch in depth. When shortening is very hot, drop large spoonfuls of the batter into the hot fat and allow the pancakes to brown on one side. Then turn them over very carefully and brown them on the other side. Drain pancakes on paper towels. Serve immediately. If you are frying these in batches, keep them warm in a moderate oven for no more than 15 minutes.

RED CABBAGE *serves four to six*

In a saucepan with a tight-fitting cover, sauté onion in butter or bacon drippings until it is tender but not brown. Stir in apples and cook the mixture for a few minutes longer. Add water, red wine vinegar, sugar, salt, pepper, and bay leaf and bring the mixture to a boil. Stir in red cabbage and cover the pan tightly. Cook the mixture over low heat, stirring occasionally, for 15 to 20 minutes. Shortly before serving, mix flour with a little water to a smooth paste and stir it into the cabbage mixture. Heat the mixture, stirring constantly, until it thickens slightly.

1 large onion, finely chopped
2 tablespoons butter or bacon drippings
2 apples, peeled, cored, and thinly sliced
1 cup water
1/2 cup red wine vinegar
2 tablespoons sugar
1 teaspoon salt
Dash of pepper
1 bay leaf
1 large head red cabbage, shredded
1 tablespoon flour

SACHER TORTE *serves twelve to sixteen*

8 egg yolks
10 egg whites
1/8 teaspoon salt
3/4 cup sugar
1 stick (1/2 cup) sweet
    butter
7 ounces semisweet
    chocolate
1 teaspoon vanilla
1 cup flour
Apricot preserves
Frosting (see below)

Preheat oven to 350° F. Grease the bottom of three 9-inch or 10-inch pans (foil pans are good). Line the bottoms with wax paper and grease the paper. When separating eggs, reserve the two extra yolks for the frosting. Add salt to egg whites and beat till peaks just form. Add the sugar a bit at a time, beating constantly. Beat a few more minutes till stiff and glossy. Meanwhile, melt the chocolate and butter over hot water. Cool a little and add vanilla. Then add this to the yolks, stirring with a wire whisk. It will be thick. Add 1/3 of the whites to the chocolate mixture and stir well. Then pour on top of remaining whites and carefully sift in flour. Fold all together with whisk, being careful not to overmix, but not leaving any white lumps showing. Pour into pans and bake 25 to 30 minutes. Turn onto rack and peel off the paper. When cake is cool, spread apricot preserves between layers and pour frosting over the cake, smoothing sides with spatula. Chill well. Serve cake at almost room temperature.

Frosting

3 ounces unsweetened
    chocolate
1 cup heavy cream
1 tablespoon corn syrup
1 cup sugar
2 egg yolks
1 teaspoon vanilla

Combine chocolate, cream, corn syrup, and sugar in a small, heavy pan and heat, stirring until sugar is dissolved and the chocolate is melted. Raise heat to medium and cook till 224° to 226° F on a candy thermometer (soft ball). Using a small wire whisk, beat the hot mixture into the egg yolks. Cool and stir in vanilla.

AN UNINTIMIDATING DINNER FOR FRIENDS
by Connie McCole

Yellow Pepper Soup

Butterflied Grilled Leg of Lamb in Mustard Marinade

Sugar Snap Peas and Red Peppers

Potatoes Arrosti with Pancetta

Creole Bread Pudding

Whiskey Sauce

serves six to eight

Connie McCole has been teaching cooking classes in San Francisco for fourteen years. Current specialty areas are Italian and timesavers, meals that can be prepared in half an hour or less. As a working wife and mother of two young boys, she understands the need to fill hungry tummies fast.

"This menu is not one of my timesavers, but it does allow you more time to enjoy your friends, since most preparation has been done in advance. I like to serve my friends meals that are unintimidating. After all, I'd like them to invite me to their table, too.

"This meal is dedicated to the memory of Yves Martin."

YELLOW PEPPER SOUP *serves six* ᴛₒ ₜᵣᵧ

Cibreo is a charming restaurant I discovered five years ago in Florence. Every day as I walked by, the restaurant was bustling with jovial patrons apparently having a wonderful time. When I tasted this soup, I began to see why.

1 carrot, peeled, chopped
1 onion, chopped
1 stalk of celery, chopped
1/4 cup of olive oil
4 yellow bell peppers,
    seeded and cut into
    large pieces
1 pound of potatoes,
    peeled and cut into
    1/4-inch slices
10 ounces beef broth
3 cups water
Freshly ground pepper
    to taste
Croutons
Virgin olive oil
Grated Reggiano
    Parmigiano cheese

In a large saucepan, cook the carrot, onion, and celery in the oil over medium heat, stirring, till all the vegetables are softened. Add the peppers, potatoes, broth, and water. Bring this to a boil, reduce heat, and let simmer for 40 minutes, or till all the vegetables are very soft. Simmer this partially covered. Puree in a blender or food processor; add a bit of pepper to taste. You don't usually need to add salt, as the cheese will balance the taste. Serve each portion with croutons, freshly made, sautéed in virgin olive oil, and a sprinkling of Reggiano.

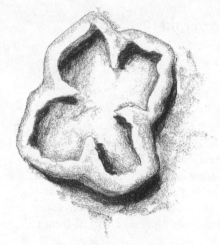

BUTTERFLIED GRILLED LEG OF LAMB IN MUSTARD MARINADE
serves eight

Mix together the mustards, sugar, water, and crushed garlic. Set aside for 15 to 30 minutes to let the flavors develop. Heat 3 tablespoons olive oil in a small sauté pan. Cook the chili peppers slowly till they are darkened but not burnt. Set aside to cool.

Finely chop the rosemary. Mix together the rosemary, mustard mixture, chili peppers and their cooking oil, the rest of the olive oil, lemon juice, pepper, salt, oregano, and vinegar.

Remove excess fat from lamb. Pierce the meat all over with a meat fork. Put the marinade into a large, strong plastic bag. Double bagging might be a good idea. Add the lamb, seal, and massage the marinade into the meat. Put the bag into a large dish, and refrigerate for 2 to 3 days, turning the bag from time to time.

Remove from the refrigerator at least 2 hours before grilling. Preheat grill, and when it is hot, remove lamb from the marinade and pat dry of any excess without totally drying the lamb. Sprinkle with salt and pepper, then grill, fell-side down for approximately 8 minutes, brushing with the marinade. Be careful not to start a fire as the marinade contains a good bit of olive oil. Turn the lamb and grill another 8 minutes for medium rare. A skewer inserted into the thickest part of the meat should feel warm to the touch when withdrawn.

1 tablespoon dry mustard
1 tablespoon Dijon-style mustard
1 teaspoon sugar
3 tablespoons water
2 large cloves garlic, peeled and crushed flat with a knife
1/2 cup + 3 tablespoons olive oil
2 dried red chili peppers, broken in half (don't discard seeds)
1/2 cup rosemary leaves, loosely packed
1/3 cup lemon juice
3 teaspoons coarsely ground black pepper
1 teaspoon salt
2 teaspoons dried oregano
3 tablespoons red wine vinegar
1 leg of lamb, boned and butterflied

SUGAR SNAP PEAS AND RED PEPPERS *serves four to six*

3/4 pound sugar snap
   peas, strings removed,
   or substitute snow peas
2 tablespoons butter
1 medium red bell pepper,
   seeded and julienned
Salt to taste

Bring a pot of water to the boil and let peas boil 1½ minutes. Drain and refresh in cold water and dry on paper towels. Heat butter in a sauté pan; add peppers and sauté, stirring till cooked but still al dente. Add peas and salt to taste.

POTATOES ARROSTI WITH PANCETTA *serves six to eight*

3 pounds new potatoes,
   scrubbed, not peeled
3 tablespoons butter at
   room temperature
Generous salt
Pepper
4 ounces pancetta (Italian
   bacon), cubed from
   thick slices
Sprigs of fresh rosemary
3 to 4 tablespoons olive oil

Parboil potatoes by placing in a large, deep pot and covering with cold water. Bring to a boil over high heat and cook till potatoes are still a bit firm when pierced with a knife, about 10 minutes for medium- to large-sized potatoes. Rinse in cold water to stop cooking, and cut in large chunks, about sixths or eighths. Butter the bottom and sides of a baking dish. Add potatoes, sprinkle with salt and pepper, pancetta, rosemary, and olive oil. Can be done ahead to this point. Roast at 450° F, being sure to turn often till potatoes are a crispy brown and the pancetta is crisp, about 25 to 30 minutes.

CREOLE BREAD PUDDING
serves eight to ten

The bread should be allowed to soak in the pudding mixture overnight before baking. I like to pop it in the oven before my friends arrive so they can be greeted by the comforting smell of something baking in the oven.

Start the raisins macerating in the whiskey. In a large bowl, combine the bread cubes with the milk and let stand, stirring occasionally, for at least 2 hours, or till the crusts are very soft. In a bowl, beat the eggs, sugar, butter, vanilla, and salt and add this to the bread mixture with the raisins and the whiskey, and stir to combine well. Transfer this mixture to a well-buttered 2½-quart gratin dish. Chill, covered, overnight. Bring to room temperature. Stir, and bake at 375° F for 1 hour, till edge is puffed and knife comes out clean. Serve warm topped with whiskey sauce.

1⅓ cups raisins macerated in 2/3 cup whiskey
8 cups sourdough bread, day-old, cut into 1/2-inch cubes
6 cups whole milk
5 large eggs
2/3 cup sugar
3/4 stick (6 tablespoons) sweet butter, melted and cooled
2 teaspoons vanilla
1 teaspoon salt
Whiskey sauce (see below)

WHISKEY SAUCE

Cream together butter and sugar and beat in eggs one at a time. Place in double boiler, add whiskey and cook, stirring continuously until slightly thickened. Serve hot in a small pitcher that has been preheated with very warm water. If sauce curdles, whisk vigorously to bring it back together.

1 stick sweet butter, softened
1/2 cup sugar
2 large eggs
3/4 cup whiskey (or to taste)

AN ITALIAN COUNTRY DINNER by Licia Demeo

Spaghetti Aglio e Òlio

Tripe Baked with Tomatoes and Rosemary

Mescluna with Balsamic Vinaigrette

Italian Country Bread

serves four to six

Licia Demeo's cooking is working-class rural and ethnic. She's a traditionalist and loves food and history simultaneously. She is presently the chef at the *Clement Street Bar and Grill* in San Francisco.

"My home cooking is classically Italian. My friends are impoverished bike messengers who always seem to be hungry when they stop by. There is always pasta followed by greens with balsamic vinaigrette. When I have enough energy, I like to make a spicy dish of oven-baked tripe and a crusty loaf of Italian bread."

SPAGHETTI AGLIO E ÒLIO (Spaghetti with Garlic and Olive Oil) *serves four to six*

The success of this dish depends on the use of high-quality spaghetti, olive oil, and Italian Parmesan. Bring 6 quarts of water and 3 tablespoons sea salt to a furious boil. Lower the spaghetti into the water. Stir to separate the strands with a cooking fork. As the pasta cooks, make the sauce. Slowly warm the olive oil in a large sauté pan. Add the garlic and cook it slowly over a low flame till transparent. Add the parsley, chili flakes, and sea salt to taste. Be careful with the salt. Add several grinds of black pepper and keep warm until pasta is ready. The pasta should be very firm but cooked through. When the pasta is cooked, strain it and toss it very thoroughly with the olive oil and garlic. Add the cheese and toss again. Serve immediately.

Sea salt
1 pound imported Italian spaghetti
1/2 cup extra virgin olive oil
2 heads organic garlic, chopped
1 bunch Italian flat-leaved parsley, chopped
1/2 teaspoon chili flakes
Freshly ground black pepper to taste
1/8 cup freshly grated Reggiano Parmigiano cheese

TRIPE BAKED WITH TOMATOES AND ROSEMARY *serves four to six*

1 carrot, roughly chopped
2 stalks celery, roughly
  chopped
1 onion, roughly chopped
1 tablespoon salt
2 pounds honeycomb
  tripe (be sure it is fresh
  from the butcher)
1/4 cup olive oil
1/3 cup chopped onion
1/3 cup chopped carrot
1/4 cup chopped celery
1/2 head chopped organic
  garlic
1/4 cup chopped Italian
  parsley
3 teaspoons fresh rose-
  mary, finely chopped
2 cups dry white wine
4 cups canned Italian
  tomatoes, seeded
  and chopped
1 cup rich beef broth (not
  a demiglace), must be
  homemade
Rind of Reggiano
  Parmigiano cheese
Chili flakes to taste
Salt to taste
1/4 cup grated Reggiano
  Parmigiano cheese

Bring 3 quarts of water to a boil with the roughly chopped carrot, celery, onion, and salt. Place the pre-rinsed tripe into the boiling water. Lower heat and simmer for 35 minutes. Remove tripe from water and cool. Discard vegetables. Cut tripe into 2-inch squares. Set aside.

Warm olive oil in a terra-cotta baking dish. Add onions, stir till translucent over a medium flame. Add carrots, stir for 4 minutes. Add celery and stir till translucent. Add garlic and Italian parsley. Cook gently for a few moments more, then stir in the tripe and rosemary. Stir the tripe around until well combined with the herbs and vegetables. Raise heat and add the white wine. Reduce. Add the tomatoes. Let them bubble before adding the broth and cheese rind. Simmer 10 minutes. Cover pan with heavy foil and a tight-fitting lid. Bake on middle shelf of moderate oven (350° F) for 2 hours. It should melt in your mouth when done. Add chili flakes and salt 1/2 hour before done. Serve with freshly grated Parmesan and crusty bread.

MESCLUNA WITH BALSAMIC VINAIGRETTE *serves four*

Mescluna is a mixture of greens including mi-zuna, arugula, baby red mirella, baby red mus-tard, and frisée. It may also include baby green onions and chervil. The mixture may vary, but it always has an exciting variety of bitter, pep-pery, spicy, and mild greens. They have so much flavor that only the simplest dressing is required. Mescluna may be purchased by the pound in health food stores that specialize in produce. There is also a seed mixture for mescluna, which may be used to grow your own.

Gently rinse the greens in cool water. Spin dry. Place in a bowl large enough to toss them with ease. Sprinkle balsamic vinegar, olive oil, and the rest of the ingredients over the greens and gently mix with your hands. There should be just enough olive oil to coat the greens, a balance of salt and acidity, and the greens should be mixed well with the other ingredients.

4 large handfuls mescluna
Balsamic vinegar
Extra virgin olive oil
    with character (I like
    Ardoino or Colavita)
1 clove young garlic,
    minced
Pinch of finely chopped
    rosemary, or
Few leaves basil
    enchiffonade
Sea salt to taste
A generous amount of
    freshly ground pepper

ITALIAN COUNTRY BREAD
makes one loaf

1 package yeast
1 cup warm water
1¼ cups white durum
  wheat flour,
  unbleached
1 tablespoon salt
2 tablespoons olive oil
1/8 cup wheat germ
1½ cups whole wheat
  flour

In a medium-sized bowl, dissolve the yeast in 1/2 cup warm water. Stir in the white flour. Turn onto a floured board and knead till springy and elastic. Add more flour if needed. Put the dough into a small, oiled bowl covered with a wet towel. Place the bowl away from drafts and leave overnight.

Add 1/2 cup warm water, salt, and olive oil to the sponge. Let it sit 15 minutes before stirring in wheat germ and whole wheat flour gradually till the dough becomes very firm and impossible to stir.

Sprinkle some white flour on the board and turn dough vigorously till smooth as a baby's skin and elastic. Test by pressing with your finger; the indentation should spring back. Also, air bubbles will appear on the surface. Put the dough in an oiled, medium-sized bowl covered with a wet towel and place away from drafts. Let rise till double in bulk. Punch down and shape into one long loaf. Roll the dough into a rectangular shape using a rolling pin. Then roll up tightly. Shape it with your hands so that the ends are tapered. Pinch the seams and put them facing down on your baking sheet. Allow to rise for 40 minutes. Slash the top of the loaf diagonally with a razor blade. Place in a 450° F oven. After 15 minutes lower to 375° F and bake 40 minutes more or till the loaf sounds hollow when you knock its bottom.

A CONVIVIAL MENU
by Annie Somerville

*Butternut Squash and Leek Soup
with Gruyère Cheese and
Thyme*

*Mushroom and Winter-Vegetable
Ragout with Soft Polenta*

*Comice Pears and Walnuts with
Romaine Hearts, Watercress, and
Radicchio*

serves six

Annie Somerville began cooking in San Francisco at the Zen Center and continued to train and learn the ways of the kitchen at Tassajara Zen Mountain Center. She is currently executive chef at *Greens* restaurant.

"I spend most of my time at Greens, and when I'm not at Greens, I'm somewhere else thinking of Greens! So I can honestly say that I rarely have the time to cook for friends at home. These are recipes for dishes we serve to friends and customers at the restaurant. I like to think that these recipes convey a sense of warmth, ease, and conviviality that friends feel when having a meal together."

BUTTERNUT SQUASH AND LEEK SOUP WITH GRUYÈRE CHEESE AND THYME *serves six to eight*

Stock:
Tops of 2 medium leeks, rinsed and chopped
1 carrot, peeled and chopped
1 medium potato, chopped
2 celery stalks, chopped
2 bay leaves
A small handful of fresh herbs (marjoram, oregano, thyme, and parsley)
4 cloves garlic
A few black peppercorns
A few pinches salt
5 cups cold water

Soup:
2 tablespoons butter
Whites of 2 medium leeks, sliced and rinsed
4 cloves garlic, minced
Salt to taste
1/2 teaspoon dried thyme
1/2 cup white wine
2 medium butternut squash (or other flavorful squash), peeled, seeded, and cut into small cubes (approximately 4 cups cubed)
Freshly ground black or white pepper
1/4 pound Gruyère cheese, grated
1 small bunch fresh thyme, chopped

This is a hearty yet elegant soup. It is relatively easy to make, and the flavors are very complementary. Any flavorful winter squash can be substituted for butternut.

Prepare the stock beginning with the leeks. Cut the leeks in half and slice the white ends of the leeks for soup. Rinse and set aside. Chop the green leek tops, rinse, and combine with other stock ingredients in a large pot. Cover with the cold water and cook over moderate heat until the stock begins to simmer. Turn down heat and simmer for 30 minutes. Strain stock, discard cooked vegetables, and set liquid aside to cook with the soup later. Melt the butter in a thick-bottomed soup pot. Add the white parts of the leeks, garlic, and a few pinches of salt and dried thyme. Cook the leeks until tender, add the wine, and cook until the wine has reduced. Add the cubed squash and cover with stock. Be careful not to use all of the stock at this point as too much stock will dilute the flavor of the soup. Cook over medium heat until the squash takes on a rather smooth consistency. Thin the soup with more stock if necessary, to desired consistency. Season to taste with salt and freshly ground pepper. White pepper is very good in this soup. Serve the soup and sprinkle with grated Gruyère cheese and chopped fresh thyme.

MUSHROOM AND WINTER-VEGETABLE RAGOUT WITH SOFT POLENTA *serves four to six*

I particularly enjoy using fall and winter vegetables in ragouts and stews. If wild mushrooms are available, use them, as their wonderful flavor enhances this dish. Be sure the ragout vegetables are of similar size so they cook evenly.

To prepare the mushroom stock combine all stock ingredients and bring to a boil. Simmer over low heat while sautéing vegetables for the ragout. Cook for 30 minutes, strain stock, and discard vegetables.

Quick Mushroom Stock:
3 ounces dried shiitake mushrooms
A few sprigs fresh herbs
1/2 medium yellow onion, sliced
4 cloves garlic
2 cups cold water
1/4 cup mushroom soy sauce or soy sauce
A few pinches of salt

Allow 20 minutes to cook the ragout. In a thick-bottomed sauté pan, sauté onion in butter and olive oil with garlic and a few pinches of salt and black pepper until they are soft. Add 1/2 of the wine and reduce. Then add the mushrooms, followed by the turnips, fennel, and peppers. Season with a few splashes of mushroom soy sauce. Add more butter and olive oil as necessary, the remaining wine, and just enough mushroom stock to make a sauce. Cook the vegetables until tender and flavorful. Be careful not to overcook the ragout, as the vegetables should be tender, yet firm. Finish seasoning with fresh herbs, salt, and pepper. Add crème fraîche or sour cream to lightly bind the sauce. Serve with soft polenta.

Note: If using fresh shiitake mushrooms, use only the cap for the ragout. Save the stems and add to stock. Do not wash shiitake, porcini, or

Ragout:
1 medium yellow onion, large dice
2 tablespoons butter
2 tablespoons olive oil
4 cloves garlic, minced
Salt and freshly ground black pepper to taste
1 cup red wine
1 pound mushrooms, cut in thick slices (include fresh shiitake, chanterelle, or porcini mushrooms if available; see note below)
1 large turnip or 4 small turnips, cut into 1/2-inch cubes if large, or into halves or quarters if small

(continued next page)

2 fennel bulbs, cut in thick
slices
1 medium red pepper, cut
in thick slices
1 medium yellow pepper,
cut in thick slices
Mushroom soy sauce or
soy sauce to taste
1/2 cup freshly chopped
herbs (Italian parsley,
marjoram, oregano,
and chives)
1/4 cup sour cream or
crème fraîche to finish
ragout
Soft polenta (see below)

1 cup polenta
4 cups boiling salted
water
1/4 cup butter
Salt and black pepper
to taste
1/2 pound grated
Parmesan cheese

chanterelle mushrooms. If using chanterelles or
porcinis, clean them with brush or damp cloth.

Soft Polenta

Allow 20 minutes to cook the polenta. It can
easily be done while cooking the stock. When
the polenta is done, leave over low flame and stir
occasionally until ready to serve. Thin with hot
water if it begins to thicken.

Make the polenta in a heavy-bottomed pan.
Whisk polenta into boiling water and continue
to whisk vigorously until polenta dissolves.
Turn down the heat and continue to stir so polenta does not stick to the bottom of the pan.
Cook over medium heat until the grains dissolve
completely and the polenta is smooth. This will
take about 20 minutes. Add butter and salt and
pepper to taste. Add 1/2 of the cheese just before
serving and sprinkle the rest of the cheese over
the polenta when it is served.

COMICE PEARS AND WALNUTS WITH ROMAINE HEARTS, WATERCRESS, AND RADICCHIO
serves six

This salad is a fall and winter favorite. If watercress or radicchio are not available, substitute chicory, escarole, or other bitter greens.

Preheat oven to 375° F. Toast walnuts for 8 to 10 minutes, until they begin to brown. Set aside to cool.

Prepare salad greens, beginning with the romaine lettuce by peeling away and discarding the tough outer leaves. Leave the small inner leaves whole and cut the larger inner leaves as necessary. Prepare the radicchio by discarding only the tough outer leaves and separating the inner leaves. Trim the large stems from the watercress and save the small sprigs for the salad. Rinse the greens and spin dry. Toss the salad greens, pears, and walnuts with walnut-sherry vinaigrette. Sprinkle with freshly ground black pepper and serve on chilled plates.

1/2 cup walnuts
2 heads romaine lettuce
1 small head radicchio
1 to 2 bunches watercress
2 ripe Comice pears, cored and sliced
Walnut-sherry vinaigrette (see below)
Freshly ground black pepper

Walnut Sherry Vinaigrette
To make the vinaigrette, combine the vinegar, salt, and shallot. Whisk in the oils to emulsify. Pour over greens and toss.

3 tablespoons sherry vinegar
1 small shallot, minced or thinly sliced
Salt to taste
4 tablespoons light olive oil
4 tablespoons walnut oil

A WINTER DINNER FOR DEAR FRIENDS
by Laura Chenel

Assorted Crostini

Marinated Salmon with Orange and Fennel

Grilled Duck Breast and White Beans

Salad of Mixed Greens with Selection of Goat Cheeses

Winter-Fruit Compote with Vanilla Ice Cream and Biscotti

serves six

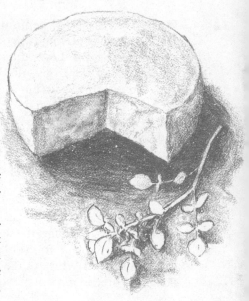

Laura Chenel created an American goat cheese industry when she opened this country's first authentic French-style goat cheese factory in 1979. Over the years she has been a strong and innovative force behind the growth and development of that still-infant industry. She has coauthored two books: *Chèvre! The Goat Cheese Cookbook* (Peaks Pike Publishing Company, 1983) and *American Country Cheese* (Peaks Pike Publishing Company, 1989).

"This is a hearty meal, designed to warm the diners' bodies and souls. It spans nearly four hours and is accented by much lively discussion, laughter, friendship, and warmth. It is accompanied by a fire in the hearth and the soft glow of many candles on the table.

"When I indulge in an occasion such as this, it is meaningful and special to me. My guests become my family for the evening. The intensely pleasurable feelings of warmth and comfort begin with the preparation of the meal, grow to a crescendo during the evening, and linger softly to fill the days thereafter."

ASSORTED CROSTINI

Slice a baguette 1/4 inch thick and toast till golden. Top with any or all of the following:

Thinly sliced aged goat cheese (Tome), drizzled with olive oil, placed in the oven for 3 to 5 minutes, then topped with shaved, sautéed garlic.

Olive paste and fresh goat cheese, placed under the broiler 1 to 2 minutes, topped with chopped basil.

Roasted red pepper and "goatzarella," placed under the broiler 1 to 2 minutes, then drizzled with olive oil, topped with freshly ground black pepper.

Chopped dried tomatoes and "goatzarella" or fresh goat cheese, placed under broiler 1 to 2 minutes, then topped with freshly ground black pepper and chopped basil.

MARINATED SALMON WITH ORANGE AND FENNEL *serves six*

12 ounces fresh salmon
 filet
1½ cups Simi Chenin
 Blanc
3 cloves garlic, thinly
 sliced
1/2 fresh jalapeño pepper,
 thinly sliced
3 tablespoons grated
 orange zest
1/4 cup fresh fennel,
 thinly sliced
1/8 cup cilantro, chopped
Abundance of freshly
 ground pepper
2 cups olive oil
Juice of 1 orange
1/2 cup white wine
 vinegar
3 fresh mandarin oranges,
 peeled, sectioned, and
 chopped into 1/4–inch
 dice
1 large fennel bulb,
 chopped into 1/4–inch
 dice
Fresh fennel weed from
 top of bulb
2 tablespoons cilantro,
 chopped

Cut salmon into 6 equal portions, 2 ounces each. Marinate for several hours in next seven ingredients. Remove from marinade and quickly sauté, skin-side down first, in very hot sauté pan, just till done but still quite soft inside. Length of time depends upon thickness of filet. Mix olive oil, orange juice, and vinegar into marinade, then pour over salmon, reserving enough to cover mandarin orange and fennel. Allow salmon to cool in refrigerator about one hour. Meanwhile, marinate fennel and orange in remaining marinade at room temperature. To serve, arrange a bed of orange/fennel salad in the center of each plate, top with a sprinkling of fennel weed and cilantro, then place a salmon filet atop the salad. Decorate salmon with a light sprinkling of the two herbs.

GRILLED DUCK BREAST AND WHITE BEANS *serves six*

Cook the beans in the water until just done, not mushy, with bay leaves, 3 cloves garlic, cayenne pepper, and parsley stems. When cooked, mix in goose fat. Let sit overnight. Next morning, drain the beans in a colander and remove the herbs. Gently cook 6 cloves of garlic in the olive oil until softened, and add the garlic and most of the olive oil to the beans along with a generous amount of black pepper, the salt, 1/2 cup parsley, 1/8 cup cilantro, and vinegar. Julienne Swiss chard and sauté in reserved olive oil until wilted, then add to beans. Mix well to combine.

Trim most of the fat from the duck breasts, leaving a small amount of fat that you slash in two or three places with a sharp knife. Marinate in 4 cloves of garlic, thinly sliced, 1/4 cup parsley, chopped, 1/6 cup cilantro, chopped, a generous grind of black pepper, and enough wine to cover. Let sit about 12 hours in the refrigerator.

When ready to serve, remove duck breasts from marinade and press ample amounts of coarsely ground black pepper into both sides of breasts. Grill quickly on a very hot grill until quite done on the outside but still rare on the inside. Heat beans over low flame until their temperature is somewhere between warm and hot. Make a pile of beans on each plate and decoratively arrange thinly sliced duck breast around beans.

2 cups white beans
4 cups water
3 bay leaves
13 cloves garlic
1 dried cayenne pepper
1 handful parsley stems
1/2 cup goose fat
1/2 cup olive oil
Freshly ground black
  pepper
1 teaspoon salt
3/4 cup parsley
1/8 cup cilantro
1/4 cup red wine vinegar
2 cups red and green
  Swiss chard
6 duck breasts
1/6 cup cilantro
1/2 bottle Côtes du Rhône
  wine

SALAD OF MIXED GREENS WITH SELECTION OF GOAT CHEESES
serves six

6 handfuls small-leafed
    lettuces such as arugula,
    oak-leaf, or red-leaf
Parsley
Cilantro
Watercress
2/3 cup fruity extra virgin
    olive oil
2 teaspoons prepared
    Dijon-style mustard
1/3 cup balsamic vinegar
Freshly ground black pepper

Rinse lettuces and greens and spin dry. Chop parsley and cilantro and strip watercress from stems. Prepare vinaigrette by whisking olive oil into mixture of mustard, vinegar, and a generous amount of pepper. Toss greens with dressing just before serving.

Accompany with three or four goat cheeses of various ages such as Taupinière, Crottin, Tome, Pyramide. Serve with walnut bread, see page 228.

WINTER-FRUIT COMPOTE WITH VANILLA ICE CREAM AND BISCOTTI

1 cup dried prunes, pitted
1 cup mission figs
1 cup dried apricots
Enough muscat eau-
    de-vie to cover
1 cup dried cherries
Enough raspberry eau-
    de-vie to cover
1 cup water
1 cup fruity red wine
    such as Beaujolais
1/4 cup sugar
Thin slivers lemon peel of
    1 lemon
1 tablespoon crystallized
    ginger, slivered
3 mandarin oranges, cut
    into half rounds
1 cup muscat raisins
1 cup roasted walnuts
Vanilla ice cream
Biscotti

Soak prunes, figs, and apricots in muscat eau-de-vie for 12 to 18 hours. Soak cherries in raspberry eau-de-vie. Combine water, Beaujolais, sugar, lemon peel, and ginger in a saucepan and bring to a boil. Remove fruits from eau-de-vie with slotted spoon and add to sugar syrup. Cook until tender, about 15 to 20 minutes, then remove from syrup and place in bowl. Add eau-de-vie remaining from soaked fruit to sugar syrup and reduce. To bowl of cooling fruit add oranges, raisins, and walnuts. Mix in reduced sugar syrup and allow to cool completely.

To serve, scoop some vanilla ice cream into each bowl. Cover with compote and serve with biscotti. There will probably be more compote than needed for this occasion, but it is delicious the next day, and for several days thereafter.

A WINTER MEXICAN DINNER PARTY
by Heidi Insalata Krahling

Guacamole with Tortilla Chips*

Salsa Verde

Chipotle Salsa

Pork Stew with Tomatillos and Greens

Orange Sopapillas

Chocolate Spice Cake

Cajeta

Piloncillo Vanilla Bean Ice Cream

serves ten

*Recipe not included

Heidi Insalata Krahling is a highly regarded Bay Area chef who enjoys cooking the cuisines of Mexico and the Mediterranean.

"This dinner is designed for my friends who know and share my passion for Mexican food – the kind of dishes that are big on taste and satisfy your soul. I usually include a romaine lettuce salad, fried plantain, and black beans. Not exactly low in calories; one doesn't count them when eating the foods of Mexico."

SALSA VERDE *yields 1½ quarts*

5 pounds tomatillos
   (peeled of outer husk)
1 yellow onion, diced and
   sautéed in olive oil
3 cloves of garlic, minced
   and sautéed in olive oil
2 jalapeño peppers,
   chopped
1 bunch cilantro, chopped
1/2 tablespoon dried
   oregano
3/4 tablespoon cumin
1/2 cup water (more
   or less to adjust
   consistency)
Salt and pepper to taste
A splash of vinegar, if
   needed for tartness

Blanch tomatillos for about 10 minutes until soft. In a blender, puree all ingredients together. Adjust seasoning and consistency. This recipe must be made to taste. All fresh ingredients can vary in flavor.

CHIPOTLE SALSA *yields 3½ cups*

2 canned chipotle chilies
1 tablespoon toasted
   sesame seeds, ground
   in spice grinder
1 cup salsa verde
   (see above)
1/2 tablespoon salt
2 cups pear or plum
   tomatoes, drained
1 bunch cilantro, chopped

Put chilies in food processor fitted with metal blade and puree until smooth. Add the rest of the ingredients and pulse until combined and chunks are gone.

PORK STEW WITH TOMATILLOS AND GREENS *serves ten*

Place pork and stock in a medium-sized stockpot and bring to a boil, slowly. Skim the grayish foam that rises to the top when simmering. Add the next 3 ingredients and simmer until pork is very tender (about 1 hour). Strain stock and reserve. Discard herbs and garlic. In a large sauté pan melt 1/4 cup lard. Add onions and garlic and sauté until soft and golden. Add the tomatillos, jalapeños, and 1/2 of reserved cooking liquid. Simmer until tomatillos are soft. Add greens, cilantro, and cumin, and simmer for about 10 minutes.

Remove from heat. Puree the mixture in the food processor or blender. Set aside.

In a large sauté pan, melt remaining 1/4 cup of lard. When hot, add pork cubes and fry until crispy and brown. Add pureed mixture and simmer for about 15 minutes. If stew is too thick, thin with remaining stock to desired consistency. Salt and pepper to taste.

*Epazote is also known as Mexican tea, wormseed, goosefoot, or Jerusalem oak and is widely used as a green herb in Mexican cooking.

5 pounds cubed pork shoulder, free of fat
5 cups pork or chicken stock
5 cloves garlic
1 bay leaf
1/2 bunch fresh epazote*
1/2 cup lard
3 onions, diced
1/2 cup garlic, roughly chopped
4 pounds tomatillos (peeled of outer husk)
4 jalapeño peppers, cut in half and seeded
1¾ pounds greens, your choice (baby kale is good)
2 bunches cilantro, roughly chopped
1 tablespoon toasted cumin seed (or to taste)
Salt and pepper to taste

ORANGE SOPAPILLAS *serves ten*

1 package dry yeast
  (1 tablespoon)
1/4 cup warm water
1½ cups milk
1 tablespoon orange
  flower water
Zest of 1 orange
2 tablespoons honey
3 cups all-purpose flour
2 cups whole wheat
  pastry flour
1 teaspoon salt
3 tablespoons butter
Peanut oil for frying

Dissolve yeast in water. Combine milk, orange flower water, zest, and honey in a mixing bowl.

In a second mixing bowl, combine flours and salt. Cut in the butter until mixture resembles coarse meal. Add the yeast mixture and milk mixture and work with hands until a smooth dough is formed. Place in a greased bowl, turning to grease top, and cover with plastic. Proof in the refrigerator for 4 hours or overnight.

On a lightly floured surface (just enough to keep from sticking), roll out dough to 1/8 inch thick. Cut in 3-inch squares and then again diagonally into triangles. Fry 2 or 3 at a time in 350° F oil. When they begin to puff, gently flip and continue frying until golden on both sides.

Serve hot with honey.

CHOCOLATE SPICE CAKE *serves ten*

Butter and flour a 9-inch-round cake pan 2 inches deep. Line with parchment paper.

Melt butter and chocolate over a bain-marie. Add egg yolks, ancho puree, and cinnamon to the chocolate mixture.

In a mixer, whip the whites to a soft peak. Add the sugar and continue to whip for 1 minute. Fold the whites into the chocolate mixture. Add the almonds. Pour into prepared pan.

Bake at 350° F for 50 minutes or until middle is firm to the touch. Remove from the oven and cool for 2 minutes. Turn out on a buttered cake round covered with parchment for 5 minutes, until bottom is cool. Then turn over on serving dish. Dust with powdered sugar and serve with cajeta and piloncillo ice cream.

*Ancho puree: Soak approximately 10 ancho chilies in hot water until they are soft. Discard stem and seeds and puree the meat of the chili until smooth. Sieve puree.

7 tablespoons butter, cut into small pieces
9 ounces bittersweet chocolate, cut into small pieces
7 egg yolks
3 tablespoons ancho puree*
1/2 teaspoon cinnamon
7 egg whites
1/4 cup sugar
1/2 cup almonds, toasted and chopped
Powdered sugar
Cajeta (see next page)
Piloncillo vanilla bean ice cream (see next page)

CAJETA (Goat Milk Caramel Sauce)

1 cup sugar
4 cups fresh goat's milk
1 tablespoon light corn
    syrup
1 cinnamon stick
1/4 teaspoon baking soda

In a heavy pan, caramelize 1/2 cup sugar until dark brown but not burnt. Add remaining ingredients and bring to a boil. The mixture will foam up again, then take on a caramel-brownish color as it reduces to a heavy cream consistency. Cool before using. Makes approximately 1½ cups.

PILONCILLO VANILLA BEAN ICE CREAM *makes one quart*

2 cups milk
2 cups heavy cream
4 ounces piloncillo sugar,
    chopped into small
    pieces*
3 ounces white sugar
Pinch of salt
1 vanilla bean, split
6 egg yolks, beaten

Heat milk, cream, sugars, salt, and vanilla bean slowly to just below boiling. Remove vanilla bean and scrape out inside of pod into cream mixture. Pour hot cream mixture into beaten yolks slowly, then place over a barely simmering water bath and cook until mix thickens and lightly coats the back of a spoon. Pour mixture through a sieve into a bowl and chill. Freeze in an ice cream freezer according to manufacturer's instructions.

*A Mexican brown, unrefined sugar found in Latin markets.

A WINTER SUPPER FOR SOMEONE SPECIAL
by Robert C. Schneider

Salad of Winter Greens with Persimmon and Water Chestnuts

Lasagne with Dungeness Crab, Fennel, and Chanterelles

Fresh Citrus Mélange

serves eight

Robert C. Schneider has been a professional chef for the past twelve years. He is presently working on an institutionally oriented cooking manual to facilitate Project Open Hand's nationwide expansion.

"This meal was originally created as an after-theater supper for a dear friend's birthday celebration. A year later it was recreated at the same friend's home to introduce Ruth Brinker to Gerry Jampolsky and Diane Cirincione of the Center for Attitudinal Healing.

"The lasagne is a bit unusual in that it calls for somewhat rich and elegant ingredients, particularly the crab meat and the fresh chanterelles, but it is assembled in the traditional layered-casserole manner to allow the different flavors to blend and bake in. Be careful in your timing so nothing overcooks and each element maintains its identity."

SALAD OF WINTER GREENS WITH PERSIMMON AND WATER CHESTNUTS *serves eight*

2 bunches arugula
1 bunch mizuna (young
   Japanese mustard
   greens)
2 bunches watercress
2 fuyu (Japanese)
   persimmons
8 fresh water chestnuts

Vinaigrette:
2 tablespoons vinegar
   (balsamic, sherry,
   spiced, or a mixture
   is good)
6 tablespoons extra virgin
   olive oil or walnut oil
1 teaspoon dry mustard
1 tablespoon poppy seeds
1 teaspoon honey
   (optional)
Salt and pepper to taste

Rinse greens, removing all stems, and spin dry. Place in a large glass salad bowl.

Remove cap from tops of persimmons and slice into thin wedges with a sharp knife. Remove persimmon seeds as you slice alongside them. You may peel persimmon wedges if you like, but usually the skins are tender enough to serve.

Peel fresh water chestnuts by slicing off the top and bottom of each with a heavy knife and then using a paring knife to peel the remaining edges. Slice water chestnuts 1/8 inch thick.

Combine all vinaigrette ingredients in a jar with a tightly sealing lid. Shake well until ingredients are combined and oil and vinegar have emulsified.

Arrange persimmon wedges in a circular pattern on top of the greens and pile the water-chestnut slices in the center. Immediately before serving pour dressing over all, toss, and serve.

LASAGNE WITH DUNGENESS CRAB, FENNEL, AND CHANTERELLES
serves eight

Put the cream in a small saucepan and reduce by half over medium heat. Keep your eye on the cream so it doesn't boil over.

Meanwhile, prepare the herbs and vegetables. Slice the fennel crosswise into 1/4-inch slices. Cut the tomatoes in half, crosswise, remove the seeds, and chop coarsely. Cut the stems off the chard and slice into a 1/2-inch chiffonade. Cut mushrooms into broad, thin slices. Chop peeled shallots medium fine. Remove stems from tarragon leaves and chop coarsely.

In a large skillet, braise the fennel slices in 1½ inches of lightly salted water for 3 minutes. Add the Swiss chard, cover, and continue to braise until the fennel is crisp-tender and all the chard is softened, another 2 to 3 minutes. Drain and set aside. In the same skillet, sauté the shallots in the olive oil for 2 to 3 minutes, until soft. Add the mushrooms and continue to sauté until the mushrooms release their liquid, perhaps another 2 to 3 minutes. Add the sherry and cook another 2 to 3 minutes. Drain the shallots and mushrooms and set aside, returning the liquid to the pan. Place over high heat and add the chopped tomatoes and fresh tarragon. Cook until tomatoes are very soft and most of the liquid has evaporated. Add the reduced cream and season with salt and pepper. Cook for about 2 to 3 minutes more and remove from heat. Sauce should be of a nice coating consistency.

Place 3 tablespoons of the sauce in the bottom of a lasagne pan, similar in dimensions to the pasta sheets. Cover with the first sheet of uncooked pasta dough. Top with the drained chard and fennel in one layer, spoon on 6 tablespoons sauce, and sprinkle with Parmesan cheese. Cover with

3 cups heavy cream
2 medium-sized fennel bulbs
1½ pounds ripe tomatoes
1 bunch red Swiss chard
1 pound wild mushrooms (preferably chanterelles, dog tooth, *Boletus edulis*, or any flavorful counterpart)
5 shallots
3 branches fresh tarragon
3 tablespoons olive oil
1/2 cup dry sherry
Salt and pepper
4 sheets of fresh pasta approximately 9 by 12 inches
Freshly grated Parmesan cheese
1½ pounds freshly cooked Dungeness crab meat

(continued next page)

the second sheet of pasta and top with the shallot–wild mushroom mixture. Again spoon over some sauce and a little grated cheese and cover with the third sheet of pasta. Next, layer the fresh crabmeat with a generous amount of sauce, and finally, add the fourth sheet of pasta, the rest of the sauce, and more grated Parmesan.

Cover the lasagne with a sheet of parchment paper and some foil over that. Crimp around the edges to seal securely. Bake in a 325° F oven for 35 minutes or until hot throughout. Cut into eight equal portions to serve.

Note: When using fresh pasta, be careful that the dough does not dry out. Always keep the pasta sheets covered with a damp towel and use one sheet at a time.

FRESH CITRUS MÉLANGE
serves eight

Cut very thin strips of zest about 1¼ inches long from all the citrus until you have about 1/3 cup. Make a syrup by combining sugar and water in a small saucepan and bringing to a boil. Boil for about 5 minutes. Add strips of zest to sugar syrup and cook briefly. Remove the zest strips and allow to cool.

Peel all the citrus, being careful to remove all the bitter white pith without breaking the sections of the fruit. Slice all the citrus crosswise into 1/4-inch-thick slices with a serrated knife. Arrange slices on a platter in a festive pattern of colors and sizes. Lightly drizzle with sugar syrup and garnish with the strips of zest like party streamers.

*Lavender gems are a citrus variety, somewhat like a lemon in appearance, but sweet to the taste.

1 white grapefruit
2 ruby grapefruit
2 blood oranges
2 mandarin oranges
2 tangerines
1 lime
1 lavender gem*
1 cup sugar
1 cup water

A NEW YEAR'S DAY DINNER by Chuck Phifer

New Year's Paella

*Watercress and Endive Salad
with Radishes*

Lemon Sherbet

serves eight

Nebraska-born Chuck Phifer is a graduate
of the California Culinary Academy and is
currently chef/co-owner of *Eddie Rickenbacker's*
in San Francisco.

*"This communal dish in the center of the table with its sheer abundance, warm sunny
colors, and incredible aroma is truly a meal fit for friends. Although paella is a meal in
itself, we like to serve it with a salad of the season, oven-warmed breadsticks with sweet
butter, and plenty of good, cold beer. After dinner, lemon sherbet and coffee."*

NEW YEAR'S PAELLA *serves eight*

Bring the stock to a boil, add saffron, simmer 10 minutes, and set aside.

In a large paella pan or other large pan, heat the olive oil. Add the garlic and sauté just till it begins to color. Add the onions and sauté to soften. Add the peppers and cook slightly, then remove the vegetables from the pan and set aside. Add chicken and brown, remove from pan. Add sausage chunks and brown, remove from pan. Add the squid and toss briefly. Add rice, tomatoes, stock, salt, sausage, chicken, the reserved vegetables, peas, olives, and parsley, reserving some of the parsley for garnish.

Stir, cover, and bring to a boil. Remove cover and arrange rockfish pieces on top. Replace cover and cook about 5 minutes more. Uncover and add mussels, cover and cook 5 minutes. Add shrimp, cover, and cook until mussels open, shrimp are cooked, and rice is tender. Add more stock or water at any point if the rice appears too dry. The rice should be moist, not soupy.

Let the paella stand covered about 5 minutes before serving. Sprinkle with remaining parsley. Place pan on a pad in center of table and remove lid with a flourish.

8 cups good fish or chicken stock
1 tablespoon saffron threads
3 tablespoons olive oil
6 cloves garlic, chopped
2 medium onions, chopped
1 red bell pepper, chopped
1 green bell pepper, chopped
8 pieces chicken, boned (I like to use thighs)
8 chorizo or other spicy sausages, cut into chunks
8 ounces or more squid, cleaned and cut into rings
4 cups rice
4 medium-sized tomatoes, peeled and cut into chunks
1½ teaspoons salt or more to taste
1 cup shelled green peas
1/2 cup sliced black olives
Chopped parsley
1½ pounds rockfish, cut into chunks
2 pounds mussels, rinsed and debearded
1 to 2 pounds large shrimp, peeled and deveined

WATERCRESS AND ENDIVE SALAD WITH RADISHES
serves eight

8 bunches watercress,
  rinsed, dried, and
  stemmed
4 medium-sized heads
  Belgian endive, cut into
  rings
2 bunches radishes, rinsed
  and sliced thinly
Walnut oil
Sherry vinegar

Combine cress, endive, and radishes and dress at the table with walnut oil and good sherry vinegar. Dress at the last minute and serve immediately as the cress wilts rapidly.

LEMON SHERBET *serves eight*   entered

1 quart milk
1/4 teaspoon salt
1⅓ cups sugar
1⅓ cups lemon juice
1⅓ tablespoons grated
  lemon zest

Mix first three ingredients and stir to dissolve sugar. Slowly add juice and zest, stirring constantly. Place in your ice cream freezer and freeze according to your machine's instructions.

AN EASTERN EUROPEAN DINNER
by Amaryll Schwertner

Sour-Cherry Soup

Game Bird Forcemeat in Pastry

Grilled Marinated Fallow Deer

Walnut Crêpe Cake

serves eight

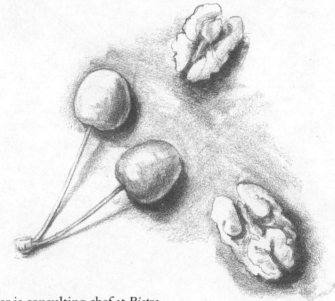

Amaryll Schwertner is consulting chef at *Bistro Bistro* near Washington, D.C. In the Bay Area she has worked at *Sante Fe Bar and Grill*, *Zuni Cafe*, and the *Premier Cru Café*.

"This dinner was one that a very dear friend, Peter Seigler, loved especially. I dedicate this menu with pleasure to his palate, to his spirit, and to his special appetite for living. Peter empowered himself and all of his friends with his outspoken positive spirit and his many candid opinions."

SOUR-CHERRY SOUP *serves eight*

1½ cups dried sour
   cherries
3 cups homemade
   cherry cider
3 cups fruity red wine
2 cups water
1/2 cup sugar (or less
   to taste)
Salt to taste (very little)
Zest and juice of 1 lemon
2 egg yolks
1 cup light cream

Soak cherries in mixture of cider, wine, and water. Bring cherries and liquid to a slow boil, then add the sugar, salt, lemon zest, and juice. Mix the egg yolks with the cream and add gently to the heated cherry liquid. Stir until the soup slightly thickens. Serve hot. (Can also be served chilled as a dessert soup.)

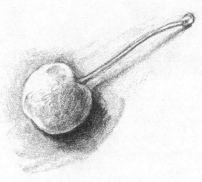

GAME BIRD FORCEMEAT IN PASTRY *serves eight*

Chill the bowl, flour, and fats thoroughly. Cut the fat into the salted flour very quickly. Whisk the egg yolk with the water and work quickly into the flour and the fat. Allow to rest in the refrigerator for several hours. Roll out the pastry on a floured board. Cut into two rounds, with the bottom being larger than the top, and allow to chill again.

Roast all of the birds until just rare. The cooking times will vary with the size of each bird. Allow birds to cool and take all the meat from the bones. Brown the bones, add water, and make a stock. Reduce the stock until it is a concentrated essence, about 1 cup. Grind the veal and pork together with the fatback into an ice-bath bain-marie. Add the cream, the seasoning, and the chilled, reduced stock. Cut the meat from the birds into 1/2-inch pieces and fold into the forcemeat mixture. Spoon the chilled mixture onto the larger of the two pastry rounds. Place the top round over the preparation and seal and decorate the edges. Cut a vent into the top of the pastry and glaze it with an egg-and-water wash.

Bake on a sheet pan at 425° F until the pastry begins to color. Reglaze if necessary. Bake until a meat thermometer inserted into the center reads 160° F. Allow to rest for 1/2 hour and serve warm.

Pastry:
2 cups good-quality pastry flour
1/2 pound sweet butter (or less butter, augmented by chilled goose fat or suet from beef)
Pinch of salt
1 egg yolk
1 tablespoon acidulated water (water with lemon juice)

Forcemeat:
2 whole guinea fowl
1 large pheasant
2 pigeons
2 quail
2 duck legs
1/2 pound veal
1/2 pound pork
1/2 pound pork fatback
3 tablespoons heavy cream
Salt and pepper to taste
1 tablespoon spice blend to suit your taste
Chilled and reduced stock from bird bones
1 egg
3 tablespoons water

GRILLED MARINATED FALLOW DEER *serves eight*

1 saddle of venison

Marinade:
**2 cups Côte Rôtie
    Guigal 1983
Several juniper berries
Several black peppercorns
Bay leaves
Coarse salt
1 organic orange, sliced
    with peel**

Sauce:
**1 shallot, minced
1 cup meat stock
1 tablespoon cold butter**

Combine all marinade ingredients and marinate venison for one or two nights, turning occasionally.

Roast or grill the meat over a medium-high heat and cook to medium rare. Oven temperature should be 425° F, and meat thermometer should read 150° to 165° F when done.

A sauce is made by reducing the marinade with the shallots and stock to a glaze or by whisking in a tablespoon of cold butter to bind the sauce.

WALNUT CRÊPE CAKE *serves eight*

entered

Mix the first five ingredients to a smooth, thick batter. Allow to rest overnight. Stir in the carbonated water just before frying.

Heat the crêpe pan first. Then, with a brush or paper towel, apply a thin film of clarified butter. Ladle on a small amount of batter and disperse to a very even layer, covering the pan by turning your wrist and allowing the batter to spread itself all the way to the edges of the pan. Turn and very lightly cook the other side. The pancakes should be thin and bubbly in places, but firm enough to hold their shape.

For the walnut filling, brown the walnuts in the oven until they release their perfume (5 to 7 minutes), then chop them in a food processor with the sugar and lemon zest. The mixture should be ground fine, but not so far as a flour.

Lay a crêpe down on a dish and brush with a light amount of port or brandy and thinned apricot or raspberry preserves. Sprinkle on a small amount of the nut-sugar mixture, then repeat the process until a cake has been formed. Macerate the raspberries in port and spread the fruit as a sauce on the plate. To serve, slice the cake in wedges.

Crêpes:
3 eggs
1¼ cups flour
1 teaspoon sugar
Pinch of salt
1 cup milk
1 cup carbonated water
Clarified butter for frying

Walnut Filling:
1½ cups walnuts
2 tablespoons raw sugar
Zest of 1 lemon
Port or brandy
Apricot or raspberry
    preserves
1 pint (or more) fresh
    raspberries

INDEX

Alaskan salmon with ginger and black
pepper, 57
albacore, grilled, with oregano pesto, 102
American foie gras and roasted apple
with ginger sauce, 33
"ancho" chili butter, 74
anchovies, grilled, with mint, 180
antipasto, 167
apple cobbler with heavy cream, 66
applesauce, 146
apple-walnut kuchen, 232
apricot tart, 198
arista (pork loin) with rosemary, garlic,
pepper, and fennel seeds, 50
artichokes
gratin of baby, 16
risotto with, 49
roasted baby, 184
arugula salad
with orange, 209
with pear and hazelnut, 162
with spring scallions and onions,
prosciutto and sieved eggs, 44
asiago dressing, 140
Asian cabbage slaw, 90
asparagus
with baked salmon and raspberry
mayonnaise, 40
with penne, 28
risotto, 14
avocado and chicken salad, 135

balsamic vinaigrette, 171, 265
barbecued foods. *See also* grilled foods
orange-rum chicken, 109
red torpedo onions, 109
basil dressing, 94
beans
baked limas, 150
black, with tomatoes and fresh basil
dressing, 94
stewed pintos with herbs, 116
beet salad, 85
berries in lemon mousse, 128
berry cobbler, 207
berry compote, 77
berry pie, 132
berry sauce, 20
biga, for Pugliese bread, 53
bisque of Drakes Bay oysters and wild
watercress, 200
black beans, with tomatoes and fresh
basil dressing, 94
black bean sauce, 113

blackberry pie, 132
black risotto with squid, 181
blinis
corn, with smoked salmon, crème
fraîche, tobiko, and chives, 242
cornmeal, with smoked sturgeon and
caviar, 121
blueberry pie, 132
bok choy, carrot, and red pepper,
sauté of, 97
bracciole (meat rolls), 171
bread
garlic, 95
glazed piñon, 118
grilled sourdough, 45
Hopi blue corn French, 191
Italian country, 266
pizza, 76
Pugliese, 52–53
three-grain quick, 151
walnut, 228
bread pudding
Creole, 261
with fresh fruit sauce, 106
pumpkin, 246
broccoli, Italian, 19
buckwheat dill muffins, 187
burgers, pita, 83
butter
"ancho" chili, 74
herb flower, 192
pasilla chili, 74
sage, 243
butternut squash and leek soup with
Gruyère cheese and thyme, 268
butternut squash-praline soufflé with
rum lemon sabayon, 165

cabbage
Asian cabbage slaw, 90
red, 255
red and green cabbage slaw, 65
cajeta, 282
cake
chocolate decadence, 188
chocolate spice, 281
orange Génoise with strawberries in
red wine, 42
strawberry shortcake, 58
walnut crêpe, 295
camarones (shrimp) al queso di punta, 174
caramel sauce (goat milk), 282
carrot, red pepper, and bok choy, sauté
of, 97

cassis sauce, 237
catfish, steamed, in black bean sauce, 113
caviar, and smoked sturgeon with
     cornmeal blinis, 121
celery root puree, 57
cheese
   asiago dressing, 140
   cream cheese and chili dip, 93
   croutons, 245
   fontina cheese, potatoes with, 227
   goat cheese and lentil spread, 39
   Gorgonzola, pine nuts, and green
      onions with soft polenta, 108
   Gruyère cheese, 226, 268
   mixed green salad with goat
      cheeses, 276
   ricotta gnocchi, 169
cherry compote, 46
cherry, soup of sour, 292
chicken
   and avocado salad, 135
   barbecued orange-rum, 109
   Chinese shredded-chicken salad, 112
   grilled Oregon blackberry, 138
   pepper-stuffed breast of, 11
   roast, with rosemary and lemon under
      skin, 197
   roasted half, with pan gravy, 130
   roasted young, with sage butter and
      grilled shiitake mushrooms, 243
   royal, 114
chili and tequila sauce, 176
chili butter, "ancho," 74
Chinese pear-apple compote with candied
     ginger à la mode, 26
Chinese shredded-chicken salad, 112
chipotle salsa, 278
chocolate, marquise of, 80
chocolate decadence cake, 188
chocolate frosting, 256
chocolate sauce, 172
chocolate spice cake, 281
cioppino, 163–64
citrus mélange, fresh, 287
cobbler
   mixed berry, 207
→ warm apple, with heavy cream, 66 ·
cole slaw, red and green, 65
collard greens, braised, 131
compote
   cherry, 46
   fresh berry, 77
   warm Chinese pear-apple, 26
   winter-fruit, 276
coriander-ginger light cream soup, 23

corn, grilled, with "ancho" chili
     butter, 74
corn blinis with smoked salmon, crème
     fraîche, tobiko, and chives, 242
Cornish game hens, spit-roasted, 206
cornmeal blinis with smoked sturgeon
     and caviar, 121
corn pudding, 198
coulis, tomato, 187, 220
couscous
   curry, with fresh chives, 25
   salad of, with romaine leaves, 69
crab cakes
   on green salad, 18
   San Francisco, 64
crab lasagne with fennel and chanterelles,
     285–86
cranberry syrup, 246
cream cheese and chili dip, 93
cream of cucumber soup, 134
cream sauce, hot, 232
creamy cepe polenta, 186
crème Anglaise, 246
crème fraîche, 16
Creole bread pudding, 261
crisps
   plum, 119
   rhubarb-strawberry, 98
crostini, assorted, 273
croutons, 163
   cheese, 245
   tapenade with, 101
cucumber soup, cream of, 134
curry couscous with fresh chives, 25
custard, lemon sponge, 20

deep-dish pie
   pear-apple, 153
   quince, 216
deer, grilled marinated fallow, 294
dessert. *See also* cake, cobbler, compote,
     ice cream, pie, pudding
   apple-walnut kuchen, 232
   apricot tart, 198
   berries in lemon mousse, 128
   butternut squash-praline soufflé with
      rum lemon sabayon, 165
   fresh fruit with English cream and
      mint, 221
   grilled peaches with wild blackberries,
      202
   honey-basted pears with chocolate
      sauce, 172
   lemon mousse with cassis sauce, 237
   lemon sherbet, 291

dessert *(continued)*
  lemon sponge custard with fresh berry
    sauce, 20
  marquise of chocolate, 80
  mélange of fresh citrus, 287
  Meyer lemon sorbet, 54
  orange dessert, 86
  papaya-lime granita, 251
  peaches with white wine and vanilla
    bean ice cream, 141
  plum Napoléon with sabayon
    mousseline sauce, 124
  puff pastry barquettes with wild
    strawberries, 182
  raspberry tart, 198
  strawberries in rum cream, 136
  strawberries with sweetened crème
    fraîche, 16
  strawberry shortcake, 58
  strawberry soufflé, 30
dessert sauces
  cajeta (goat milk and caramel
    sauce), 282
  cassis sauce, 237
  chocolate, 172
  cranberry syrup, 246
  English cream, 221
  fresh berry, 20
  fresh fruit, 106
  hot cream, 232
  praline, 110
  raspberry, 80
  rum-lemon sabayon, 165
  sabayon mousseline, 124
  whiskey, 261
  whiskey crème Anglaise, 246
dill dressing, 65
dip, cream cheese and chili, 93
dressings. *See also* vinaigrette
  asiago, 140
  dill, 65
  fresh basil, 94
  sesame and walnut oil, 25
duck
  braised legs of, with onions and
    cabbage, 156–57
  clay pot roast, with olives and
    garlic, 215
  grilled breast of, with white beans, 275
  roast breast of, with herb-buttered
    noodles, 105
duck liver, with roasted apple and ginger
    sauce, 33
Dungeness crab lasagne with fennel and
    chanterelles, 285–86

egg pasta, 210–11
eggplant, sautéed, with scallions and red
    pepper, 151
eggplant and red pepper salad, 73
eggs
  holiday, with white truffles, 226
  shirred, with ham, 146
  sieved, 44
endive and spinach salad with feta cheese,
    cherry tomatoes, and mint, 152
English cream, 221

fall vegetables, 206
fennel, mushroom, Parmesan, and white
    truffle salad, 155
fennel à la barigoule, 34
fennel and citrus salad, 249
figs, warm, with prosciutto, 194
Finnish pancake, 8
fish
  Alaskan salmon with ginger and black
    pepper, 57
  albacore, grilled, with oregano
    pesto, 102
  baked salmon and asparagus with
    raspberry mayonnaise, 40
  grilled anchovies with mint, 180
  grilled salmon and radicchio, 180
  salmon marinated with orange and
    fennel, 274
  salmon in parchment, 29
  steamed catfish in black bean sauce, 113
  swordfish braised with baby leeks and
    tarragon, 15
foie gras, American, 33
fontina cheese, potatoes with, 227
forcemeat, game bird, 293
French bread, Hopi blue corn, 191
frosting, chocolate, 256
fruit, fresh, with English cream and
    mint, 221
fruit compote, 276
fruited muffins, 6

game bird forcemeat in pastry, 293
game hens
  smoked, 70
  spit-roasted Cornish, 206
garlic and potato soup, 45
garlic bread, 95
Génoise, orange, with strawberries in red
    wine, 42
gnocchi, ricotta, 169
goat cheese and lentil spread, 39
Gorgonzola, pine nuts, and green onions
    with soft polenta, 108

granita, papaya-lime, 251
gratin
   of baby artichokes, 16
   of potatoes, 197
greens, salad of bitter, 214
grilled foods
   albacore with oregano pesto, 102
   anchovies with mint, 180
   blackberry chicken, 138
   corn with "ancho" chili butter, 74
   duck breast with white beans, 275
   eggplant and red pepper salad, 73
   fallow deer, 294
   lamb, 259
   peaches with wild blackberries, 202
   quail with mustard glaze, 185
   radicchio and pancetta, 192
   salmon, 19, 180
   shiitake mushrooms, 243
   shrimp, 230
   sourdough bread, 45
   tomato sauce, 101
   zucchini, 102
Gruyère cheese, 226, 268
guinea fowl, in pastry, 293

ham, and shirred eggs, 146
hazelnut pie crust, 195
herb flower butter, 192
honey-basted pears with chocolate
   sauce, 172
Hopi blue corn French bread, 191

ice cream
   fresh lemon verbena, 194
   piloncillo vanilla bean, 282
   strawberry swirl, 59
   vanilla bean, with peaches and white
      wine, 141
Italian broccoli, 19
Italian country bread, 266

Japanese soba noodles, 89

kuchen, apple-walnut, 232

lamb
   grilled leg of, in mustard marinade, 259
   pita burgers made of, 83
lasagne
   with Dungeness crab, fennel, and
      chanterelles, 285–86
   with lobster and chervil, 219
leek and potato timbale, 244
leek sauce, 248
lemon buttermilk pie with
   strawberries, 178
lemon curd, 148

lemon meringue pie, 12
lemon mousse
   with cassis sauce, 237
   fresh berries in, 128
lemon sherbet, 290
lemon sorbet, 54
lemon sponge custard, 20
lemon verbena ice cream, 194
lentil and chard soup with tomato
   concasse, 168
lentil and goat cheese spread, 39
lettuces vinaigrette, 158
lima beans, baked, 150
lime-ginger vinaigrette, 236
lime-papaya granita, 251
lime sour cream, 231
lobster
   and chervil with lasagne, 219
   mousseline, 35
   and ravioli salad, 79
   risotto, 127
   stock, 219

Maine lobster mousseline, 35
Mandarin steak salad, 56
marinade
   for fallow deer, 294
   mustard, for lamb, 259
   orange-rum, for barbecued chicken, 109
   for roast squab, 24
   for salmon with orange and fennel, 274
   for shrimp, 230
   for vegetables à la Grecque, 126
   for vegetable julienne, 90
mashed potatoes, 131
   red, with green onions, 97
mayonnaise, raspberry, 40
meat rolls (bracciole), 171
meringue, 12
mescluna with balsamic vinaigrette, 265
Meyer lemon sorbet, 54
mousse
   lemon, with cassis sauce, 237
   lemon, with fresh berries, 128
muffins
   buckwheat dill, 187
   fruited, 6
mushroom and fall vegetable
   ragout, 269–70
mushrooms, grilled shiitake, 243
mushroom soup, 234
mushroom tart, 201
mussels in white wine, 10
mustard glaze, 185
mustard marinade, 259

Napoléon, plum, with sabayon
  mousseline sauce, 124
noodles
  herb-buttered, 105
  Japanese soba, 89
Norwegian salmon, sautéed, with tomato
  coulis and tarragon, 220
nougat, with candied fruits and pureed
  mint, 37

onions, barbecued red torpedo, 109
orange and arugula salad, 209
orange dessert, 86
orange Génoise with strawberries in red
  wine, 42
orange-rum chicken, barbecued, 109
orange sopapillas, 280
oregano pesto, 102
Oregon blackberry chicken, 138
Oriental smoked game hens, 70
oven-fried potatoes, 11
oven-roasted vegetables with rosemary
  and garlic, 139
oysters, bisque of Drakes Bay, 200

Pacific salmon, grilled, 19
paella, New Year's, 289
pancakes
  Finnish, 8
  potato, 254
pancetta
  grilled radicchio and, 192
  potatoes arrosti with, 260
  with rabbit and mushrooms, 250
papaya-lime granita, 251
pasilla chili butter, 74
pasta
  egg, 210
  fettuccine with herb butter and roast
    duck breast, 105
  lasagne with lobster and chervil, 219
  penne with asparagus, 28
  pumpkin-stuffed, 210–11
  spaghetti with garlic and olive oil, 263
  spaghettini with grilled tomato
    sauce, 101
  sun-dried tomato, 205
pastry
  hazelnut pie crust, 195
  game bird forcemeat in, 293
  pâte brisé, 239
  puff pastry barquettes with wild
    strawberries, 182
  tart shell, 198
pastry cream, 182

peaches
  grilled, with wild blackberries, 202
  with white wine and vanilla bean ice
    cream, 141
pear-apple pie, 153
pears
  honey-basted, 172
  salad of, with arugula and hazelnut, 162
  seckel, poached in red wine with burnt
    caramel, 159–60
  with walnuts, romaine hearts,
    watercress, and radicchio, 271
peas and red peppers, 260
penne with asparagus, 28
peperonata, 51
pepper (red), bok choy, and carrot
  sauté, 97
pepper oil, 204
pepper-stuffed chicken breasts, 11
persimmon, water chestnut, and winter
  greens salad, 284
pesto, oregano, 102
pheasant, in pastry, 293
pie
  berry, 132
  dark roast winter squash, with
    hazelnut crust, 195
  deep-dish pear-apple, 153
  deep-dish quince, 216
  lemon buttermilk, 178
  lemon meringue, 12
  winter-harvest, 239–40
piñon bread, glazed, 118
pinto beans, stewed, with herbs, 116
pita burgers, 83
pizza bread, 76
plum crisp, 119
plum Napoléon with sabayon mousseline
  sauce, 124
plum soup, 68
polenta, 230
  baked, with Gorgonzola, pine nuts,
    and green onions, 108
  creamy cepe, 186
  soft, 270
pomegranate, bitter greens, and
  cucumber salad, 214
pork
  arista (pork loin) with rosemary,
    garlic, pepper, and fennel seeds, 50
  pork chops smothered in mushrooms, 96
  pork stew, with tomatillos and
    greens, 279
  roast, 175
  spicy pork stew, 231

potatoes
with fontina cheese, 227
garlic mashed, 18
gratin of, 197
leek timbale and, 244
mashed, 131
mashed red, with green onions, 97
new, with lemon butter, 64
oven-fried, 11
potatoes arrosti with pancetta, 260
Spanish potato tortilla, 5
potato pancakes, 254
praline sauce, 110
prawns
spicy, 92
spot, in spicy peanut sauce, 88
prosciutto, warm figs and, 194
pudding
bread, with fruit sauce, 106
corn, 198
Creole bread, 261
pumpkin bread, with whiskey crème
Anglaise, 246
puff pastry barquettes with wild
strawberries, 182
Pugliese bread, 52–53
pumpkin bread pudding with whiskey
crème Anglaise, 246
pumpkin-stuffed pasta, 210–11

quail
grilled, with mustard glaze and braised
Swiss chard, 185
in pastry, 293
quince pie, deep-dish, 216

rabbit
braised, with thyme and mustard
seeds, 235
with pancetta and mushrooms, 250
saddle of, with black and rose
peppercorns, 123
radicchio
grilled, with pancetta, 192
grilled salmon and, 180
ragout, mushroom and fall
vegetable, 269–70
raspberries, in fresh berry compote, 77
raspberry mayonnaise, 40
raspberry pie, 132
raspberry sauce, 80
raspberry tart, 198
ravioli and lobster salad, 79
red cabbage, braised, 255
red peppers and sugar-snap peas, 260
red torpedo onions, barbecued, 109
reindeer, roasted loin of, 201
rhubarb-strawberry crisp, 98

rice dishes
asparagus risotto, 14
black risotto with squid, 181
lobster risotto, 127
risotto with artichokes, 49
tabbouleh variation, 82
rice-paper shrimp rolls, 22
rice wine and butter sauce, 24
ricotta gnocchi, 169
risotto. *See also* rice dishes
asparagus, 14
with artichokes, 49
black, with squid, 181
lobster, 127
rocket salad with spring scallions and
onions, prosciutto and sieved egg, 44
roebuck, roasted loin of, 201
romaine lettuce
hearts of, with asiago dressing, 140
leaves of, with couscous salad, 69
with walnuts, watercress, and
radicchio, 271
rouille, 163
rum cream with strawberries, 136

sabayon, rum-lemon, 165
sabayon mousseline sauce, 124
Sacher torte, 256
sage butter, 243
salad
arugula, pear, and hazelnut, 162
arugula and orange, 209
Asian cabbage slaw, 90
beet, 85
bitter greens with pomegranate and
cucumber, 214
with chicken and avocado, 135
Chinese shredded-chicken, 112
comice pear and walnut, with romaine
hearts, watercress, and radicchio, 271
confetti, 193
couscous with romaine leaves, 69
endive and spinach, 152
fennel, mushroom, Parmesan, and
white truffle, 155
fennel and citrus, 249
garden, with balsamic vinaigrette, 171
green, with crab cakes, 18
green, with lime-ginger
vinaigrette, 236
green, with sesame and walnut oil
dressing, 25
grilled eggplant and red pepper, 73
hearts of romaine with asiago
dressing, 140
lettuces vinaigrette, 158
lobster and ravioli, 79
Mandarin steak, 56

salad *(continued)*
    mescluna with balsamic vinaigrette, 265
    mixed green, with goat cheeses, 276
    roasted squab, with mixed greens, 218
    rocket, with scallions and onions,
        prosciutto and sieved eggs, 44
    tomato, cucumber, and red onion, 132
    watercress and endive, 290
    wild-green, 117
    winter greens, with persimmon and
        water chestnuts, 284
salad dressing. *See also* vinaigrette
    asiago, 140
    dill, 65
    fresh basil, 94
    sesame and walnut oil, 25
salmon
    Alaskan, with ginger and black
        pepper, 57
    baked, with asparagus and raspberry
        mayonnaise, 40
    with ginger and black pepper, 57
    grilled, with radicchio, 180
    grilled Pacific, 19
    marinated with orange and fennel, 274
    in parchment, 29
    sautéed Norwegian, with tomato coulis
        and tarragon, 220
    smoked, with corn blinis, 242
    Thai soup with, 204
salsa
    chipotle, 278
    fresca, 177
    verde, 278
San Francisco crab cakes, 64
Santa Rosa plum and white wine soup, 68
sauce. *See also* dessert sauce
    black bean, 113
    chili and tequila, 176
    grilled tomato, 101
    hot cream, 232
    leek, 248
    lime, 36
    lobster, 35
    raspberry mayonnaise, 40
    rice-wine and butter, 24
    roasted apple with ginger, 33
    rouille, 163
    spicy peanut, 88
    tomato, with Italian field
        mushrooms, 170
    walnut, 212
sauerbraten, 253
sauté
    of bok choy, carrot, and red pepper, 97
    of eggplant with scallions and red
        peppers, 151

Norwegian salmon with tomato coulis
    and tarragon, 220
scallops
    with leek sauce, 248
    shiso-wrapped kabobs of, 192
sesame-ginger vinaigrette, 89
shellfish
    camarones al queso di punta, 174
    cioppino, 163
    crab lasagne with fennel and
        chanterelles, 285–86
    lasagne with lobster and chervil, 219
    lobster mousseline, 35
    lobster risotto, 127
    marinated and grilled shrimp, 230
    mussels in white wine, 10
    paella, 289
    rice-paper shrimp rolls, 22
    scallops with leek sauce, 248
    shiso-wrapped scallop kabobs, 192
    spicy prawns, 92
    spot prawns in spicy peanut sauce, 88
sherbet, lemon, 290
sherry vinegar-shallot vinaigrette, 18
shirred eggs with ham, 146
shiso-wrapped scallop kabobs, 192
shortcake, strawberry, 58
shrimp
    camarones al queso di punta, 174
    grilled marinated, 230
    rice-paper shrimp rolls, 22
smoothie, strawberry-orange, 4
soba noodles, 89
sopapillas, orange, 280
sorbet, Meyer lemon, 54
soufflé
    butternut squash-praline, 165
    strawberry, 30
soup
    bisque of Drakes Bay oysters, 200
    butternut squash and leek, 268
    chilled tomato and red bell pepper, 32
    cream of cucumber, 134
    double coriander-ginger light
        cream, 23
    green garlic and potato, 45
    lentil and chard, 168
    Santa Rosa plum and white wine, 68
    sour cherry, 292
    Tarpon Springs, 122
    Thai, with salmon, 204
    wild mushroom, 234
    yellow pepper, 258
sour cream, lime, 231
sourdough bread, grilled, 45
spaghetti aglio e olio (spaghetti with
        garlic and olive oil), 263

spaghettini with grilled tomato
    sauce, 101
Spanish potato tortilla, 5
spice cake, chocolate, 281
sponge roll, whole wheat, 147
spread, goat cheese and lentil, 39
squab
    roast, with rice-wine and butter
        sauce, 24
    salad of, with mixed greens, 218
squash pie with hazelnut crust, 195
squid, black risotto with, 181
steak salad, Mandarin, 56
stew
    pinto bean and herb, 116
    pork, with tomatillos and greens, 279
    spicy pork, 231
strawberry-orange smoothie, 4
strawberry-rhubarb crisp, 98
strawberry shortcake, 58
strawberry soufflé, 30
strawberry swirl ice cream, 59
strawberries
    in fresh berry compote, 77
    in red wine with orange Génoise, 42
    in rum cream, 136
    with sweetened crème fraîche, 16
Swiss chard, braised, 185
swordfish, braised with baby leeks and
        tarragon, 15
syrup, cranberry, 246
Szechuan pepper oil, 204

tabbouleh variation, 82
tapenade with croutons, 101
Tarpon Springs soup, 122
tarts
    apricot, 198
    fresh tomato, 104
    raspberry, 198
    wild mushroom, 201
tatziki, 83
tchoutchoukaa, 84
Thai soup with salmon, 204
timbale, leek and potato, 244
tomato and red bell pepper soup with
        caviar, 32
tomato concasse, 168
tomato coulis, 187, 220
tomato pasta, 205
tomato sauce and Italian field
        mushrooms, 170
tomato tart with basil, 104
tomatoes
    with black beans and fresh basil
        dressing, 94
    fresh, 75

sliced fresh, with cucumbers and red
        onions, 132
torte, Sacher, 256
tortilla, Spanish potato, 5
tripe, with tomatoes and rosemary, 264
truffles, white
    with holiday eggs, 226
    salad of, with fennel, mushrooms, and
        Parmesan, 155
tuna, grilled albacore, with oregano
        pesto, 102

vanilla bean ice cream, 282
vegetables
    à la Grecque, 126
    celery root puree, 57
    fall, 206
    Italian broccoli, 19
    marinated vegetable julienne, 90
    mushroom and fall vegetable
        ragout, 269-70
    oven-roasted, with rosemary and
        garlic, 139
    sautéed eggplant with scallions and red
        pepper, 151
    sauté of bok choy, carrot, and red
        pepper, 97
    sugar-snap peas and red peppers, 260
    zucchini pillows with sweet peppers, 41
vinaigrette, 284
    balsamic, 171, 265
    lettuces, 158
    lime-ginger, 236
    sherry vinegar-shallot, 18
    toasted sesame-ginger, 89
    walnut-sherry, 271

walnut bread, 228
walnut crêpe cake, 295
walnut sauce, 212
walnut-sherry vinaigrette, 271
water chestnut, persimmon, and winter
        greens salad, 284
watercress and endive salad with
        radishes, 290
whiskey crème Anglaise, 246
whiskey sauce, 261
whole wheat sponge roll, 147

yellow pepper soup, 258

zucchini
    pillows with sweet peppers, 41
    grilled golden, 102

30
59
83

95
106
169
210
212
232

66 Apple Cobbler
68 Plum wine soup
101 Tapenade
118 Banana nut bread
141 Ice cream
212 Walnut Sauce

271 Vinegrette

64

153
119
98
do